T0329993

The Cost of Living Crisis

To Nisreen, Danny, Ryan and Ivy

The Cost of Living Crisis

Implications for Economic Theory and Public Policy

Imad A. Moosa

Professor of Economics and Finance (retired)

Edward Elgar
PUBLISHING

Cheltenham, UK • Northampton, MA, USA

Published by
Edward Elgar Publishing Limited
The Lypiatts
15 Lansdown Road
Cheltenham
Glos GL50 2JA
UK

Edward Elgar Publishing, Inc.
William Pratt House
9 Dewey Court
Northampton
Massachusetts 01060
USA

A catalogue record for this book
is available from the British Library

Library of Congress Control Number: 2024944306

This book is available electronically in the **Elgar**online
Economics subject collection
https://doi.org/10.4337/9781035338238

ISBN 978 1 0353 3822 1 (cased)
ISBN 978 1 0353 3823 8 (eBook)

Printed and bound in Great Britain by
TJ Books Limited, Padstow, Cornwall

Contents

Preface

The cost of living crisis is an important topic that is worthy of a book for at least two reasons. The first reason is that the crisis is making life difficult, except for those at the right tail of the income distribution, which makes the topic of interest for the average person who does not have to be an economist to understand the causes, consequences and cures of the crisis. This is why this book contains a simplified analysis and clarifications – for example, that inflation is neither a necessary, nor a sufficient condition for the eruption of a cost of living crisis. A crisis of this sort has two dimensions, inflation and wage stagnation, both of which are endemic under a neoliberal economic system. It follows that a cost of living crisis may arise because of inflation or recession, and this is why it is severe under hyperinflation and stagflation.

The second reason, which pertains to those with formal training in economics, is that the crisis has implications for economic theory and public policy. The crisis can be used to debunk the myth that inflation is always and everywhere a monetary phenomenon, as Milton Friedman once (famously) said. This is because it is crystal clear that the resurgence of inflation has been caused by supply-side (cost-push and profit-push) factors, which are either ignored or justified by the followers of Friedman who tend to use some sort of twisted logic. The first macroeconomic policy implication is that central bankers have no control over inflation because they have no control over the money supply, and because inflation is not a monetary problem, except under the extreme conditions of hyperinflation. The second implication is that the policy of raising interest rates to curb inflation is not only ineffective but also counterproductive because interest payments represent a cost of production, in which case raising interest rates aggravates, rather than alleviates, inflation.

The analysis presented in this book, which should be accessible to those without formal training in economics, is based on simulated as well as actual data taken from various sources, official and otherwise. I use simulated data generated in Excel because (and this is my humble opinion) simulation is more powerful than formal empirical analysis based on the con art of econometrics. Simulation is much easier to understand than any of those seemingly sophisticated but realistically useless econometric estimation and testing methods. The actual data used in the analysis cover a large number of countries, with a particular emphasis on three: Australia, the UK and the US. This emphasis stems from the fact that I am more familiar with these countries than others, having lived and worked in all of them. Australia is the country I call home.

Writing this book would not have been possible without the help and encouragement I received from family, friends and colleagues. My utmost gratitude must go to my wife, Afaf, who bore most of the opportunity cost of writing this book. I would also like to thank my colleagues and friends, including John Vaz, Kelly Burns, Vikash Ramiah, Liam Lenten, Brien McDonald and Nirav Parikh. I would like to thank my friends and former colleagues at Kuwait University, including Ebrahim Merza, Anwar Al-Shriaan, Khalid Al-Saad and Nabeel Al-Loughani.

In preparing the manuscript, I benefited from the exchange of ideas with members of the Table 14 Discussion Group, and for this reason I would like to thank Bob Parsons, Greg O'Brien, Greg Bailey, Bill Breen, Paul Rule, Peter Murphy, Bob Brownlee, Jim Reiss and Tony Pagliaro. I am grateful to Greg Bailey in particular for providing feedback on some chapters and for the advice I received from him while I was preparing the book proposal. My thanks also go to friends and former colleagues who live far away but provide help via means of telecommunication, including Kevin Dowd (whom I owe big intellectual debt), Razzaque Bhatti, Ron Ripple, Bob Sedgwick, Sean Holly, Dan Hemmings, Ian Baxter, Basil Al-Nakeeb and Mike Dempsey. Last, but not least, I would like to thank Alex Pettifer, the Editorial Director of Edward Elgar, who encouraged me to write this book. I am also grateful to the rest of the crew at my favourite publisher, including Caroline Cornish, Nina Booth and Finn Halligan.

Naturally, I am the only one responsible for any errors and omissions that may be found in this book. It is dedicated to my daughter, Nisreen, my son, Danny, my grandson, Ryan, and my granddaughter, Ivy.

Imad A. Moosa
March 2024

Abbreviations and acronyms

ACCC	Australian Competition and Consumer Commission
AI	Artificial Intelligence
AUKUS	Australia-United Kingdom-United States
ATM	Automated Teller Machine
BBC	British Broadcasting Corporation
BIS	Bank for International Settlements
BP	British Petroleum
BTU	British Thermal Unit
CEO	Chief Executive Officer
COP	Conference of the Parties
COVID	Coronavirus Disease
CPI	Consumer Price Index
DD	Demand Deposits
DIY	Do It Yourself
ECB	European Central Bank
EDF	Électricité de France
EU	European Union
FAO	Food and Agriculture Organization
FMCG	Fast-Moving Consumer Goods
FRED	Federal Reserve Bank of St Louis
G20	Group of Twenty Countries
GDP	Gross Domestic Product
GSCPI	Global Supply Chain Pressure Index
ILO	International Labour Organization
IMF	International Monetary Fund
IPO	Initial Public Offering
IPPR	Institute for Public Policy Research
IRI	Information Resources Inc.
ITV	Independent Television

MMF	Money Market Funds
NATO	North Atlantic Treaty Organization
NHS	National Health Service
NXP	Next eXPerience
OECD	Organisation for Economic Co-operation and Development
OLD	Other Liquid Deposits
PC	Personal Computer
PCE	Personal Consumption Expenditure
PDI	Personal Disposable Income
PIMCO	Pacific Investment Management Company
PS	PlayStation
QTM	Quantity Theory of Money
RAF	Royal Air Force
RAW	Real Average Wages
RBA	Reserve Bank of Australia
RMW	Real Minimum Wages
TUC	Trades Union Congress
UAE	United Arab Emirates
UHC	Universal Healthcare
UK	United Kingdom
UN	United Nations
UNDP	United Nations Development Programme
US	United States
VAT	Value Added Tax
WTI	West Texas Intermediate

1.   The cost of living crisis: an overview

1.1   THE CONCEPT OF A COST OF LIVING CRISIS

The "cost of living" can be defined as the income or level of spending needed to maintain a certain quality of life while paying for housing, food, energy and healthcare (that is, essential items). This definition is by no means unique because a variety of definitions can be found in the literature and even in dictionaries. For example, the *Cambridge Dictionary* defines the cost of living as "the amount of money that a person needs to live", implying that "living" requires the consumption of certain (essential) goods and services. Porter (2022) defines the cost of living as "the amount of money required for covering necessary expenses to maintain a certain lifestyle standard in a particular place and time". In this definition, "necessary expenses" include housing, food, taxes, healthcare, clothing, education, entertainment and transportation. Another definition is that the cost of living is "the amount of money you're likely to pay for basic expenses and to maintain a certain lifestyle standard in the city of your choice" (Herrity, 2023). In this definition "basic expenses" include rent or mortgage payments, food, clothing, educational expenses, healthcare, transportation and taxes.

In general, the cost of living is the cost of covering essential items, the goods and services characterised by a low elasticity of demand. Entertainment is certainly not one of these items – people struggling to cope with the current crisis talk about rent, food and energy, not about entertainment (certainly not about spending $1000 to watch Taylor Swift in action). This point is made by Dales (2022) who argues that "what's particularly worrying is that while households can choose not to buy a second-hand car, they have to buy food, fuel and utilities", which means that "a lot of this surge in inflation can't be avoided". The problem with the definition put forward by Herrity (2023) is the phrase "in the city of your choice". Someone who lives comfortably in a particular city cannot claim to be in a cost of living crisis by moving voluntarily to a more expensive city on the same income. The definition suggested by Jacobs et al. (2014) is that the cost of living is the expense households incur to buy the goods and services that are necessary to maintain a certain standard of living. In turn, they define the standard of living as "the utility that a household derives from consuming goods and services".

We have to keep in mind that the classification of goods and services into necessary and luxury items is not precise, as we have seen from the various definitions of the cost of living that we have come across so far. Baxter and Moosa (1996) present a comprehensive analysis of this issue, referring to the classical work of Adam Smith, David Ricardo and Alfred Marshall, as well as the more recent work of Richard Stone, Gerard Debreu and Angus Deaton. For example, Alfred Marshall (1890) described what he called the "necessaries for efficiency" in the England of his time as follows:

> A well-drained dwelling with several rooms, warm clothing, with some changes of underclothing, pure water, a plentiful supply of cereal food, with a moderate allowance of meat and milk, and a little tea, etc., some education and some recreation, and lastly, sufficient freedom for his wife from other work to enable her to perform her maternal and her household duties.

What is surprising about Marshall's description of "necessaries for efficiency" is the inclusion of "some recreation", which may be needed for a pleasant life. However, people do not die or suffer because of the lack of recreation. Furthermore, one can always find free recreation such as bush walking and swimming in the sea.

Baxter and Moosa (1996) distinguish between "basic needs" and other non-durable consumption expenditures, identifying basic needs items as four categories that can be found in the official UK classification of consumer expenditure, which are primarily intended to satisfy consumers' physiological needs. These categories are food, clothing and footwear, housing, and energy products. They also demonstrate that "basic needs" consumption expenditure has different characteristics from those of expenditure on other non-durable items such as alcoholic drinks, tobacco, household goods and services, and entertainment. It remains true, however, that the lists of necessary and luxury items vary across time and space.

It follows that a cost of living crisis is a state of affairs where the cost of everyday living essentials rises more quickly than average household income, typically in the form of wages and salaries. It can also be defined as a situation in which real disposable income declines, where the word "disposable" is the portion of income available for spending on goods and services (that is, what is paid by the employer to the employee less taxes and contributions to superannuation, national insurance, Medicare, etc.). The word "real" means disposable income adjusted for inflation – hence, it is a measure of the purchasing power of nominal disposable income (that is, the amount of goods and services that can be bought with the dollar amount representing nominal income). What matters for living standards is not how much money people earn, but how much goods and services they can buy with the amount of money they earn.

The cost of living is typically measured in terms of a price index that represents the general price level (as opposed to the price of a particular good or service). The most commonly used index is the consumer price index (CPI), which is a weighted average of the prices of goods and services bought by the average consumer. Inflation is the period-to-period percentage change in cost of living. The annual inflation rate in a particular month is measured as the percentage change in the CPI in that month relative to the same month in the previous year. For example, the CPI in the US rose from 298 in October 2022 to 307.6 in October 2023, which puts the inflation rate in October 2023 at 3.2%.

However, the CPI is not the only measure of the cost of living, and for some economists it is not the best measure. Jacobs et al. (2014) put forward some reasons why the CPI "might not fully reflect household concern about cost-of-living inflation". In particular, they argue, the CPI is a measure of the average inflation rate across households, which is different from the inflation rates experienced by individual households whose consumption baskets differ from the average basket used to calculate the CPI. Some households experience higher inflation rates than the average for all households, because they spend proportionately more on high-inflation items, while other households experience below-average inflation, because they spend proportionately more on low-inflation items. Furthermore, the CPI is calculated on the basis of a fixed basket of goods and services, which means that it does not take into account the effect of substitution when consumers try to alleviate the adverse effect of rising prices by shifting their spending from higher-inflation to lower-inflation items. While these observations are valid, other measures of the cost of living (such as the personal consumption expenditure price index) are subject to the same problems. More worrying than the points raised by Jacobs et al. (2014) is perhaps the proposition that governments have the power and incentive to under-report the inflation rate. One of these incentives is to give the impression that things are not as bad as what they really are (on the tendency to under-report inflation, see Moosa, 2020).

Even though a cost of living crisis is typically associated with rising inflation rates, inflation may be neither a necessary nor a sufficient condition for a crisis to surface. The current crisis has definitely been triggered by resurgent inflation, but inflation will not trigger a cost of living crisis if incomes are indexed, in the sense that they rise in tandem with the cost of living (as measured by the CPI). A cost of living crisis may not be associated with inflation but rather with recession and unemployment because a person who loses their income as a result of redundancy will not be able to buy essential goods and services. In 2009, when the inflation rate was low, there was a cost of living crisis (even though no one called it that) for the unemployed who lost their jobs in the great recession that followed the global financial crisis. In 2020 and

2021, people were laid off as a result of the COVID-19 pandemic, which gave rise to a cost of living crisis in the absence of inflation.

1.2 THE TIMING OF THE CURRENT CRISIS

Even though there is never a good time for a crisis, the timing of the current crisis is particularly cruel, coming as countries around the world continue to feel the economic, social and political impacts of the COVID-19 pandemic. The current crisis, which started in early 2022 or late 2021, coincides with tax increases, energy price hikes, social security cuts, heightened military expenditure, and stagnating nominal wages. These are elements of an extremely difficult environment, particularly for the families already struggling to get by. It also comes some 40 years after the adoption of neoliberalism as the guiding philosophy, promoting privatisation, liberalisation, deregulation, deindustrialisation and financialisation. Neoliberal policy prescriptions have been undermining the ability of the economy to boost aggregate supply and unleashed a wave of debt accumulation and significant cuts in public services.

In crises, there is a particularly important role for social security systems, which can provide protection from poverty, but this crisis comes at a time when social security systems have been moving from bad to worse as governments, for one reason or another, find it more logical to spend money on fighting unnecessary wars, or financing proxy wars, than helping the people in need. For example, Patrick and Pybus (2022) identify indicators of the decline of the British social security system as the five-week wait for a first universal credit payment, high levels of debt deductions, and restrictions on benefit entitlement (the benefit cap and the two-child limit), which they describe as "poverty producing, perversely doing the very opposite of what a social security system should". They go on to say the following:

> Families living on a low income have struggled to navigate the pandemic, and now face a punishing round of budgetary pressures, which come on top of the recent ending of the £20 uplift to Universal Credit and the failure to uprate benefits in line with current rates of inflation.

Although this is a description of the British social security system, the same is observed in other countries where neoliberalism has taken over as the guiding philosophy, intended to benefit the 1% at the expense of the 99%. The crisis comes at a bad time because no policy maker, not even those in charge of consumer protection, seems to care about the fact that energy companies, pharmaceutical companies, big tech, and multinationals operating in the food sector have all been raking in billions of dollars in profits while people are suffering.

Another reason why this crisis comes at a bad time is that those in charge of monetary policy do not know what they are doing or, as described by Papadimitriou and Wray (2021), "still flying blind", opting to deal with the crisis by using interest rate hikes, thereby aggravating the hardship faced by ordinary people living on after-tax wages and salaries. Central bankers boost their ego by claiming control over inflation as a result of using an "aggressive" interest rate policy, irrespective of the pain inflicted on those who have variable rate mortgages. In the process, well-paid central bankers even claim bonuses to enrich themselves at the expense of people struggling to navigate through the crisis. Even elected politicians claim credit for victory over inflation, which is an illusion. In November 2023, Rishi Sunak said that he would stick to his plan on reducing inflation, claiming "success" in halving the rate (Hatton, 2023). He even said the following: "On me personally if inflation isn't halved" (Baker, 2023).

This is an illusion and pure fantasy on the part of the British prime minister. It is a heroic statement because Sunak should know that most of the inflation in the UK is due to external factors, beyond his or the Bank of England's control. By far the biggest driver of UK inflation is soaring food, fuel and energy prices. The Bank of England estimates that around 80% of inflation is due to global shortages and the jump in the prices of goods set on global markets, such as oil. Given that 80% of the current bout of inflation is due to soaring goods and commodities prices, which are set on international markets, the Bank of England cannot do much to reduce inflation. After all, raising interest rates will do nothing to boost the supply of natural gas, or to reduce the cost of goods shipped from Asia (RSM, 2022).

In reality, raising interest rates is not an effective means of reducing the inflation rate, particularly when inflation is caused by cost-push and profit-push factors. It remains to say that those who blame inflation on Vladimir Putin should not claim credit for reducing the inflation rate, because if Putin is the cause, then he is the only one capable of reducing inflation! In Chapter 4 we will find out why the inflation rate came down in 2023 compared to 2022 without any anti-inflationary action taken by Putin.

1.3 A HISTORICAL PERSPECTIVE

This is by no means the first cost of living crisis, which is why some observers compare it with previous crises. However, the comparison is typically based on inflation rates, which is inadequate as a proper comparison must cover wages and public services as well. The problem is that while historical data are available on inflation, historical data on wages are not available for a long period of time.

Gregory (2022a) describes the cost of living crisis in Britain in 1795, the year that witnessed a poor wheat harvest, resulting in chronic shortages. The wheat (hence bread) shortage coincided with upheaval resulting from the French Revolution and the subsequent wars with the French Republic. As a result, the price of bread doubled and a number of bread riots broke out across the country as people went hungry. Burial figures from that period show a significant increase in 1795, implying a rise in the death rate. Even though the crisis eased slightly in 1796, as a result of a successful domestic harvest, bread prices continued to fluctuate wildly towards the end of the 18th century, bringing continued hardship for many years thereafter (see also Stern, 1964).

Gregory (2022b) also describes the 1800 cost of living crisis in Britain when inflation was running at 36%. The reason for high inflation in 1800 was 20 years of Napoleonic Wars, which drained the country's resources while growing demand was triggered by the industrial revolution. The economy struggled to supply ample arms, food and fuel to the army and navy, and shortages emerged across all sorts of everyday goods. As a result, the prices of clothing, beverages, candles, coal, meat, dairy and cereals (the items purchased by the common person) went up sharply. The prices of these items had been rising for decades as population growth and a declining mortality rate led to continuously growing demand. Gregory makes an explicit mention of the failure of wages to keep up with inflation even though she describes the crisis as an "inflation crisis".

A famine is an extremely severe cost of living crisis. A well-known cost of living crisis of this sort was the Irish potato famine, which lasted from 1845 to 1852 and had a major impact on the Irish society (for example, Kinealy, 1994). One cause of the famine was the infection of potato crops by blight throughout Europe during the 1840s. Another reason was single-crop dependence, represented by heavy reliance of the tenant farmers of Ireland (then ruled as a British colony) on potato as food, and this is why the infestation had a catastrophic impact on the population of Ireland. The impact of the famine was exacerbated by a new Whig administration in London, which pursued a laissez-faire economic doctrine and firmly believed that the Irish lacked moral character (this is the culture of blaming the victim).

Wohl (1990) refers to the "pseudo-scientific literature of the day" in which "the Irish were held to be inferior, an example of a lower evolutionary form, closer to the apes than their 'superiors', the Anglo-Saxons". Large amounts of food were exported from Ireland during the famine while London refused to block food exports, thereby contributing to anti-British sentiment. The potato famine was aggravated by the inadequacy of relief efforts provided by the British government, coupled with the illusion that the free market would put an end to the famine. In 1846, a victory for the advocates of free trade was enshrined by the repeal of the Corn Laws, which had protected domestic grain producers from foreign competition. The repeal of the Corn Laws failed to put an end to the crisis, since the Irish did not have the money needed to purchase foreign grain. The Irish potato famine left, as its legacy, deep and lasting feelings of bitterness and distrust towards the British.

The British administration in India engineered a famine in 1770, followed by severe ones in 1783, 1866, 1873, 1892, 1897 and during World War II (1943–44). Following the advent of the British rule, most of the famines were a consequence of monsoonal delays as well as the exploitation of the country's natural resources by the British for their own financial gain. The World War II famine was engineered by Winston Churchill, who ordered the diversion of the supplies of medical aid and food intended for the starving victims to the already well-supplied soldiers fighting in Europe. When the Delhi government sent a telegram to Churchill, painting a grim picture of devastation, his response was: "Then why hasn't Gandhi died yet?" He also declared that he hated Indians because "they are a beastly people with a beastly religion" and blamed the famine on the victims because they "breed like rabbits" (Chakraborty, 2014). The famine of 1770 in Bengal was far deadlier than the Black Plague that terrorised Europe in the 14th century.

More recent crises are discussed by Dales (2022) who compares between the current crisis and the crises of the 1970s and 2008, arguing that the previous episodes were worse than the present one. The reasoning used by Dales to justify his view that the crisis of the 1970s was worse than the current crisis is that inflation was much higher in the 1970s. The crisis of 2008 (or 2009) arose in the absence of high inflation because the loss of income resulting from the great recession led to the same result – that people could not afford to buy things. He refers to a "crumb of comfort" that "the inflationary squeeze on our ability to spend won't be as big as in the 1970s or in the years after the Global Financial Crisis" and to the good news that "we have been through worse". This is gross misrepresentation of the facts on the ground, and it is no consolation for a struggling son in 2023 to know that his father struggled even more in the 1970s.

The UK figures used by Dales to support his proposition relate to inflation and wage growth. After the two oil price shocks in the 1970s, CPI inflation was much higher than in the current episode, reaching 25.3% in August 1975 and 15.6% in April 1980. Wage growth was also higher, but it was not high enough to prevent real wage growth of −7.6% in June 1977 and a cumulative fall in the level of real wages by 9.5%. The worst bout of falling real wages materialised in the aftermath of the global financial crisis, even though inflation was not high. At its lowest in February 2009, real wage growth was −8.6%. Over a six-year period between February 2008 and March 2014, real wages fell by 13.5%, which coincided with an unemployment rate that ranged between 6% and 8%, compared with 4% in the current crisis. This means that the number of people with zero real disposable income (as a result of unemployment) reached 2.56 million in the aftermath of the global financial crisis, compared to 1.38 million in the current crisis.

However, some observers believe that this comparison is not valid, even misleading. For example, Roberts (2022) argues that "in the 1970s, we didn't have to choose between heating and eating". In a letter to *The Guardian*, she said the following:

> I feel quite angry about the present comparisons. We didn't need food banks, there was no talk of "heating or eating". But then the gap between the haves and have-nots was not so wide. I believe that the 70s were the time of greatest financial equality since the second world war. That changed in the 80s and has never gone back.

The significance of the 1980s is the victory of neoliberalism, symbolised by the destructive "reforms" introduced by Margaret Thatcher for the benefit of the 1%. One important difference was that utilities were still publicly owned in the 1970s before neoliberalism enabled wholesale privatisation and deregulation. People did not have to pay for healthcare and education. Governments could intervene to protect the vulnerable, but not anymore. This issue is discussed by Elliott (2023) who refers to the statutory price caps introduced by the government of Ted Heath in comparison to Rishi Sunak's government that wants a voluntary store scheme to meet Sunak's pledge to halve inflation. Back in the 1960s and 1970s, it was widely believed and accepted that price controls were needed to prevent a small number of firms using their market power to exploit consumers and extract consumer surplus. These days price controls represent a no-go zone, a taboo as far as the government is concerned.

Six US post-war inflationary episodes are identified by Rouse et al. (2021) who compare them with the current episode. These episodes, characterised by an inflation rate of more than 5%, occurred in 1946–48, 1950–51, 1969–71, 1973–82 and 2008. The immediate post-war episode occurred during the period July 1946–October 1948, caused mainly by the elimination of price controls, supply shortages and pent-up demand. The second episode, which was associated with the Korean War, occurred over the period December 1950–December 1951. The 1950s episode was triggered by a jump in demand as households (reminded of rationing and supply shortages during World War II) rushed to purchase goods when supply was limited as a result of shifting some production facilities to the production of military goods. The third episode (March 1969–January 1971) was caused by a booming economy, but inflation fell following President Nixon's introduction of a freeze on wages and prices. In Episode 4 (April 1973–October 1982), the US experienced its longest stretch of heightened inflation because of two surges in oil prices. Episode 5 (April 1989–May 1991) occurred when Iraq invaded Kuwait, leading to a jump in oil prices. Episode six (July 2008–August 2008) is represented by two months of above 5% inflation caused by rising oil prices. One barrel of West Texas Intermediate crude oil cost more than $140 in July 2008 compared to $70 just a year earlier. Rouse et al. reach the conclusion that the closest historical crisis to the current one is the first one because both are characterised by supply chain disruptions and a spike in consumer demand after a period of temporary suppression.

1.4 INFLATION-DRIVEN VERSUS UNEMPLOYMENT-DRIVEN CRISES

Figure 1.1 displays monthly observations of the cost of living (proxied by the CPI) in the US, going back to January 1947. As the CPI rises, the purchasing power of money declines, which can be seen in the diminishing value (purchasing power) of one dollar. This means that a dollar could only buy 7 cents worth of goods and services in October 2023 compared to January 1947. Figure 1.2(a) shows the inflation rates corresponding to the CPI depicted in Figure 1.1 (measured as the percentage change in the CPI relative to the same month in the previous year). While central bankers claim that the 2023 decline in the inflation rate was due to the effective use of interest rate hikes, it will be argued and demonstrated that this claim is bogus and that other causes have led to reversal of the direction of the inflation rate. It is interesting to note that even though the inflation rate was negative during the period March 2009–October 2009, that period witnessed a cost of living crisis because of widespread unemployment and the loss of income.

In Figure 1.2(b) we can see annual observations of the US inflation rate going back to 1913, showing the high inflation rates in the 1920s and the deflation (the decline of the general price level, which corresponds to negative inflation rates) of the 1930s. If anything, there was a bigger cost of living crisis in the 1930s than the 1920s, even though the inflation rate was negative in the 1930s. The 1920s were boom years, while the 1930s were years of depression. The cost of living crisis of the 1930s was caused not by inflation but by mass unemployment during the great depression.

Cost of living crises that occur as a result of unemployment can be seen by observing a time series on US real personal disposable income (PDI), as shown in Figure 1.3. In this case, a cost of living crisis is associated with a negative growth rate of real PDI, which may or may not be associated with inflation. The behaviour of PDI provides a visual comparison between the current crisis and the crisis of the 1970s. The dip in PDI during the current crisis is far bigger than the dip of the 1970s, which shows that the current crisis is far worse. Table 1.1 reports the months that witnessed a year-on-year drop in PDI of 2% or more with the associated inflation rate. In most (but not all) cases, the

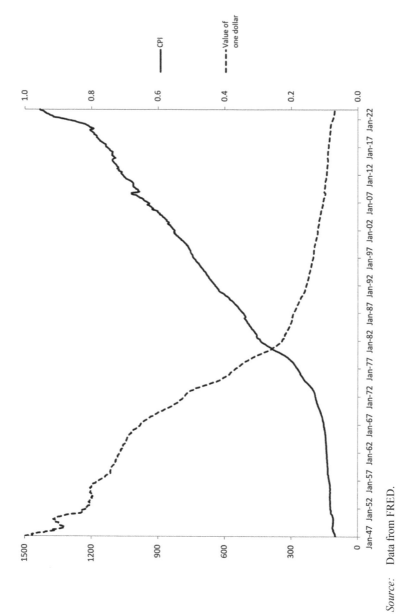

Source: Data from FRED.

Figure 1.1   *CPI and value of one dollar (US, monthly observations)*

(a) Monthly Observations

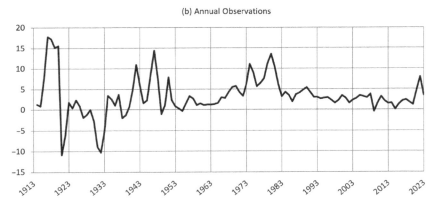

(b) Annual Observations

Source: Data from FRED and Federal Reserve Bank of Minneapolis.

Figure 1.2   *CPI inflation rate (US, monthly and annual observations)*

decline in PDI is associated with high inflation because real PDI is disposable income adjusted for inflation. In 1974, comparable drops in real PDI were associated with high inflation (December and November) and low inflation (October).

The severity of a cost of living crisis is determined by the rate of decline of PDI and the inflation rate. It is possible, therefore, to construct an index for the severity of a crisis in a particular month as the sum of the absolute values of the growth rate of PDI and the inflation rate, converted into an index such that the highest score takes the value of 100. We can see that March 2022 was by far the worst in terms of the severity of the crisis. Eight out of the top nine

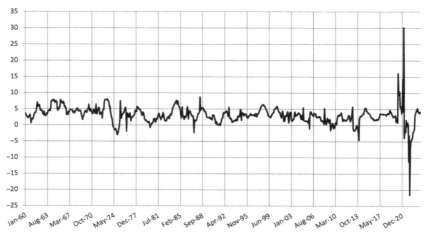

Source: Data from FRED.

Figure 1.3   Growth rate of US real personal disposable income

most severe months were in 2022. The table shows clearly that this crisis is by far worse than the crisis of the 1970s.

The most severe cost of living crises are the products of hyperinflation, which occurs when inflation runs at an extremely high (and typically, but not necessarily, accelerating) rate, to the extent that it spirals out of control. Hyperinflation brings with it a severe cost of living crisis because real income drops to almost zero very quickly. Figure 1.4 shows what would have happened to real income calculated from a constant nominal income of 100 in some of the worst hyperinflations in history. The worst ever hyperinflation hit Hungary during the period August 1945–July 1946 where the daily inflation rate peaked at 207%. At that rate, real income would have dropped to less than 1% of its original value in five days. The second worst was the hyperinflation of Zimbabwe (March 2007–November 2008) where the daily inflation rate peaked at 98%. At that rate, real income would have declined to less than 1% of its original value in seven days. In the least bad of these hyperinflations (Poland, January 1923–January 1924), real income would have lost half of its original value in 18 days. The following is what Victor Klemperer, a German scholar, wrote about how he saw the hyperinflation of the 1920s (Bisno, 2023):

"How long will we still have something to eat? Where will we next have to tighten our belts?" Meat would soon reach 3 billion marks per pound. Butter was twice that sum. A pound of potatoes and a glass of beer, staples of the German diet, came in at 50 million and 150 million marks, respectively. It was best just to forget about

Table 1.1   Severity index of cost of living crises (US data)

Month/Year	Growth Rate of PDI	Inflation Rate	Severity Index
March 2022	−21.5	8.5	100.0
January 2022	−11.2	7.6	62.6
December 2013	−4.6	11.8	54.6
April 2022	−7.4	8.2	51.9
February 2022	−3.1	12.2	50.9
September 2022	−2.3	12.1	47.9
June 2022	−4.6	8.4	43.4
July 2022	−4.3	8.2	41.8
August 2022	−3.8	8.0	39.0
December 1974	−2.6	8.9	38.4
November 1974	−3.0	8.5	38.2
April 1987	−2.3	8.2	35.0
May 2022	−4.7	4.1	29.5
November 2013	−2.4	5.2	25.3
July 2021	−2.1	3.7	19.2
April 2021	−3.9	1.2	17.1
October 1974	−2.3	1.5	12.7

Source: Author's own.

grains, their importation having all but ceased. A pound of rye bread cost more than 100 billion marks by November 1923.

Bisno (2023) tells a story about Betty Scholem, a Berlin resident who wrote the following in a letter she sent to her son on 15 October 1923: "Conditions have taken a catastrophic turn here … . This letter cost 15 million marks to send and it will be 30 million beginning the day after tomorrow." She and her husband estimated their expenses in the billions as the monthly inflation rate approached 30,000%. This story and similar stories from other episodes of hyperinflation describe the characteristics of a cost of living crisis on steroid.

When the economy is experiencing stagflation, a cost of living crisis would materialise as a result of rising prices and declining (or vanishing) nominal wages. This state of affairs was present in the 1970s when major economies were experiencing inflation and unemployment at the same time. On this occasion, the cost of living crisis had arisen primarily as a result of resurgent inflation. We have already seen a comparison between the present crisis and the crisis of the 1970s. On the surface, a crisis caused by inflation and unem-

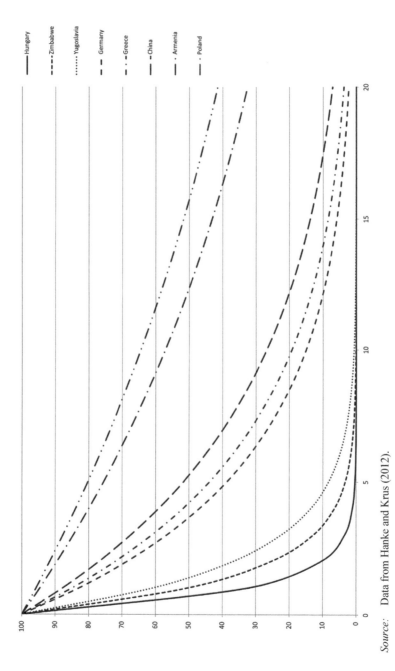

Source: Data from Hanke and Krus (2012).

Figure 1.4   *Erosion of real income under hyperinflation*

ployment should be more severe than a crisis caused by inflation only, which means that the crisis of the 1970s is worse than the present one. However, we have seen that this is not the case because there was a better social safety net in the 1970s than the present time. This again shows that the severity of a cost of living crisis is determined by other factors besides inflation.

1.5   IMF-INSTIGATED CRISES IN DEVELOPING COUNTRIES

Some cost of living crises in developing countries have been caused not by domestic inflation or domestic policy in general, but by the neoliberal principles implicit in the Washington Consensus, which are imposed on those countries by the International Monetary Fund (IMF) as a condition for receiving IMF loans. The conditionality provision of the IMF invariably leads to riots as the cost of living soars in response to the marketisation of the production of essential goods through liberalisation, privatisation and the removal of subsidies. Conditionality is also a common reason for reducing government services, rising unemployment and social instability.

Table 1.2 shows some examples of IMF-instigated cost of living crises, which are described in detail by Moosa and Moosa (2019) and by Woodroffe and Ellis-Jones (2000). The difference between the current crisis and the crises listed in Table 1.2 is that the current crisis is globalised whereas those listed in Table 1.2 are localised. However, the similarities are startling. In Chapter 5, it will be argued that a major cause of the current crisis is the adoption by developed countries of neoliberalism, a set of doctrines that are used to justify a brutal economic system that works for the benefit of a minority at the expense of the majority. The IMF has been imposing neoliberalism on developing countries through the principles of the Washington Consensus as embodied in the conditionality provision.

Countries requesting loans from the IMF are expected to abide by the neoliberal principles of the Washington Consensus that include privatisation, liberalisation and deregulation, which inevitably lead to a higher cost of living resulting from the exorbitant prices set by the profit-maximising firms producing essential goods and services. Under the present crisis, people are feeling the pinch because of rising prices of food, energy and other essential items. This is exactly what happened in the cost of living crises produced by following IMF recommendations, which lead to loss of jobs, deprivation of the services provided by the public sector, higher prices, and lower wages. In Bolivia in 2000, people faced a 200% rise in the price of water because of privatisation. In Egypt in 1977, the removal of subsidies led to a quadrupling of the price of bread. In Costa Rica in 2000, the privatisation and selling of the electricity sector to foreign investors led to a sharp increase in the price of

Table 1.2   *Examples of cost of living crises caused by IMF conditionality*

Country	Year	IMF Conditionality Prescription
Argentina	2000	Cuts in social security expenditure, including unemployment benefits and severance pay
Argentina	2018	Abolishing half of government departments
Bolivia	2000	Privatisation of all remaining public enterprises, including the water industry, leading to a 200% hike in water prices
Brazil	2000	Boosting privatisation programmes and enhancing the liberalisation of external trade
Colombia	1999	A "structural reform agenda", including policies to downsize the public sector, mainly through privatisation and reduced public sector spending
Costa Rica	2000	Boosting private sector participation in areas previously reserved for the public sector and allowing a greater role for foreign investors in electricity generation, insurance and banking
Ecuador	2000	Introduction of "reforms", including dollarisation of the economy, wage restraint and the removal of subsidies, as well as "important structural reforms" in the labour market and the oil sector, privatisation, and a "more liberal trade regime"
Egypt	1977	Removal of state subsidies on basic foodstuffs, including bread
Egypt	2017	Introducing major cutbacks to subsidies and instructing bakeries to reduce the sales of subsidised bread as part of a series of austerity measures
Honduras	2000	Privatisation of telecommunications and electricity distribution and "reform" of the social security and pension system
Kenya	2000	Macroeconomic and structural "reforms", civil service "reform" and privatisation
Morocco	1984	"Economic stabilisation", involving, among other measures, the withdrawal of subsidies on basic goods
Nigeria	2000	Structural "reforms" to tackle serious deficiencies in the provision of power, telecommunications and oil products

Country	Year	IMF Conditionality Prescription
Paraguay	2000	Proceeding with the "necessary changes" in the civil service and the social security system, as well as a reduction in the minimum wage
South Africa	2000	Structural "reforms" in the areas of labour market, trade liberalisation and privatisation to attract foreign investment and enhance "efficiency"
Tunisia	1984	Removal of food subsidies, as part of the "economic stabilisation programme", leading to a sudden doubling of bread prices
Tunisia	2018	Measures aimed at reducing the budget deficit, including higher service and consumption taxes, leading to a general hike in the prices of goods and services
Zambia	2000	Limiting credit to public enterprises and completing the transition to a market economy, including the privatisation of the remaining public utilities and the operations of the oil sector

Source: Author's own.

electricity. In 2000 in Paraguay, people suffered a reduction or a total loss of income as a result of "necessary changes" in the civil service and the social security system, as well as reduction in the minimum wage. In 2018 in Sudan, people had to cope with a sudden sharp rise in the prices of bread, sugar and electricity. In all cases involving "reform" of the oil sector, people end up paying sharply higher prices for petrol at a time when they lose income or accept lower income as a result of privatisation.

1.6   DIMENSIONS OF THE CRISIS: A SIMULATION EXERCISE

A cost of living crisis is characterised by declining real wages, which means that a crisis has two dimensions, prices and wages. Prices are those of the goods and services that wage earners consume, proxied by the CPI or one of its components, such as a price index for food. Wages here pertain to disposable income, what is left after taxes. This is why a crisis may be caused by prices rising faster than wages or rising prices and falling wages.

In this section a simulation exercise is conducted to examine three propositions about interaction between wages and prices. The first proposition is that a cost of living crisis arises only if inflation outpaces nominal wage growth, which means that high inflation is neither a necessary nor a sufficient condition for a cost of living crisis to be present. To substantiate this proposition, we simulate the general price level (CPI) and average wages over 40 periods under four scenarios for average wages: (i) staying unchanged, (ii) growing approximately at the same rate as the inflation rate, (iii) growing at a lower rate than inflation, and (iv) growing at a higher rate than inflation. The simulation results are shown in Figure 1.5, which displays the trajectory of real wages under the four scenarios. Under scenarios 1 and 2, the real wage rate declines, implying the presence of a cost of living crisis. Under scenarios 3 and 4, there is no crisis because nominal wages grow either at the same rate or a higher rate than the inflation rate, which respectively implies stable and rising real wages. A corollary of the first proposition is that the severity of the cost of living crisis is determined by the difference between the growth rates of prices and wages.

In reality, real wages do not rise or fall consistently as shown in Figure 1.5. Hence, a second simulation is conducted over 160 periods, divided into four intervals (0–40), (41–80), (81–120) and (121–160). The results of this simulation are exhibited in Figure 1.6, showing that real wages fall sharply in the interval (0–40) (as in scenario 1), stabilise in the interval (41–80) (scenario 2), rise in the interval (81–120) (scenario 4), and fall moderately in the interval (121–160) (scenario 3). This means that this hypothetical economy experiences cost of living crises during the intervals (0–40) and (121–160).

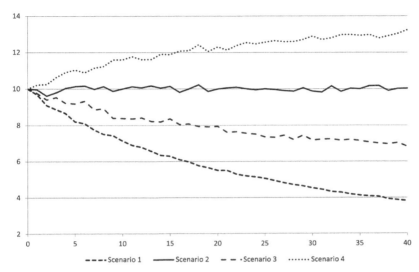

Source: Data simulation.

Figure 1.5   *Real wages under four scenarios (simulated data)*

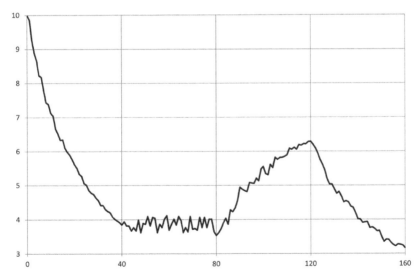

Source: Data simulation.

Figure 1.6   *Real wages under changing CPI behaviour (simulated data)*

Proposition 2 is that hyperinflation produces the most severe cost of living crisis because under hyperinflation prices rise at such a high rate that wages cannot catch up, leading to a rapid decline in real wages. To confirm this proposition, the price level is simulated under four scenarios where inflation runs at 50%, 40%, 30% and 20% per period, while keeping nominal wages constant at 10. Figure 1.7 shows the simulation results for the general price level and real wages under the four scenarios. We can see that real wages drop very quickly, but more quickly under scenario 1 at an inflation rate of 50% per period. However, Figure 1.8 shows that if nominal wages grow at 30% per period, then there is no cost of living crisis when the inflation rate is 20% or 30% because at these inflation rates, real wages are either stable or rising.

Proposition 3 is that a cost of living crisis is mostly related to the prices of essential items, which means that a crisis will not materialise if the prices of essentials fall, even if the overall price level rises. For this purpose we run a simulation in which the nominal wage is kept constant, the price of essentials falls at the rate of 0.1% per period, while the price of non-essentials rises by 0.3% per period. For simplicity, we assume that the general price level is the average of the prices of essentials and non-essentials. Figure 1.9 shows the results of simulating real wages over 40 periods. We can see that while real wages in terms of the general price level fall, they actually rise in terms of the price of essentials. Hence, there is no cost of living crisis because people can cut down on the consumption of non-essential items.

1.7   CONCLUDING REMARKS

A cost of living crisis is a state of affairs where most people cannot afford to buy essential goods and services, which are required for "living". It is important to emphasise that in a cost of living crisis, most people (not all people) cannot afford to pay for living essentials. Therefore, a cost of living crisis could result from rising prices, stagnant or declining incomes, or a combination thereof. In an extreme case, a cost of living crisis arises when people lose their incomes, in which case they cannot afford to buy essential goods and services, even under conditions of price stability. A cost of living crisis on steroid occurs when a country experiences hyperinflation.

The current cost of living crisis is a product of rising prices producing declining or stagnant real wages. It is global, in the sense that it encompasses developed and developing countries. However, not all cost of living crises are global. A crisis could hit one country experiencing rising prices and/or stagnant wages and/or high unemployment. In this case, the crisis is localised, resulting from bad economic policy, natural disasters or political instability. A cost of living crisis may even be personalised for someone who cannot

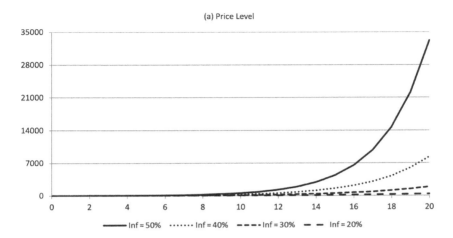

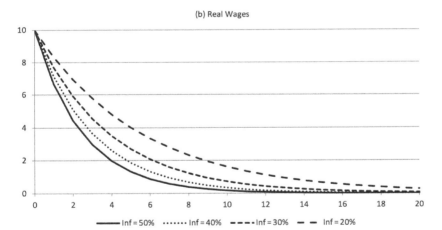

Source: Data simulation.

Figure 1.7   *Real wages under hyperinflation with constant nominal wages (simulated data)*

afford to buy living essentials because of the loss of income as a result of redundancy or illness.

Localised crises can also result from policies imposed on particular countries from the outside. This is a typical characteristic of the cost of living crises that have been experienced by developing countries requesting assistance from the IMF, which requires satisfying conditions that invariably lead to cost

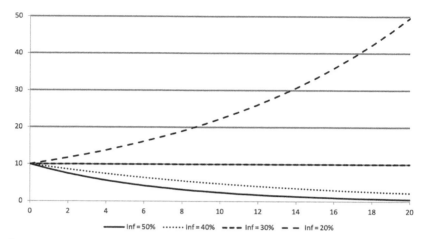

Source: Data simulation.

Figure 1.8   *Real wages under hyperinflation with growing nominal*
                  wages (simulated data)

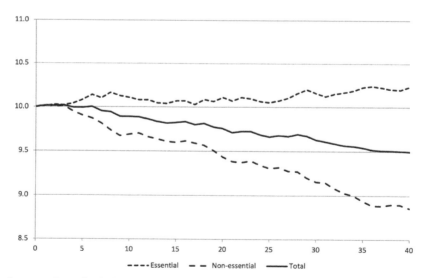

Source: Data simulation.

Figure 1.9   *Real wages in terms of essential and non-essential items*
                  (simulated data)

of living crises and even riots. This scenario is not exclusive to developing countries because it has happened to Greece as a result of the austerity measures imposed by the European Union. Austerity, as a source of cost of living crises, has been experienced by many developed countries, not because of the imposition of conditions by an external party but by a government that follows the rules of neoliberalism.

It is rather strange that in the midst of the current crisis, the Organisation for Economic Co-operation and Development (OECD) has been calling for "bold reforms" that are similar to those recommended by the IMF over decades, even though IMF-prescribed "reforms" have proved to be a source of misery in the countries at the receiving end. The OECD's *Economic Outlook 2023* states that strong and sustainable growth requires scaling back and better targeting of fiscal support. The OECD also recommends that central banks "need to maintain restrictive policies until inflationary pressures start abating". Additionally, the OECD notes that "the world economy needs ambitious structural policy reforms including reenergising labour and product markets, removing cross-border trade barriers, promoting competition and adapting competition policies to the digital era". These are the very policies that have led to the aggravation and globalisation of the current cost of living crisis.

Two issues implicit in the OECD's recommendations will be discussed in the coming chapters. In Chapters 4 and 5, we will discuss the causes of the current crisis, which is typically blamed on Vladimir Putin and the coronavirus. It will be argued that a major contributor to the current crisis is some 40 years of neoliberalism, which has produced both rising prices (for example, by sustaining profit-push inflation) and stagnant real wages (resulting from the transfer of income from labour to capital). The second issue stems from the OECD's recommendations that central banks "need to maintain restrictive policies", meaning that central banks will have to raise interest rates further or maintain them at high levels. In Chapter 8, it will be argued that interest rate hikes cannot and did not produce the fall in inflation rates in 2023. Unlike what central bankers and politicians claim, interest rate hikes do not lead to the containment, but rather to the aggravation, of the crisis.

2. The cost of living crisis as a global phenomenon

2.1 INTRODUCTION

In this chapter we examine the current cost of living crisis as a global phenomenon. It is global in the sense that it has hit every country because it is propelled by global factors. Even though the crisis can be characterised as being global, it is not an "equal opportunity agent", in the sense that it has not affected countries equally. Rather, one can observe cross-country variation with respect to the severity of the crisis. The degree of severity is determined by domestic factors such as the productive capacity of the economy and the extent of deindustrialisation, as well as the availability of a social safety net, a welfare state and universal healthcare. A unique factor that has made the crisis more severe in the UK than in other European countries is Brexit, which is believed to have contributed to the escalation of inflation and restricted the availability of goods imported from the European Union.

Five global factors are identified by A. Taylor (2022) as the causes of the crisis – what he calls "5 problems behind the cost of living crisis": the COVID-19 pandemic, the war in Ukraine, slowdown of the Chinese economy, climate change and inflation contagion (the phenomenon that inflation in one country is transmitted through trade and financial flows to its trading partners). Obviously, these five "problems" are global in nature. Likewise, Timmins and Thomas (2022) identify seven causes of the crisis: (i) rising energy prices globally, (ii) shortages of goods as a result of the pandemic, (iii) rising shipping costs, (iv) rising wages due to tightness of labour markets, (v) climate change, (vi) trade barriers, and (vii) the end of pandemic support. One of these factors, rising shipping costs, re-emerged as an important cost-push factor in late 2023 as a result of the Israeli attack on Gaza, which prompted Yemen to attack ships heading for Israel through the Red Sea. Shipping costs went up because of rising insurance premiums and because of the diversion of some ships to the longer route around Africa.

As stated before, one reason for different degrees of severity is the capacity of the economy to cope with a crisis of this sort. In this chapter we examine the crisis and its effects on developed and developing countries collectively, but we take a special look at the crisis in the UK. We start with an examination of the crisis in developed countries.

2.2 THE COST OF LIVING CRISIS IN DEVELOPED COUNTRIES

We start by examining data on CPI inflation in OECD countries and country groups over the period October 2017 to November 2023. Figure 2.1 displays the inflation rates for four countries and two country groups. The inverted V-shaped formation implies a similar pattern of rising followed by declining inflation rate. The same pattern can be observed by looking at Table 2.1, which shows the rise and fall of inflation for a larger number of countries and country groups. The table reports lows and highs of the inflation rate measured as the percentage change in the CPI in a particular month relative to the same month of the previous year.

The most striking observation is that the rise in inflation started way before the outbreak of the war in Ukraine, in which case current inflation cannot be blamed squarely on Vladimir Putin. In most cases, the resurgence of inflation started in 2020, which means that it is associated with the COVID-19 pandemic and the resulting disruption of the production of goods and services. In two countries, Czechia and Hungary, the resurgence of inflation started in 2018 before the advent of the pandemic. In all cases, the peak of inflation was reached in late 2022 or early 2023, which means that the war in Ukraine did aggravate the situation. Duration refers to the number of months between the lows and highs of inflation, ranging between 59 months in Hungary and 16 months in Luxembourg. In most cases, however, duration is about 24 months.

Figure 2.2 displays the percentage change in energy and food prices where we can observe similar behaviour as in Figure 2.1 (the rise and fall of food and energy price inflation). One can plausibly suggest that the decline in the CPI inflation rate has happened because of the decline of inflation in food and energy, not because of the use of interest rate policy. This proposition is plausible because the demand for energy and food is interest insensitive. It is noteworthy, however, that a declining inflation rate does not imply the containment of the crisis because prices are still rising (and real incomes declining), albeit at progressively lower rates.

Inflation is one side of the cost of living crisis, the other side being wage growth. A cost of living crisis would not arise if wages grew as fast as or faster than inflation, such that real wages remain constant or rise over time. This proposition was illustrated by using a simulation exercise in Chapter 1. Figure 2.3 shows the growth of real average wages (RAW) and real minimum wages (RMW) over time in 12 OECD countries, based on data provided by the OECD. The situation does not look good in any of the 12 countries. In

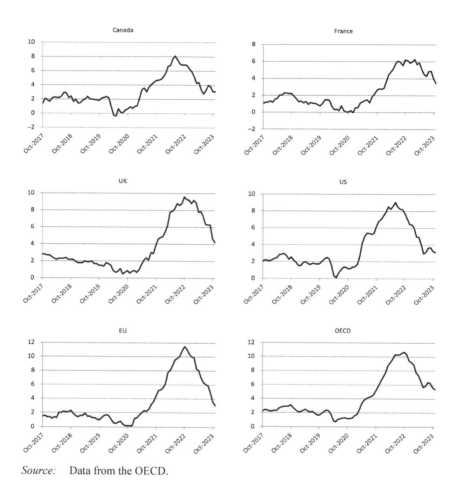

Source: Data from the OECD.

Figure 2.1   CPI inflation in selected OECD countries (all items)

Australia, sustained growth in real average and minimum wages was followed
by a decline in 2021 and 2022. In Belgium, real minimum wages have been
declining since 2009. In Canada, real minimum wages declined in 2021 and
2022. In France, real average wages went down in 2021 while real minimum
wages remained flat. In Greece, real average wages have been declining since
2010 whereas real minimum wages declined between 2009 and 2013, and
also in 2021 and 2022. In Ireland, real minimum wages declined in 2021 and
2022 whereas real average wages declined in 2022. In Japan, real minimum
wages have been rising but real average wages have been almost flat. In the

Table 2.1   *The rise and fall of inflation (2017–23)*

	Low (%)	Month-Year	High (%)	Month-Year	Duration (months)
Austria	0.6	05-2020	11.2	01-2023	32
Belgium	0.3	01-2021	12.3	10-2022	21
Canada	-0.4	05-2020	8.1	06-2022	25
Czechia	1.7	03-2018	18.0	09-2022	54
Denmark	0.0	10-2020	10.1	10-2022	30
Estonia	-1.7	05-2020	24.8	08-2022	27
Finland	-0.3	04-2020	9.1	11-2022	31
France	0.0	12-2020	6.3	02-2023	28
Germany	-1.0	07-2020	8.8	11-2022	28
Greece	-2.3	12-2020	12.1	06-2022	18
Hungary	1.9	02-2018	25.7	01-2022	59
Ireland	-1.5	10-2020	9.2	10-2022	24
Italy	-0.6	09-2020	11.8	11-2022	26
Latvia	-0.7	11-2020	22.2	09-2022	22
Lithuania	0.2	12-2020	24.1	09-2022	21
Luxembourg	-0.1	02-2021	7.4	06-2022	16
Netherlands	0.7	08-2020	14.5	09-2022	25
Norway	0.7	11-2020	7.5	10-2022	23
Poland	0.7	01-2019	18.4	02-2023	49

	Low (%)	Month-Year	High (%)	Month-Year	Duration (months)
Portugal	−0.7	05-2020	10.1	10-2022	29
Slovak Republic	0.7	01-2021	15.4	02-2023	25
Slovenia	−1.2	05-2020	11.0	08-2022	27
Spain	−0.9	05-2020	10.8	07-2022	26
Sweden	−0.4	04-2020	12.3	12-2022	33
Switzerland	−1.3	06-2020	3.5	08-2022	26
United Kingdom	0.5	08-2020	9.6	10-2022	26
United States	0.1	05-2020	9.1	06-2022	25
European Union	0.2	12-2020	11.5	10-2022	22
Euro area	−0.3	12-2020	10.6	10-2022	22
G7	0.2	05-2020	7.8	06-2022	25
OECD (Europe)	1.2	10-2020	16.6	10-2022	24
OECD (Total)	0.7	05-2020	10.7	10-2022	29

Source: Author's own.

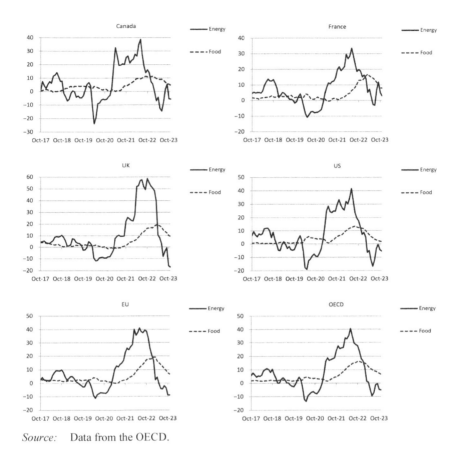

Source: Data from the OECD.

Figure 2.2   CPI inflation in selected OECD countries (energy and food)

Netherlands, real average wages have been flat since 2010, whereas real minimum wages were flat and went through sharp decline in 2021 and 2022. In New Zealand, real minimum wages declined in 2021. In Spain, real average wages have been flat since 2010, whereas real minimum wages went down in 2021 and 2022. In the UK, real average wages have been through weak growth since 2008, whereas real minimum wages declined in 2022. In the US, there has been strong growth in real average wages, but real minimum wages have been consistently declining since 2010.

In Table 2.2 we observe the average compound growth rates of real average and minimum wages over the period 2001–22 and in 2022 only. We can see that real minimum wages declined in all countries in 2022, with the exception

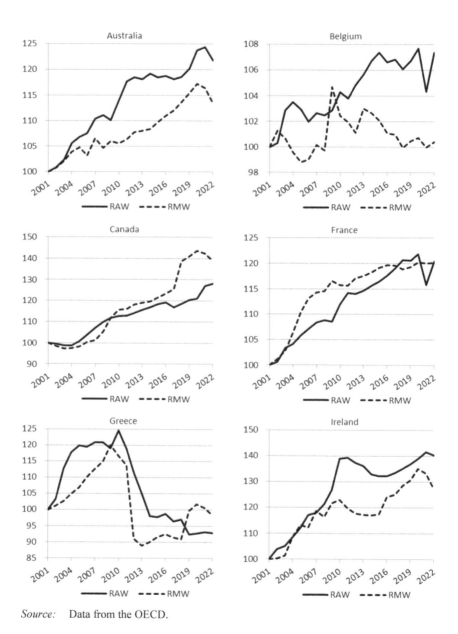

Source: Data from the OECD.

Figure 2.3   Real average and minimum wages in selected OECD
               countries (2001 = 100)

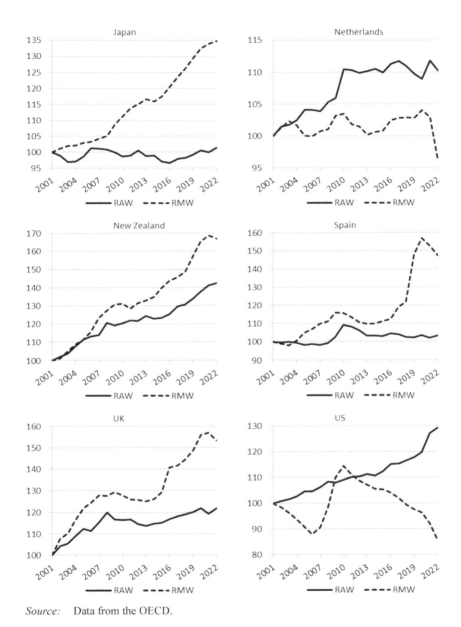

Source: Data from the OECD.

Figure 2.3 *(continued)*

Table 2.2   *Growth rates of real average and minimum wages (%)*

Country	Real Average Wages (RAW)		Real Minimum Wages (RMW)	
	2001–22	2022	2001–22	2022
Australia	0.94	−2.10	0.60	−2.59
Belgium	0.34	2.90	0.02	0.43
Canada	1.19	0.69	1.58	−2.28
France	0.89	3.94	0.88	0.07
Greece	−0.35	−0.32	−0.08	−2.22
Ireland	1.63	−0.82	1.16	−4.51
Japan	0.07	1.45	1.43	0.62
Netherlands	0.47	−1.40	−0.18	−6.53
New Zealand	1.69	0.89	2.47	−1.16
Spain	0.16	1.41	1.87	−3.42
UK	0.94	2.14	2.05	−2.26
US	1.23	1.71	−0.75	−7.41

Source: Author's own.

of Belgium, France and Japan where the growth rate was less than 1%. In the US, an already low real minimum wage went down by 7.4% in 2022, simply because the nominal minimum wage has been flat for a long period of time. In Figure 2.4, we can see that the US has the lowest minimum wage relative to the average wage, and this is why poverty is more rampant in the US than in other OECD countries.

It follows that the current crisis is not only due to resurgent inflation but also to stagnant wages. Surely stagnant real wages cannot be blamed on Putin, like almost everything else, but the phenomenon can be attributed to the dominance of neoliberalism as the guiding economic philosophy. Neoliberalism has been instrumental in the transfer of income from the poor to the rich and from labour to capital. This is why it will be argued in Chapter 5 that neoliberalism is more responsible for the crisis than Putin.

2.3   THE COST OF LIVING CRISIS IN THE UK

Now we consider in detail the dimensions of the cost of living crisis in the UK, which seems to be in a worse shape than other European countries. For example, Williams (2022) acknowledges the effect of the "chaotic international backdrop" but he highlights the unique difficulties encountered by UK households who faced (at the beginning of the crisis) "the twin shocks of the

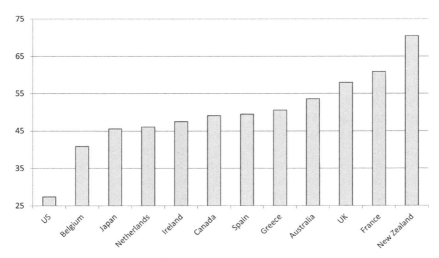

Source: Data from the OECD.

Figure 2.4 *Minimum relative to average wages in 2022 (%)*

energy price cap rising and a historic increase in taxation in April [2022]". Partington and Kirk (2022) attribute the cost of living crisis in the UK to "a snapback in demand for goods and services after lockdown, when prices fell sharply, as well as the impact from supply chain disruption due to Covid-19 hitting factory production and global trade". While these factors are equally valid for other OECD countries, the UK has a specific problem, Brexit-related disruptions. We will come back to the effect of Brexit later on.

In addition to Brexit, this crisis comes at the wrong time following the rapid dismantling of public services and reduction in income support, and when the government pushed for an increase in national insurance contributions. This is another reason why the crisis has particularly hit the poor who are faced with the problem of managing, with the same level of nominal income, a larger menu of more expensive essentials. Poor households have been particularly hit because inflation is concentrated in energy and food, given that the poor spend a larger proportion of their incomes on these items than discretionary, less essential items. Partington and Kirk (2022) cite a report prepared by the Resolution Foundation stating that, on average, the lowest-income families spend twice as much proportionally on food and housing bills as the richest. They also quote Dave Innes, head of economics at the Joseph Rowntree Foundation (a poverty charity), as saying the following: "If you're already spending mainly on essentials, where are you going to cut back if prices are going up?" The Foundation estimates that low-income single-adult households could be forced to spend 54% of their income on gas and electricity (Butler, 2022).

Even though the crisis has enriched the owners of supermarkets who have raised the prices of food items by more than the inflation rate, some supermarket owners have been complaining that they are losing the customers who can no longer buy the same amounts of the same items as before the advent of the crisis. For example, Monroe (2022) quotes the managing director of Iceland (a supermarket chain) who, in an interview with ITV, stated that his stores were losing customers, not to other competitors or better offers, but to food banks and hunger, to starvation and charity. Monroe tells a story about "an elderly gentleman who confessed he had eaten a teaspoon of toothpaste for his dinner in order to fool himself into thinking he had chewed, swallowed, tasted and digested something". A frequent observation in British supermarkets is the tendency of shoppers to remove some items from the shopping basket at checkout when the total comes to more than the pre-allocated budget.

Other observations, according to Monroe (2022), include "juggling late and delayed benefit payments, knocking a bit off each bill to keep the wolves from the door, shopping around for the cheapest school uniform that won't fall apart in the washing machine, and scrutinising the shelf-edge labels for the 'price per 100g' of each product, ignoring the brightly coloured offers". As a result, he suggests that the CPI should be replaced with a new price index, "one that will document the disappearance of the budget lines and the insidiously creeping prices of the most basic versions of essential items at the supermarket". In other words, Monroe proposes the modification of the CPI to include the very basic and essential items (for example, rice and potato as opposed to ready meals and wine bottles).

Let us now consider the numbers published by the Office for National Statistics. Figure 2.5 displays the overall CPI inflation (all items) as well as the percentage change in the indices for rent, food, restaurants and cafes, motor fuel, and gas. We can readily see that inflation in the UK picked up in early 2016 and peaked in November 2017, the period immediately following the Brexit vote in 2016, which led to depreciation of the pound. The current inflation started in May 2021 and peaked in March 2023. We can readily observe remarkable correspondence between overall inflation and food price inflation, as indicated by a correlation coefficient of 0.93. Gas price inflation is more strongly correlated with the overall inflation rate than motor fuel price inflation.

In Table 2.3 we can see that the average annual compound growth rate of the CPI (overall inflation) was exactly equal to the rate of food inflation over the period 2013–23, even though food prices rose much faster than the overall CPI in 2022 and 2023. We can also see the big decline in the prices of gas and motor fuel in 2023. Again, this indicates that it was not the use of interest rates

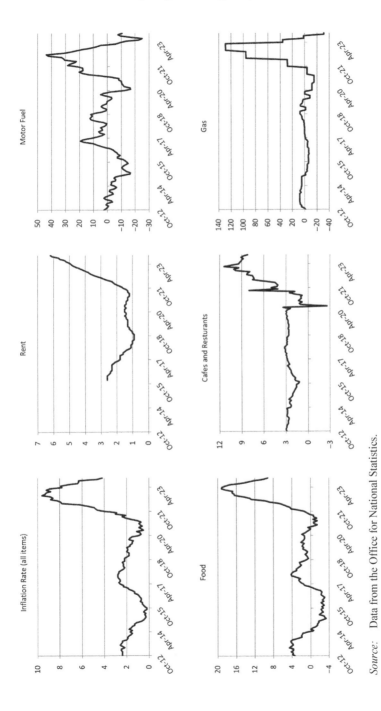

Source: Data from the Office for National Statistics.

Figure 2.5   *Indicators of UK CPI inflation*

Table 2.3   *Indicators of UK inflation (%)*

	Inflation	Food	Restaurants and Cafes	Motor Fuel	Gas
November 2013	1.9	2.8	2.8	−3.6	6.3
November 2014	1.1	−1.7	2.4	−5.9	5.1
November 2015	0.4	−2.4	1.2	−12.9	−6.4
November 2016	1.5	−2.1	2.8	7.4	−4.6
November 2017	2.8	4.2	3.1	3.5	0.1
November 2018	2.2	0.5	2.6	8.9	7.6
November 2019	1.5	2.1	2.9	−2.9	−8.7
November 2020	0.6	−0.5	0.8	−10.0	−15.4
November 2021	4.6	2.5	4.2	28.5	28.1
November 2022	9.3	16.5	9.8	17.2	128.9
November 2023	4.2	9.2	8.2	−10.6	−31.0
Average (compound)	2.7	2.7	3.7	1.1	4.8

Source: Author's own.

that brought the inflation rate down in 2023, neither was it a vindication of the promise made by the prime minister that he would halve the inflation rate (Baker, 2023; Hatton, 2023).

Even though it is common these days to blame it all on Vladimir Putin, UK inflation can be blamed in part on David Cameron and Boris Johnson because Cameron initiated the Brexit referendum and Johnson was an instrumental campaigner for the "yes" vote. It is now widely believed that Brexit has contributed significantly to the resurgence of inflation in the UK. On 31 May 2022, an opinion poll was conducted asking the question whether or not Brexit had contributed to the cost of living crisis in the UK. In response, 67% of the participants thought that Brexit had made their cost of living higher, compared with 5% who said it had made it lower (Clark, 2022).

The view that Brexit has aggravated inflation in the UK, which is expressed by most of the survey participants, is shared by former officials of the Bank of England. For example, in June 2023, Mark Carney, the former Bank governor, claimed that Brexit reduced the UK economy's capacity to produce goods and services, resulting in the "weaker pound, higher inflation and weaker growth we're experiencing". He also said that Brexit was a "unique adjustment", implying that it explained why inflation was higher and more enduring in the UK than in the Eurozone (Bourne, 2023).

The adverse effect of Brexit on the cost of living in the UK was transmitted through several channels. The first channel is the health and safety checks on imports from the EU, which were reintroduced in January 2021 when the UK exited the EU's internal market and customs union. Ziady (2023) notes that Brexit has already contributed to Britain's high inflation by introducing friction into the country's most important trading relationship, given that the EU is the source of 28% of the food consumed in the UK. In August 2023, the British government delayed health and safety checks on food imports from the EU for the fifth time in three years amid fears that the extra controls would push up food prices and disrupt vital supplies. Bakker et al. (2023) found that Brexit was responsible for about a third of UK food price inflation since 2019, adding nearly £7 billion to Britain's grocery bill. Their results show that between December 2019 and March 2023, food prices rose by 25% and that in the absence of Brexit this figure would have been 8%.

Another channel of transmission is the Brexit-triggered depreciation of the pound. Keegan (2023), who believes that Brexit is the reason why inflation is so much higher in the UK than in other countries, notes that the 2016 Brexit referendum was followed by a dramatic depreciation of the pound, which led to higher import prices in pound terms, particularly the price of food imported from the EU. As a matter of fact, Keegan believes that "Brexit is the biggest act of self-harm this country has imposed upon itself since the English civil war of 1642–51." He sarcastically describes the adverse effects of Brexit as follows:

> For the Conservatives, Brexit "freedom" involves an increasingly bitter civil war within the party and the freedom to demonstrate that Brexit is a disaster. Quite apart from the manifest economic damage, Brexit also offers the freedom to queue at ports and airports, disrupt parcel services, enjoy empty shelves, stop your children from enjoying educational opportunities abroad, and severely limit how much time you can spend in the EU, even if you own property there.

The third channel of transmission is a tighter labour market. Askew (2023) quotes the former deputy governor of the Bank of England, Charlie Bean, as saying that the labour market in the UK was "much tighter" than on the continent, reflecting the exodus of half a million workers during the COVID pandemic. Bean also suggested that "Brexit has made it harder for firms to suck in the extra labour they need at short notice from abroad." Labour short-ages create inflationary pressure as businesses have to compete for labour by offering higher salaries, which feed into the economy. Brexit has made it harder for EU nationals to work in Britain at a time when the pandemic forced thousands of foreign workers to go back home. Brexit-triggered inflation also arises from the observation that post-Brexit, British companies face less pres-sure to reduce prices or enhance productivity, both of which are inflationary. This is why Bean concludes that "the UK is on a path to long-term decline, as

Brexit reduces trade and economic growth". Keegan (2023) believes that "the solution is to rejoin the EU", not that this would stop UK inflation but it would perhaps make things less bad.

2.4   THE COST OF LIVING CRISIS IN DEVELOPING COUNTRIES

Globalisation has brought with it the very unpleasant situation that a crisis somewhere in the world becomes a global crisis by spreading to every corner of the world. Typically, a global crisis has more adverse effects on low-income developing countries than developed countries, since developing countries lack the resources required to deal with a crisis. In this respect, this crisis is not different. It is affecting consumers in low-income developing countries where food and energy comprise a larger share of a typical household budget, magnifying the impact of higher food and energy prices. Several developing countries in Asia and Africa that are reeling under high debt servicing costs, capital outflows, and diminishing availability of credit from foreign lenders are in deeper trouble than others. A stark and growing divide has emerged between countries that can access financing at reasonable terms and those that cannot, exposing the latter to high risk of a fiscal crisis.

The war in Ukraine has disrupted energy and food markets, inflicting disproportionately more pain on developing countries. In a study of 159 developing countries commissioned by the United Nations Development Programme (UNDP), Molina et al. (2022) find that rising prices of key commodities have devastated the poorest households. The crisis, according to the UNDP study, "may have pushed over 51 million people into extreme poverty at $1.90 a day, and an additional 20 million at $3.20 a day, with hotspots in Sub-Saharan Africa, particularly in the Sahel, the Balkans and the Caspian Basin". One source of pain is rising prices, the other being rising interest rates, which exert an adverse effect on developing countries via two channels. The first is the risk of triggering further recession-induced poverty that will exacerbate the crisis even more. Depleted reserves and high levels of sovereign debt make it more difficult for developing countries to access global financial markets. The Molina et al. (2022) study concludes that developing countries "face challenges that cannot be solved without urgent attention by the global community". A UNDP official, Achim Steiner, describes the situation succinctly as follows (UNDP, 2022):

> Unprecedented price surges mean that for many people across the world, the food that they could afford yesterday is no longer attainable today … . This cost-of-living crisis is tipping millions of people into poverty and even starvation at breathtaking speed and with that, the threat of increased social unrest grows by the day.

This sentiment is shared by the UN Secretary General, António Guterres, who expresses the view that "a global cost-of-living crisis is affecting billions of people", warning that "governments are drowning in debt", that "soaring interest rates are squeezing developing countries dry", and that "over 40 per cent of people living in extreme poverty are in countries with severe debt challenges" (United Nations India, 2023). Guterres goes on to praise "efforts to help developing economies survive this financing crisis", particularly the G20 debt service suspension initiative and the distribution of special drawing rights by the IMF. In reality, the IMF itself has caused severe cost of living crises in developing countries by deploying its notorious conditionality provisions. We will come back to this point.

To understand how people around the world are experiencing and coping with the cost of living crisis, GeoPoll (2022) conducted a survey in August 2022 in nine countries from Latin America and the Caribbean, Africa, the Middle East and Asia. The survey showed double digit increases in the prices of essential items during the period between February and August 2022. Table 2.4 displays the highest percentage rise in prices in the nine countries. Some of the findings of the survey are as follows:

- Runaway price increases have not been confined to food products. Most respondents across countries are feeling the pinch in almost every aspect of their lives.
- One in four respondents says that they or a household member has gone to sleep hungry in the previous seven days because food was inadequate.

Table 2.4   Highest percentage rises in essential items in the Geopoll survey

Item	Country	Percentage Rise
Wheat	Kenya	73
Rice	Nigeria	65
Dairy	Jamaica	47
Cooking Oil	South Africa	85
Gas	Guatemala	65
Fruit	Tunisia	43
Vegetables	Tunisia	40
Meat/Egg/Fish	Guatemala	68
Sugar	Turkey	52
Fertiliser	Sri Lanka	17

Source: Author's own.

It is even worse in Kenya and Nigeria where the number rises to 44% and 36%, respectively.

- The majority of respondents in all nine countries agree that food prices have risen significantly in the previous six months, illustrating the scope and severity of the crisis.
- Most respondents (72%) said that rising prices have reduced their family's standard of living at least "somewhat". More than a third (39%) said that it has reduced their standard of living "by a lot".
- The economic crisis in Sri Lanka has led to a popular uprising and ousting of the president in July 2022. As the situation continues to deteriorate, most Sri Lankans participating in the survey said that declining incomes had left them unable to deal with the crisis. Some 90% of the respondents said that they were worse off financially than they had been six months earlier and more than half said that they were much worse off.
- Declining incomes and rising prices in Kenya have worsened the financial situation for 47% of the respondents.
- Government-financed income increases in Turkey do not appear to have been adequate to offset the country's highest inflation in decades.
- More than three out of every four respondents in South Africa (77%), Kenya (79%) and Nigeria (80%) said that they felt extremely concerned about rising prices.
- Skyrocketing food prices in Pakistan, where the average household spends more than 40% of its income on food, have pushed many families to the brink.

The cost of living crisis has created food insecurity, most notably in the developing world. In a food security update, the World Bank (2023) notes that "domestic food price inflation remains high". The update contains specific figures: inflation higher than 5% is experienced in 61.9% of low-income countries, 76.1% of lower-middle-income countries, 50% of upper-middle-income countries and 57.4% of high-income countries. In real terms, food price inflation exceeded overall inflation in 74% of the 167 countries where data are available. Figure 2.6 displays food price inflation in the ten hardest hit countries, as reported by the World Economic Forum (2023).

In response to soaring inflation, governments in developing countries are left with a daunting choice between increasing spending to support their populations, thereby burying themselves deeper in debt, and implementing austerity measures that may trigger social unrest. The International Rescue Committee (2022) reports on the dire situation in five countries that were in a bad shape even before the advent of the crisis. In Afghanistan, the crisis came on top of an economic collapse that ensued following the shift in power in August 2021. The economy has been crippled by actions taken by the US and its allies to

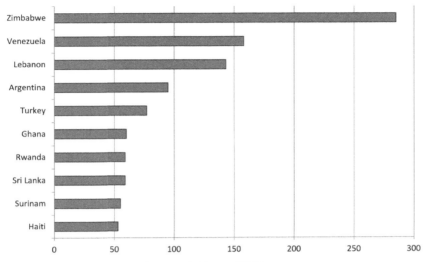

Source: Data from the World Economic Forum (2023).

Figure 2.6   *Top ten food price inflations (% in 2022)*

isolate the Taliban by cutting off Afghanistan from the international financial system. While less money is flowing into Afghanistan, the prices of basic household items rose 50%, while prices of food staples like grain and rice nearly doubled in 2021. In Lebanon, where people cannot access their bank accounts, rising prices and falling wages force consumers to turn to the black market for fuel and medicine. In Pakistan, the cost of living crisis coincided with devastating floods, pushing the economy over the brink. The situation has been made worse by the political turmoil caused by a US-orchestrated conspiracy against the former prime minister, Imran Khan. The economic fallout from the Ukraine war and a series of climate-induced disasters have left Somalia on the brink of famine. In Venezuela, the crisis came on top of devastating economic sanctions imposed by the US and supported by its allies, leading to a rapid shrinkage in the size of the economy.

The dire economic situation in Afghanistan and Venezuela was not caused by Putin and his invasion of Ukraine, but by the sanctions imposed on the two countries – this is not to say that the war in Ukraine has not contributed to the crisis. On 11 February 2022, President Biden issued an executive order to "block" (effectively seize) $7 billion of Afghanistan's reserves in the US and move them into one account at the New York Federal Reserve, allocating $3.5 billion for potential distribution to the families of the September 11 victims. The West's biggest contribution to Afghanistan's food insecurity is the sanctions on Afghani banks. Sanctions prevent Afghans from having a normal working economy and hamper remittances, leading to a significant increase in the cost of importing food. The dire situation in Afghanistan would have materialised irrespective of whether or not Putin had invaded Ukraine. The same goes for Venezuela, as crippling economic sanctions led to a cost of living crisis even before the advent of the current crisis. It is interesting to note that sanctions have been imposed on Afghanistan allegedly because the Taliban do not allow girls to go to school and on Venezuela because Madura is pursuing socialist policies that hurt ordinary people. In both cases, the ulterior motive is punishment for refusal to say "how high" when America says "jump".

2.5   CONCLUDING REMARKS

The cost of living crisis is global because resurgent inflation is global, resulting primarily from global factors operating in a globalised world. In the introduction to this chapter, the seven causes of the crisis, as envisaged by Timmins and Thomas (2022), were listed. Here, some elaboration is warranted on the seven reasons why the cost of living is going up around the world. Five of the seven factors constituting the reasons are global, which puts them out of the control of domestic policy makers, implying that the use of interest rates to curb inflation is a silly idea, to say the least. Rising wages do not constitute a global factor, because wages have been rising in some countries and stagnant in others as we shall see in Chapter 5. Rising wages cannot be a global factor, because (amongst other reasons) countries have different minimum wage legislations. This point is also relevant to the alleged price-wage spiral, which is taken by central banks as a justification for the use of interest rates to curb inflation and for demanding "restraint" from workers aspiring for higher wages to cope with the crisis. On this occasion, the price-wage spiral is a myth that will be debunked in Chapter 4. The end of pandemic support is not a global factor because countries have taken different actions with respect to pandemic support. Furthermore, it is not clear how ending pandemic support causes inflation, given that it implies declining incomes, which relieves pressure on prices.

The global nature of the cost of living crisis is evident in four studies commissioned by the European Parliament (2022), all of which appear in one document entitled "Inflation as a Global Challenge". In the first paper, "Tackling Global Inflation at a Time of Radical Uncertainty", it is suggested that "inflation is boosted by the interplay of global and domestic factors", which involve both aggregate demand and supply with different intensity in different countries. In a subsequent chapter, we will consider the issue of whether the current inflation is caused by supply or demand factors, reaching the conclusion that it is mostly driven by supply factors. The second paper deals with global monetary spillovers, in which it is suggested that inflationary pressures have triggered a largely synchronised tightening of monetary policy around the world. This means that central banks all around the world are using the faulty policy of interest rate hikes. In Chapter 8, it will be argued that interest rate hikes are not only ineffective in curbing inflation, but also that they are inflationary. In the third paper, it is argued that high inflation in the euro area is due to both internally generated demand pressures and external shocks that have led to rising food and energy prices, pointing out correctly that the latter element is more important than the former. It is suggested that "central banks need to tighten monetary policy to address high inflation", which is rather odd because the current inflation is caused primarily by global cost-push factors and domestic profit-push factors, both of which cannot be tamed by raising interest rates. However, the authors correctly note that "the simultaneous rise in inflation around the world over the past year clearly suggests that common global factors are playing an important role but this doesn't necessarily imply that the determinants of inflation are exactly the same in each economy". For example, the situation in the UK has been worsened by Brexit, which is a specific factor that has affected the supply side of the economy. In the fourth paper, it is suggested that inflation has always had a strong global component, driven mostly by volatile energy prices, and that the global shock that dominates inflation is evidently the increase in energy prices. Again, this global nature of inflation renders interest rate policy incapable of dealing with it.

Likewise, Bivens et al. (2022) argue that rising inflation is a global phenomenon, which means that high inflation in the US has not been driven by any unique American policy, such as the fiscal relief offered to people during the pandemic, neither is it due to "anything else U.S.-centric". They reject the view that inflation has been caused by excess aggregate demand generated by over-stimulation, on the grounds that this explanation is not supported by observed data. They note that countries experiencing larger declines in unemployment have not seen larger inflation spikes. Again, they correctly emphasise global supply factors and reject the demand-side explanation. All of these issues will be elaborated on in the following chapters.

The global nature of the crisis does not mean that all countries have been affected equally. For example, it can be argued that Britain is in a worse shape than other European countries because of Brexit and the early adoption of neoliberalism, which has led to deindustrialisation, financialisation and a number of adverse consequences that will be discussed in Chapter 5. However, a big difference, with respect to the effect of the crisis, can be observed between developed and developing countries. Developing countries have been more adversely affected by inflation because food and energy comprise a larger share of the budget for consumers in developing countries, magnifying the impact of rising food and energy prices. The situation is made even worse by chronic indebtedness and weak fiscal positions, leaving governments with limited means to support their populations, thereby perpetuating a cycle of poverty, hunger and civil unrest. The contribution of the IMF to this vicious cycle has been documented repeatedly (for example, Moosa and Moosa, 2019).

3. Consequences of and responses to the crisis

3.1 INTRODUCTION

People all around the world are facing severe challenges as a result of the cost of living crisis. The consequences of the crisis include its adverse effects on poverty (including child poverty), homelessness, food insecurity, indebtedness and health. It has also led to an increase in the number of women resorting or returning to prostitution, and it has changed consumer behaviour. The incidence of crime has risen as a result of the crisis, and so has the incidence of suicide, drug abuse, domestic abuse and divorce. All of these consequences of the crisis will be discussed in turn.

Responses to the crisis differ across countries but they fall under two categories: (i) measures taken to help people financially to overcome the difficulties associated with the rising cost of living, and (ii) measures taken to bring inflation under control. Measures taken to help people financially are typically temporary, some of which have already come to an end, and others were promised but not or partially implemented. They include reduced prices, price caps and freezes, tax credits, cuts in sales tax of some essential items, subsidies, cash payments and more welfare spending. Measures taken to reduce inflation and bring it under control have predominantly taken the form of using monetary policy – specifically, raising interest rates aggressively to curb demand, thereby reducing pressure on the general price level. In this chapter we consider the first set of responses, while the use of monetary policy is reserved for Chapter 8.

3.2 CONSEQUENCES OF THE CRISIS: POVERTY

Poverty arises when the financial resources of a person or a household fall below their minimum needs, putting them in a position where they cannot afford to heat their homes (if they have homes), pay rent or buy living essentials. People living below the poverty line do not have the financial resources needed to meet their basic needs. The poverty line (also called "poverty threshold", "poverty limit" or "breadline") is the minimum level of income considered to be adequate in a particular country. It is calculated by estimating the total cost of necessities for the average adult. In September 2022, the World Bank updated its global poverty lines, putting the new extreme poverty line at $2.15 per person per day, which replaces the previous $1.90 poverty line (World Bank, 2022). In the US, the poverty line for a family of four is defined by an annual level of income of $30,000 (HealthCare.com, 2023). Living in poverty intensifies the risk of early death, leading to mental and physical health problems. It is associated with housing problems, homelessness, and a high incidence of being a victim and/or a perpetrator of crime.

The connection between the cost of living crisis and poverty has two aspects. The first is that, like the COVID-19 pandemic, the crisis is disproportionately hurting poorer households. In any crisis (whether it is a pandemic or a cost of living crisis) the whole community faces challenges, but not every household is hit to the same degree. Typically, individuals and households on low incomes face far worse hardship than those who happen to be more affluent. The second aspect of the connection between the cost of living crisis and poverty is that an increasing number of people who were living above the poverty line have been driven into poverty by the crisis. This may also be true of the pandemic as people were driven into poverty as a result of losing their jobs. The situation is particularly grim because the crisis comes at a time when neoliberalism has led to the erosion of the welfare state, symbolised by cuts and freezes to social security and public services, which particularly affect people on low incomes, both in and out of work. Mcrae et al. (2023) argue that poverty in the UK is not new – rather, "poverty is deeply rooted in the UK, with more than a decade of cuts meaning millions of families across the country are struggling through financial hardship". However, they acknowledge that "many more are being pushed below the breadline" because the cost of living crisis has a greater impact on low-income households.

The crisis-triggered poverty problem in the UK is indicated by spikes in the numbers turning to charities, such as food banks. Between 1 April 2022 and 31 March 2023, food banks in the Trussell Trust's UK-wide network distributed close to three million emergency food parcels to people facing hardship – this is an increase of 37% from the same period in the previous year. More than one million of these parcels were allocated to children (Trussell Trust, 2023). The impact of poverty on children is severe, with adverse effects on brain development and educational attainment. Child poverty intensifies the risk of poverty in adulthood through unemployment and low pay.

The situation is similar in Australia where, according to the Salvation Army (2023), tens of thousands of Australians are continuing to plunge into extreme poverty, with vulnerable households turning to desperate measures to cope. The results of a survey show that 93% of respondents who reached out to the Salvation Army for support were struggling to afford basic living necessities.

This means that after paying for essential living items (such as housing, food, utilities, health and fuel) the typical respondent is living on less than $6 a day to spend or save for other expenses. Nearly one in four households cannot afford to take their children to see a doctor or a dentist and one in five are unable to provide them with three meals a day. A 55-year-old mother told the Salvation Army that she had lost 40 kilograms in the previous nine months because all of her money went on "keeping a roof over my kids' heads and trying to keep them in a safe place". Another mother said the following: "I eat the leftover food from my child's meal, if there is any, or I just don't eat." She added: "I wait at the school car park from drop-off until pick-up if I'm short on fuel", and "I have sold most of my own clothing to buy my children clothes."

Blair (2023) observes signs of poverty in the changing behaviour of consumers in Australia. He talks about those who say that they have not had a piece of red meat in months due to skyrocketing supermarket prices, and others who "started sailing the high seas of piracy after deleting their streaming accounts". Some drivers are "going easy" on the accelerator, opting to "just let it coast when I see a red light ahead". For many Australians, the common ritual of indulging in a "cafe brekky" (that is, having breakfast in a cafe) has become a luxury they can no longer afford. For most people, dining out has become a thing of the past as they opt instead for more economical meal options at home.

Some horrific facts and figures are revealed by Duffy (2023) about child poverty in Australia, based on the results of the Smith Family's community attitude survey, conducted by Essential Media nation-wide. The survey found that 72% of Australians believe that child poverty has worsened due to the crisis, an increase from 56% when the survey was conducted at the height of the pandemic in December 2020. The findings also show that 81% of the respondents believe that child poverty will get even worse in the next 12 months. The Smith Family's chief executive, Doug Taylor, refers to the "almost impossible decisions about where to use their limited funds".

3.3   CONSEQUENCES OF THE CRISIS: HOMELESSNESS

One tends to think that the homeless are those who sleep rough; those whom we see sleep on the street and beg for help. In reality, those who sleep on the street represent the tip of the iceberg. Like an iceberg, the majority of those experiencing homelessness are the "hidden" homeless, those who may be staying in temporary accommodation and those who sleep in cars, caravans and garages. Also classified as homeless are the so-called "sofa surfers" – those who are allowed to sleep on someone's sofa on a temporary basis. Fondeville and Ward (2011) classify the homeless into the following categories: (i) people without a roof over their heads who sleep rough or in overnight shelters; (ii) people without a home who have a roof over their heads but who are excluded from the legal rights of occupancy and do not have a place to pursue normal social relations; (iii) people living in insecure housing who do not have a secure tenancy and/or are threatened with eviction; (iv) people living in inadequate housing conditions (with friends or relatives, in squats, in caravans or illegal campsites, in conditions of extreme over-crowding and in other generally unsuitable places). If these definitions are adopted, the number of homeless people would be much more than what the official figures lead us to believe.

In the UK, restrictions on the ability of landlords to repossess properties and evict tenants during the pandemic came to an end in May 2021, leading to a rise in evictions and therefore homelessness. Based on figures for the people living in temporary accommodation in England, Buchanan and Burns (2023) find that in March 2023, almost 105,000 households were in temporary accommodation, including more than 131,000 children, which is 10% up on the previous year. This figure for temporary accommodation, which is the highest since records began in 1998, surpasses a previous high of 101,300 reached in 2004. The figures also show that almost 14,000 households were in hotels or bed and breakfasts in the three months to March 2023. The official figures released by the Department for Levelling Up, Housing & Communities in July 2023 (covering England only) show that between January and March 2023, 37,890 households were assessed as being threatened with homelessness, and that 41,950 households were initially assessed as homeless and therefore owed a relief duty, up 10.7% from the same quarter of the previous year.

In Australia, the situation is also grim. In March 2023, more than 95,000 people sought homelessness assistance, 83% of whom cited housing or financial issues as the reason. Kelly and Butler (2023) tell the story of one of those people, a 59-year-old woman whose rent went up from $420 to $550 a week, making it unaffordable to stay in the house she had lived in for three years. She sold all of her belongings, including her car, and moved into a bus she bought, now parked outside her son's rental home in Kalgoorlie (West Australia). Between December 2022 and March 2023, the number of people seeking homelessness assistance rose by 10.2% in New South Wales, 12.9% in Queensland, and 11.1% in Western Australia. Figure 3.1 shows the numbers in each state.

The US has a notorious record of homelessness even in the best of times. The 2023 *Annual Homelessness Report*, published by the Department of Housing and Urban Development, shows that at the end of January 2023, 653,104 people (about 20 of every 10,000 people) experienced homelessness across the US. This is the highest number of people reported as experiencing homelessness on a single night since reporting began in 2007. About 29% of the people experiencing homelessness did so as part of a family with at least

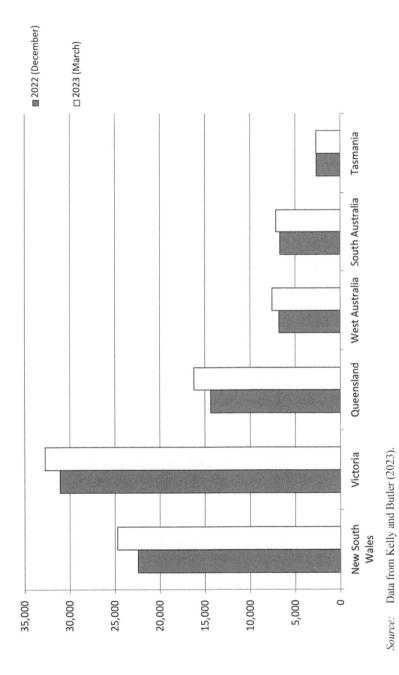

Source: Data from Kelly and Butler (2023).

Figure 3.1 *Numbers of people seeking homelessness assistance in Australia*

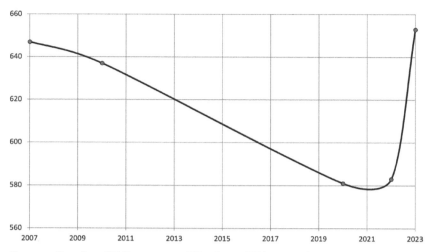

Source: Data from US Department of Housing and Urban Development.

Figure 3.2   Homelessness in the US (thousands)

one adult and one child. Figure 3.2 shows that the drop in homelessness experienced since 2007 was reversed by the cost of living crisis.

3.4   CONSEQUENCES OF THE CRISIS: CRIME

Desperate times push people to desperate measures, and a particular desperate measure is crime. Students of macroeconomics are told that the consumption function (consumption as a function of income) has a positive intercept, meaning that when income is zero, people still consume essentials, such as food and energy. How does this happen – that is, how is consumption expenditure financed when income is zero? Well, this can be done by borrowing, by depleting savings, by help from family and friends, by help from the state, and by help from charities. Crime is another source of funding, even though this is rarely mentioned in macroeconomics classes on the consumption function.

A spiralling cost of living drives people to desperation. Desperate people may steal the goods they need directly, such as food and energy, or they might steal high-value goods, sell them and use the proceeds to finance the purchase of food and energy. Speaking to *The Guardian*, Sherry Peck of the charity Safer London notes that "social injustice and inequality are the drivers of increased violence" (Dodd, 2022). In August 2022, London's mayor, Sadiq Khan, warned that the increasing cost of living could lead to more violence and make it easier for gangs to lure vulnerable young people (Dodd, 2022).

Various kinds of crime have risen in the UK as a result of the crisis, as reported by Crime Investigation (2023). These include electricity theft, gang crime, countryside theft, shoplifting, insurance fraud and scams.

The situation in the UK is summarised by Bentham (2023) as follows: "The cost of living crisis is threatening a new surge in 'high harm' burglary, car thefts and robbery." This situation, however, is not unique to the UK. In Australia, for example, Green (2023) reports that one in eight Australians has admitted to stealing, that as many as 2.4 million Australians have participated in petty crime, and that 5% of Australians have admitted to stealing at the supermarket self-checkout. Slightly fewer (4%) cheat the machines by scanning cheaper items and bagging expensive ones (for example, scanning onion and bagging avocado).

The same observation can be made of New Zealand. *The Straight Times* (2023) tells the stories of a man who strolls out of a New Zealand supermarket carrying bags stuffed with nine stolen legs of lamb, another who pushes out a shopping cart stacked with corned beef and mayonnaise, and another who smashes a security guard in the face with a bottle of milk before taking off with a basket of goods. Theft in New Zealand increased 45% in 2022 compared with 2021.

The US has seen a spike in "flash robs" involving gangs of thieves targeting luxury malls in California. A flash rob is a form of organised theft in which a large number of people enter a shop and steal merchandise, overwhelming employees by sheer numbers. For example, on 12 August 2023, thieves smashed displays and stole an estimated $60,000–$100,000 worth of merchandise from Nordstrom in the Westfield Topanga mall in Canoga Park, California (Percy, 2023). More concerning about crime in the US is the escalation of the number and rate of violent victimisations, as shown in Figure 3.3. Victimisations reflect the total number of times that persons or households become victims of crime. Violent victimisation includes rape or sexual assault, robbery, aggravated assault and simple assault (for details, see Thompson and Tapp, 2023).

3.5 CONSEQUENCES OF THE CRISIS: DOMESTIC ABUSE AND DIVORCE

The cost of living crisis is making it more difficult for the victims of domestic abuse (typically women) to leave an abusive relationship. Feeling financial pressure, victims are choosing to live with the trauma of abuse rather than to face the threat of financial destitution or homelessness or dealing with the worry of covering bills and paying for food. They have to make a difficult choice: remaining in an unsafe home or facing financial destitution or home-

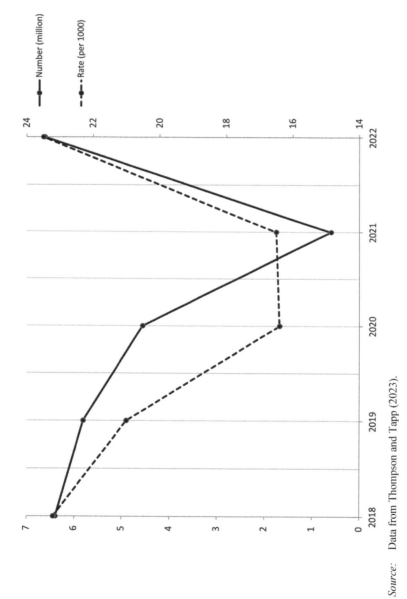

Source: Data from Thompson and Tapp (2023).

Figure 3.3   *The number and rate of violent victimisations in the US*

lessness. On the other hand, abusers are using the financial hardship triggered by the crisis as a tool for coercive control.

In the UK, Gill (2022) notes that soaring energy costs have left many women feeling trapped in abuse. She refers to a survey, conducted by Women's Aid (a British national charity working to end domestic abuse against women and children), of women who have experienced domestic abuse to find out how conditions have changed as a result of the crisis. The majority of respondents (96%) said that the crisis had a negative impact on their financial situation. Two-thirds (66%) of the survivors said that abusers were using concerns about financial hardship as a tool for coercive control. Almost three-quarters (73%) of women living (and having financial links) with the abuser said that the crisis had either prevented them from leaving or made it harder for them to leave.

As far as divorce is concerned, the crisis has led to a spike in the number of couples opting for a DIY divorce (which enables them to avoid the exorbitant fees charged by unscrupulous lawyers) and those who continue to live together after separating. In Australia, the numbers show that in 2023, 47% of separating couples attempted to negotiate their own divorce, rather than paying for legal advice, with 33% reaching a settlement without advice (Bowes, 2024). Choosing to continue living together is dictated by financial difficulties, in the sense that it has become unaffordable for a couple to rent separately or for one to pay the mortgage while the other pays rent. Even separated couples living in different places choose to live together while they are still separated. The silver lining is that rising cost of living is a factor making people think twice before deciding to separate.

3.6 CONSEQUENCES OF THE CRISIS: FOOD INSECURITY

Food security is a term that came to prominence during the COVID-19 pandemic when it was observed widely. The term refers to the physical availability of food, and to whether or not people have the resources and opportunity to gain reliable access to it. It follows that food insecurity is represented by limited or uncertain access to sufficient, nutritious food that is needed for a healthy life. The 1996 World Food Summit defines food security as a situation "when all people, at all times, have physical and economic access to sufficient, safe and nutritious food to meet their dietary needs and food preferences for an active and healthy life" (FAO, 1996). The four pillars of food security, as identified by the Food and Agriculture Organization (FAO, 2006), are availability, access, utilisation and stability of supply. A food-insecure household lacks sufficient resources to provide adequate nutrition to its members. Schmuecker and Earwaker (2022) define food insecurity as follows: "at least one household member in the last 30 days has either cut down the size of meals or skipped meals because there wasn't enough money for food or been hungry but did not have enough money for food".

People experiencing severe food insecurity skip meals or go hungry, either because they cannot afford food or because they lack access to it. The experience of food insecurity is stressful, and it is associated with numerous harmful physical and mental health outcomes in the short as well as the long run. Among children, food insecurity is also associated with adverse behavioural and learning outcomes. Children born in food-insecure households risk birth defects, and those living in food-insecure households tend to have a lower health-related quality of life as well as cognitive and behavioural problems that affect wellbeing and school performance.

Some figures that indicate the incidence of food insecurity in the UK are cited by Brown et al. (2023) who note that "early impacts of the crisis can already be seen in food security". They examine the findings of a survey conducted by the Office for National Statistics that was conducted in January 2023. The results show that 9% of the respondents said that their households had on occasions run out of food while being unable to buy more, 13% said that they or another adult in the household had skipped or cut down on the size of meals, and 8% had gone hungry. In all of these cases, the impact was most severe for people aged 16–29, and least severe for those aged 65 and over. The most frequently cited means of economising on food was eating out less (63%) and buying cheaper food (52%).

Likewise, research conducted by the Food Standards Agency highlights the growth in food insecurity. In the period April to July 2022, around 20% of the respondents were classified as "food insecure", a rise from April to June 2021, when 15% fell into this category. In 2022, the rate was particularly high for people aged 25–34 (30%), households with children under 16 years (29%), households with an annual income of less than £19,000 (43%), and people who were long-term unemployed (59%).

3.7   CONSEQUENCES OF THE CRISIS: INDEBTEDNESS

The rise in debt and arrears, a problem that has not received much attention in the literature and the media, is a deeply troubling consequence of the financial pressures felt by ordinary people. With limited availability of the financial resources needed to cover rising prices, people are increasingly resorting to debt just to get by. Recall the observation that people still consume necessary items even when their incomes fall to zero. One way to finance spending is crime, as we have seen. The other is borrowing or requesting postponement of payment, giving rise to indebtedness or aggravating the situation for those who are already in debt.

Two types of debt are identified by Schmuecker and Earwaker (2022). Households that are in arrears are those who have fallen behind on the payments that become due (which is a form of indebtedness). These households fall behind on the payment of bills and rent or on making periodic repayments on their credit cards or personal loans. The other type, personal borrowing, is that households take fresh loans to pay their bills. This is particularly bad when the interest rate charged on unsecured loans is extremely high or when penalties and punitive conditions are attached to the loans (Shylock style, as in William Shakespeare's *The Merchant of Venice*). These are typical characteristics of the loans provided by loan sharks, doorstep loans and pawn brokers. A loan shark is a person who (or an entity that) lends money at extremely high interest rates and often uses threats of violence to collect debt. A doorstep loan, also known as home credit, is an emergency short-term loan for a small sum of money. A pawn broker is an individual who, or a business that, offers secured loans to people, with items of personal property used as collateral (not much different from Shylock's collateral of a pound of Antonio's flesh).

The figures cited by Schmuecker and Earwaker (2022) paint a horrific picture of the situation in the UK. At the end of May and early June 2022, 4.6 million low-income households were in arrears, either for household expenses (such as rent, council tax or utilities) or because they have fallen behind on their loan repayments. The average amount owed by low-income households in arrears was £1600 and more than a million people were taking on debt just to cover essential items. Low-income households owed around £22 billion in debt, with £12.5 billion of new debt taken on in 2022. Of that £22 billion, £3.5 billion was owed to high-cost credit providers such as doorstep loans, pawn brokers and loan sharks. A further £2.3 billion was owed to buy now, pay later providers. Bernard (2022) describes as "very worrying" the observation that almost a fifth of low-income households were in debt to high-cost lenders.

Figure 3.4 shows the situation in the US with indebtedness represented by the credit card delinquency rate as reported by FRED. We can see that the delinquency rate reached its peak in the second quarter of 2009 in the midst of the great recession. Thereafter, it was declining as a result of the recovery from the great recession. In the third quarter of 2023, the delinquency rate started rising again.

3.8   CONSEQUENCES OF THE CRISIS: HEALTH AND WELLBEING

A cost of living crisis is also a health crisis or that it leads to a health crisis – that is, both physical and mental health. This is why Roberts and Petchey (2023) argue that the rising cost of living is more than an economic squeeze and that it is a "public health emergency, potentially on a par with the COVID-19

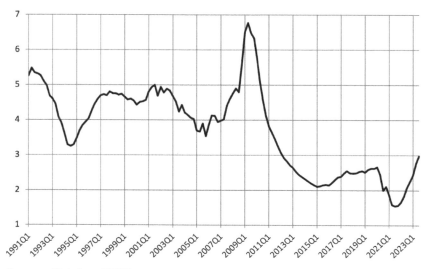

Source: Data from FRED.

Figure 3.4   *Credit card delinquency rate in the US*

pandemic". Like the pandemic, the negative effects of the crisis on health and wellbeing are felt disproportionately by those on the lowest incomes, who are likely to include lone parents, people living in deprived areas, homeless people, those with disabilities, older people and children. The threat that the cost of living crisis poses for health is primarily a product of aggravated food and energy insecurity, higher stress levels and reduced provision of health and social care. Health and income are deeply intertwined: how much money an individual makes influences their health, and vice versa. In terms of the jargon used by economists, reverse causality can be observed between health and income.

Even before the advent of the current crisis, it had been observed that children born when the economy is not in a good shape (such as a recession or stagflation) have shorter life expectancies and worse health during their lives. Adults in poor health are less able to work and less likely to be offered employment, leading to poverty. The current cost of living crisis affects people's health in a number of ways. First of all, expensive food and energy have direct effects on health. Those who cannot afford food find it inevitable to replace healthier options with cheaper, more processed food, or even go without. Consuming less healthy food items (which are higher in calories) results in rising obesity and heightened risk of long-term chronic conditions, such as diabetes and cardiovascular disease. Children exposed to poor diets early in life have worse health and weaker performance at school. Likewise, higher energy prices mean that individuals are less able to keep warm in winter or cool down in summer. Extreme weather on either side is conducive to higher mortality rates, particularly among those with pre-existing health conditions. Roberts and Petchey (2023) point out that not having the money to put the heating on means living in cold and damp conditions, aggravating the risk of heart attack and stroke, as well as arthritic and respiratory conditions. Older people, children and babies are at particularly high risk.

Rising cost of living and uncertainty about the future hurt not only physical but also mental health. This can be a vicious circle because financial vulnerability and worries are strongly associated with poor mental health, which in turn makes a difficult situation even more difficult. One cause of deteriorating mental health under the crisis is the accumulation of debt, as Bernard (2022) notes that "debt and arrears also often have a significant impact on people's mental health". According to the Money and Mental Health Policy Institute (2022), nearly half of the people with problem debt have mental health problems and 40% experience aggravation of those problems. Financial difficulties also affect recovery rates, with people 4.2 times as likely to suffer from depression after 18 months if they experience problem debt. The relation between debt and mental health problems is bidirectional: people with problem debt are significantly more likely to experience mental health problems, and people with mental health problems are more likely to be in problem debt.

To be more specific, the Money and Mental Health Policy Institute (2022) notes that financial difficulties are a common cause of stress and anxiety. Stigma around debt is conducive to the materialisation of a situation where people struggle to ask for help and may become isolated. The impact on people's mental health can be particularly severe if they resort to cutting back on essentials, such as food and energy, or if (and this is not a big if) creditors are aggressive or insensitive when they collect debt. Furthermore, people experiencing debt problems are three times as likely to think about suicide. The link between debt problems and suicide is so strong that more than 100,000 people in England attempt suicide each year for debt-related reasons.

The effects on people's physical and mental health are likely to lead to rising demand for healthcare. In the UK, this comes at a bad time when the NHS is being eroded or "effectively privatised" as noted by Roberts and Petchey (2023). According to Calnan (2023), privatisation of the NHS has come in many guises over the last decade, bringing with it not efficiency (as it is typically claimed by free marketeers) but rather fragmentation, waste, loss of patients' trust, inequities in access, the creation of a self-seeking for-profit service sector, and the potential emergence of a two-tier healthcare system. The eroded NHS is already stretched following the pandemic, as waiting lists are the longest they have been in two decades, which may be related to long-term shortages of front-line staff in both health and social care. The NHS has been undermined by a string of "reforms" over recent years, such as the Health and Social Care Act 2012 with its particular emphasis on marketisation. For example, Goodair (2023) notes that private sector firms are increasingly contracted to deliver health and social care in England. The privatisation of public services pertaining to health and social care is politically sensitive, with many fearing that the profit motive is likely to put patients and service users at risk. If you do not believe this, look at the miserable situation in the US where thousands of people die or become bankrupt every year because of unaffordable healthcare provided by the private sector.

Yet, the British government is squandering money fighting unnecessary wars, directly or by proxy. On 12 January 2024, Rishi Sunak vowed that Ukraine "will never be alone", announcing £2.5 billion of military aid, which is the UK's largest annual commitment since Russia's invasion of Ukraine in February 2022. This money would have been diverted away from the better use of alleviating the health problems associated with the cost of living crisis. While he was in Kyiv, Sunak praised the attack launched by the RAF on Yemen, a former British colony that happened to be the poorest country in the Middle East and one of the poorest in the world. Tragically, Sunak pledged that he "won't hesitate to protect lives" (The Standard, 2024). Well, a better way to save lives at home is to divert money from bombs to healthcare and social welfare. The lives lost in the UK as a result of the crisis cannot be saved by bombing poor villages in Yemen, which (by the way) is a historical tradition.

3.9   CONSEQUENCES OF THE CRISIS: SUICIDE AND DRUG ABUSE

Extreme cases, where people under financial pressure contemplate suicide, are on the rise. A report published in October 2023 by Mind.org (2023) shows that one in five people report worsening depression because of the cost of living crisis, and one in ten have developed an eating disorder as a result. More serious, however, is the finding that a large number of the people living in England and Wales have considered taking their own lives to leave behind the pain inflicted by the crisis. The results also show that people receiving universal credit (a means-tested social security payment) are more than three times more likely to consider suicide because of the crisis than those who do not receive benefits. The report tells the story of a 40-year-old man who tried to take his life twice in 2022. He said:

> I'm not feeling great about the future. I'm aware there are darker times ahead coming with the cost-of-living crisis, I'm having trauma treatment right now,

currently on a waiting list for further trauma therapy, and I've got to worry about the cost-of-living crisis. The added stress of the cost-of-living crisis impacted me hugely … . It haunts me to this day how I will survive and how I can provide for myself and my son with benefits being looked into and possibly reduced. My mental illness is severe without the cost-of-living crisis putting more stress on me.

A similar story comes from Australia where the participants in a survey were asked about the biggest risk to suicide rates in 2020, 2021 and 2022 (Walker, 2022). In 2020, 59% of the respondents identified the cost of living and personal debt as the factor. In 2022, that number jumped to 73%. The related factor of housing access and affordability also jumped from 51% in 2020 to 72% in 2022. Rolfe (2023) refers to figures published by Suicide Prevention Australia, which looks at the social and economic issues driving distress and subsequent suicide risk, showing that suicide deaths rose by 7% in 2022 across New South Wales and Victoria, representing more than half the national suicide toll between them.

The proposition that economic mishaps can be a cause of aggravated alcohol and drug consumption has been observed and examined empirically, which means that this is not a new issue that is specific to the current crisis (see, for example, Broadbent et al., 2023; Dom et al., 2016; Nosrati et al., 2019; Zolopa et al., 2021). Like suicide, addiction to alcohol and other drugs has risen, even though the effect of the crisis on the consumption of alcohol and drugs may go one way or the other because financial strain can impact people differently. Some people opt to reduce alcohol consumption because of tighter budgets. Others, on the other hand, may resort to more drinking or drug use to cope with the associated psychological distress and worry (for example, Broadbent et al., 2023; De Goeij et al., 2015). In 2023, spending on alcohol and tobacco went up by 4.1% in Queensland, but declined by 4.6% in Victoria (Alcohol and Drug Foundation, 2023).

In the UK, A YouGov poll commissioned by the Forward Trust found that nearly a third (32%) of adults have fallen into addiction or know someone who has done so. Of those whose addiction relapsed, nearly 61% said that the cost of living crisis was the most significant trigger for stress, anxiety and trauma. The poll of over 2190 adults found that 6% of the respondents had been drinking more and more since the beginning of the crisis. A quarter of those who took their alcohol intake to a higher level reported problems such as lack of sleep and stress (Keane, 2022).

3.10   CONSEQUENCES OF THE CRISIS: PROSTITUTION

The cost of living crisis has led to several changes in the world of prostitution. The first is that a significant number of women, mostly mothers, are resorting to prostitution in order to be able to feed their families. The second is that women who at one stage left prostitution have returned to the profession as they got squeezed financially. The third is that, out of desperation, prostitutes are becoming more adventurous by accepting to provide services for what might be dangerous clients whom they would not accept under normal circumstances. By doing so, they put themselves in much more perilous situations as they struggle to pay their energy bills and feed their families.

These observations have been made by several authors. Stephenson (2022) observes a significant rise in the number of women in the UK resorting or returning to sex work. In a report published by Christian Action Research and Education (2022) it is noted that "British mothers are turning to prostitution to help pay their bills as the cost-of-living crisis intensifies". Some of the women interviewed for the report said that they had taken on "webcam work", where they are paid to pose nude online, and "escort jobs" where they are paid for sex. Oppenheim (2022) suggests that "spiralling living costs are endangering sex workers' safety by forcing them to accept potentially dangerous male clients whose inquiries would have previously rejected". He quotes some sex workers saying that there are fewer clients due to people cutting back on costs, meaning that they are being forced to accept any potential customer and agree to render sexual services that they would normally refuse to render. Bryant (2023) uses the term "survival sex" and mentions "sex for rent" as a "growing problem as economic conditions tighten". Sex for rent occurs when a landlord demands sex from a tenant in return for discounted or free accommodation.

3.11   CONSEQUENCES OF THE CRISIS: CONSUMER BEHAVIOUR

The cost of living crisis has changed consumer behaviour in a number of ways. This observation is made explicitly in the October 2022 report on demand signals for fast-moving consumer goods (FMCG), which are non-durable products that sell quickly at relatively low costs. The report was published by Information Resources Inc. (IRI), which is a Chicago-based data analytics and market research company. The report notes that "consumers are displaying signs of severe 'inflation fatigue' that is forcing a range of coping behaviours not seen since the austere late 70s and early 80s" (IRI, 2022). This observation is made on the basis of examining consumer demand on 230 FMCG categories, more than 2000 product segments, and over ten million stock-keeping units across 14 markets in Europe, the US and Asia Pacific. The report, which analyses in-store purchases for the year ending in July 2022, combined with a consumer survey of 3000 global shoppers, shows that diminishing disposable income is affecting middle- and low-income consumers across the developed world. The surveyed shoppers mention the return of the packed lunch, staying in, and buying products offered at reduced prices even if they are out of date. Running down savings has become rather common to cope with far-reaching changes. An executive of IRI, Ananda Roy, makes the following comment (PR Newswire, 2022):

> It's evident that consumers' willingness to spend is suffering and the direction of travel is likely to worsen – with the likelihood of further sharp price rises given high input costs and volatile energy prices … Gone are the days of the one-stop weekly shop, we're expecting to see an increase in shopping around for must-have products and the consumption of less expensive seasonal goods. There are several difficult decisions for shoppers on the cards, and retailers and brands will do well to take a long and hard look at how they're going to respond to shopper needs.

Changes in consumer behaviour as identified by Brown et al. (2023) include the following:

- People are eating less healthy food, eating out less, and cutting back on their social lives.
- They are shopping around more.
- They have reduced spending on clothing, home improvements, electronics and furniture.
- They are cutting back expenditure by eating less fresh food, eating out less, reducing social visits, making fewer journeys, spending less on gifts, and reducing the number or cost of holidays.
- People aged 18–24 are more likely than older participants to be cutting back on dining out, social visits and holidays.
- Cost-cutting measures are more prevalent in those from minority ethnic backgrounds and those who reported finding their current financial situation "very difficult".

On the basis of the survey, more specific observations made in the IRI report include the following:

- Over half of consumers are in a crisis mode.
- Consumers are becoming better informed of fast-moving changes in the economic environment.
- Consumers are taking control of their expenses to moderate the impact of high levels of inflation across a wide range of everyday purchases, particularly food and other staples.

- They are choosing where to shop to moderate the effects of the crisis.
- They are switching to discount shops, which have spread into town centres and residential areas, offering a small but low-priced range of products compared to what is offered by big retailers.
- Shoppers think ahead to get the best value and stay within their budgets.
- Consumers are paying increasingly more attention to product labels. For example, 41% of shoppers are reading packaging labels for more information and 27% are looking more often for independent reviews of everyday products to justify purchase.
- Consumers are changing where they consume everyday products (at home, on-the-go, outside venues), taking a packed lunch, staying in for drinks with friends rather than going to a bar, showering at the gym or at work, enjoying specialty coffees at home, and replacing visits to the salon with hair styling and grooming products.
- Just over half of shoppers plan to order less cooked food to be delivered at home (51%) and 47% plan to eat out less.

In a nutshell, the cost of living crisis has made consumers more discerning in the ways they spend their money and allocate shrinking budgets. To pay for essential items, they reduce spending on less essential items, such as eating out, new clothes and "one-off treats". Households have become more careful in spending on home improvements, holidays and new appliances. Tight budgets mean that less money is available to put into savings, with adverse consequences for retirement income.

3.12   RESPONSES TO THE CRISIS

Responses to the crisis, as described in this section, are the actions that have been put in place or announced to help people deal with financial difficulties. Table 3.1 shows some of the measures that were taken in 2022 as reported by Jones (2022), the World Economic Forum (2022), H. Taylor (2022) and Mcrae (2022).

These measures have been largely inadequate. In March 2020, Chancellor Rishi Sunak's Spring Statement set out measures to tackle the cost of living crisis in the UK, including doubling the household support fund to extend it beyond its planned end and cutting fuel duty. On the other hand, Sunak announced an increase in the rate at which national insurance has to be paid from £9568 to £12,570 a year. This is why H. Taylor (2022) suggests that these measures "will not go far enough in supporting those who need it most". While the chancellor claimed that the Spring Statement was designed to "protect the economic security of people across the country", Fitzmaurice and Taylor (2022) argue that "households are likely to experience the largest drop

Table 3.1   *Responses to the crisis by country*

Country	Action (executed or planned)
US	1. Reducing prescription drug prices 2. Tax credits to encourage energy efficiency 3. An income-driven repayment plan that would cap loans for low-income borrowers 4. A loan forgiveness programme for non-profit and government workers 5. Partial cancellation of student debt
Brazil	1. Cutting fuel taxes 2. Raising social welfare payments 3. Reducing petrol prices 4. Labour subsidies 5. One-time payments of $120 for 7.5 million citizens
Japan	1. Raising average minimum wage 2. A cap on the price of imported wheat sold to retailers
Indonesia	1. Reallocating part of the fuel subsidy budget towards welfare spending, including cash handouts 2. Subsidising transport fares
India	1. Imposing restrictions on exports of food items including wheat and sugar 2. Cutting taxes on imports of edible oil 3. Cutting taxes on fuel and essential goods
Malaysia	Subsidies and cash aid
South Africa	Cutting pump prices of fuels
Saudi Arabia	Allocation of 20 billion riyals to social welfare spending
UAE	Doubling financial support to low-income families
Turkey	Raising minimum wage by 30%
Austria	Partial reimbursement for the cost of power

Country	Action (executed or planned)
France	1. Freezing gas prices at the October 2021 levels 2. Capping electricity price increases at 4% 3. Handing out €100 to low- and middle-income households to help pay energy bills
Kenya	1. Increasing the monthly minimum wage 2. Helping farmers pay for fertilisers 3. Providing fuel subsidies
Germany	1. Paying all people in regular employment a one-off rebate of €300 2. Students and welfare recipients received double their usual lump-sum payment to assist with heating private homes 3. Introducing a cheap monthly public transport pass on a temporary basis 4. A significant tax cut on fuel for three months by 30 cents for petrol and 14 cents for diesel 5. A one-off €300 payment to help with the rising cost of living, with a further €100 for each child and an additional €100 for anybody receiving state benefits
Spain	1. Cutting VAT on gas temporarily from 21% to 5% 2. Free train travel over distances up to 300 km for those buying a multi-trip ticket
Poland	1. A one-off payment for each coal-burning household 2. Smaller subsidies for different types of heating fuel such as liquefied petroleum gas
Netherlands	1. Offering the lowest-earning households a one-off energy subsidy 2. Raising the minimum wage 3. Lowering VAT on energy
Norway	Capping electricity, with the state covering most of the bills
UK	1. Giving 8 million low-income households a direct payment split into two instalments 2. Offering an energy grant for every household 3. Doubling the household support fund 4. Cutting fuel duty
Bangladesh	Introducing family ration cards

Country	Action (executed or planned)
New Zealand	1. Cutting taxes on fuel 2. Reducing public transport fares by 50% 3. Increasing the minimum wage from $20.00 to $21.20 an hour
Ireland	1. A €11 billion package of benefits and tax cuts 2. Credits for residential electricity bills 3. Farms and other businesses could claim up to €10,000 a month off their utility bills 4. Further assistance with energy bills to the most vulnerable

Source: Author's own.

in disposable income since 1956", which means that "the Spring Statement is unlikely to support those who need it most as inflation continues to soar". The Statement, they argue, represents a "failure to prioritise support to those who need it most". The prime minister at that time, Boris Johnson, acknowledged the precarious situation that many households were facing, but when he was asked whether families should eat cheaper food, not replace clothes, turn down the thermostat, or turn off the heating entirely, he said that "people obviously will face choices that they will have to make". What a comforting statement from the leader of the nation who himself was and is not affected by the crisis to any extent.

H. Taylor (2022) comments on one measure taken in Germany (tax cuts on fuel), arguing that it will do little to help the worst off. The analysis presented by Transport & Environment (2022) shows that the richest 10% of drivers will receive seven times more in fuel tax cuts than the poorest, on average, because they consume far more fuel. Still, the UK is an outlier compared to its European counterparts. This is how Taylor explains the disparity:

> With other major economies cutting the tax burden on working people, the UK is an outlier in its decision to raise National Insurance rates at this time. Overall, the measures announced by the Chancellor will not provide economic security to millions of people in the UK struggling to make ends meet in 2022, and the promise of tax cuts to come in 2024 will do little to reassure low income workers who are today already having to make compromises on day to day essentials including food and heating.

A more appropriate response to the situation in the UK is recommended by Ghelani and Clegg (2022) in order to protect low-income households. They present three options: (i) restoring the £20 weekly uplift to universal credit; (ii) increasing elements of universal credit, as though they had been uprated by 10% in April 2022; and (iii) restoring work allowances to 2015 levels to help all universal credit households in work.

The response to the crisis in developing countries is dealt with in a major UNDP study of the ramifications of soaring food and energy prices (Molina et al., 2022). The argument put forward in the UNDP study is that soaring food and energy prices impose tough challenges, in the presence of "normative and instrumental reasons to shield poor and vulnerable-to-poverty populations from risks of impoverishment and to prevent short-term shocks from translating into persistent economic deprivation". The items listed in the governmental policy toolkit for protecting people's livelihoods include one-off or time-bound income support; in-kind and quasi-cash transfers (for example, school-feeding and vouchers); blanket subsidies (for example, price caps or freezes); unemployment insurance; and tax cuts (for example, VAT or fuel tax). Actions of this sort bring with them some challenges, such as delivery capacities and fiscal sustainability. Another problem is that some actions can move in the wrong direction – for example, blanket energy subsidies can protect low-income households while encouraging more energy consumption and exacerbating income inequality, given that subsidies have pro-rich bias.

The results of surveys show that blanket subsidies and tax cuts that forego revenue are the tools most governments in developing countries have resorted to for the purpose of protecting consumers. The IMF has identified around 70 countries implementing at least one of the policy actions mentioned above, with some differences between developing and developed countries. In the former, the most common policy actions are cash transfers, vouchers and reduced utility bills, while the most used tools in developing countries are tax cuts and reliance on existing subsidies (Amaglobeli et al., 2022). Similarly, around 60 countries identified by the World Bank have introduced energy price-related measures, whereas 40 countries are maintaining existing fuel subsidies – with the bulk accounted for by developing countries (Gencer and Akcura, 2022). Finally, out of the 142 policy responses identified by Gentilini et al. (2022) across 77 countries, more than one hundred of these responses involve tax cuts and subsidies for fuel, food and fertiliser, with the lion's share of these (65%) concentrated in developing countries.

3.13   CONCLUDING REMARKS

Serious crises have serious adverse consequences and require serious responses. Unfortunately, the measures taken all around the world are not serious enough, most notably because they are minuscule and temporary. On the contrary, governments blame inflation on greedy workers demanding higher wages and punish them by lifting interest rates under the pretext of fighting inflation. In reality, what happens is that more of the incomes earned by workers go to banks, which constitutes a reverse-Robin Hood redistribution of income from workers to banks. Governments do not shy away from admitting this perverse redistribution of income, claiming that it is necessary to relieve demand pressure on prices. No government has blamed greedy businesses for raising prices to boost profit beyond reason. People are therefore squeezed between higher interest rates engineered by central banks and higher prices demanded by businesses. We will find out that higher interest rates lead to higher rather than lower inflation because interest payments are a cost of production.

Governments claim that what they are doing is the best they can do because of tight budgets. Well, tight budgets can be made "untight" by a tax on windfall corporate profit. The burden of the crisis should not fall on people only – rather, the corporate sector should bear some of the burden. Is not this what the acclaimed corporate social responsibility is all about? The same can be done by imposing a wealth tax on high net worth individuals, an idea that was floated, but never saw the light, during the pandemic. The same can be done by transferring wasteful military spending to finance welfare programmes. More lives can be saved by boosting welfare spending than spending on wars of aggression and proxy wars. Last, but not least, budgets can be made very "untight" by nationalising natural resources, which should belong to the people rather than the oligarchy and multinationals. Nothing like this can happen as long as those in charge adopt neoliberalism as the guiding philosophy.

4.   Causes of the crisis: inflation

4.1   INTRODUCTION

As far as Joe Biden is concerned, the inflation problem in the US (and the rest of the world) has been brought about by Vladimir Putin. In June 2022, Biden spoke at the Port of Los Angeles where he addressed the main issue on the minds of Americans: inflation. Parker (2022) comments on Biden's speech by saying that "in the spirit of a tried-and-true liberal, he [Biden] blamed everyone in the world for a problem that he is responsible for". However, Biden singled out Putin as the source of inflationary pressure. This is how Parker interpreted the speech:

> Apparently, our president believes that Russian President Vladimir Putin is running America. We've never seen anything like Putin's tax on both food and gas. … Putin's price hike is hitting America hard. … I'm doing everything in my power to blunt Putin's price hike and bring down the cost of gas and food.

The recent resurgence of inflation can be attributed primarily to cost-push and profit-push factors, even though it is sometimes attributed to a combination of cost-push and demand-pull factors. For example, it is believed that the COVID-19 pandemic has led to the emergence of cost-push factors (such as disruption of supply chains) and demand-pull factors, in the sense that on exit from the pandemic, suppressed demand became actual demand. The issue of whether inflation has been caused mostly by cost-push or demand-pull factors will be addressed in Chapter 8 where we reach the conclusion that this inflation has been caused primarily by cost-push factors, which is why interest rate hikes are ineffective.

In this chapter, nine possible causes of the resurgence of inflation are identified and discussed. These include the semiconductor chip crisis, the energy crisis, the food crisis, the global supply chain crisis, wage-push inflation, profit-push inflation, productivity growth slowdown, inflationary expectations and globalisation. The relevance of monetary factors, which are believed by some economists to be the (or a) source of inflation will be discussed in Chapter 6 followed (in Chapter 7) by a critique of the myth perpetuated by

Milton Friedman's proposition that inflation is always a monetary problem (the Friedmanite myth).

4.2   THE SEMICONDUCTOR CHIP CRISIS

Semiconductor chips effectively represent the "brain" of every electronic device. They are required for the production of a broad range of electronic equipment, and that is not only computers and electric cars. According to an analysis conducted by Goldman Sachs, semiconductor chips are used, one way or another, in 169 industries, including steel products, ready-mix concrete, air conditioning systems, refrigerators, and even in breweries and soap manufacturing (Howley, 2021). Other products that require semiconductor chips include graphics cards, video game consoles and household appliances. Chips are required to produce household appliances (such as refrigerators, dishwashers, washing machines and microwaves) which need semiconductors to control and regulate the flow of electricity and make appliances run more efficiently. Personal computers have central processing units that act as their brain by executing instructions and performing calculations. In mobile devices, chips are used for communication, processing, memory and display – for example, a smartphone has a chip to connect to a cellular network, a chip that enables touch screen input, and a chip that stores data.

The causes of the global chip shortage can be seen in the timeline suggested by Ashcroft (2023) who describes the shortage as a "global supply chain crisis" and attributes it to a "perfect storm of causes, including war and pandemic". In early 2020, the cause was the pandemic; in late 2020, it was trade war between the US and China; in 2021, it was cryptocurrency mining; in the summer of 2021, the shortage was aggravated by severe weather in Taiwan; and in February 2022, it was the Russian invasion of Ukraine.

The COVID-19 pandemic is thought to be the main, but not the only, cause of the global chip shortage. In the first quarter of 2020, plunging sales forced manufacturers to revise business projections downwards and slash semiconductor orders. From early 2020, the pandemic and efforts to contain it caused disruptions in supply chains and logistics, which had an adverse effect on the availability of chips. The shortage was aggravated by a significant increase in the demand for PCs and mobile phones worldwide as a result of the pandemic-driven shift to working from home. At the same time, users turned to new, chip-filled forms of entertainment to pass time during months of lockdown, ranging from gaming to cryptocurrency mining. Initially, the shortage was thought to have been caused by a temporary delay in supplies as factories shut down when the pandemic first hit. However, even though production went back to normal subsequently, a new surge in demand, driven by changing habits as a result of the pandemic, has maintained the shortage (Sweeney, 2021).

Apart from the pandemic, trade friction between the US and China was a contributory factor to the chip shortage. In September 2020, the US imposed sanctions on China's manufacturers, forcing companies with American ties to use Japanese and Korean suppliers, which were already producing at maximum capacity (for example, Massie, 2021). Another cause, identified by *The Economist* (2021), is the high demand for general-purpose graphics processing units for use in cryptocurrency mining. Patel (2021) identifies as another cause the severe winter storm that hit Texas in February 2021, forcing the closure of three plants owned by Samsung, Infineon and NXP Semiconductors. Yet another cause is the series of fires that hit semiconductor plants around the world (for example, Shivdas, 2021).

As a cause of the chip shortage, the effect of the Russia-Ukraine war was transmitted via more than one channel. The first is that Ukraine produces about half of the global neon supply, a noble gas needed for the production of chips (Financial Times, 2022). On the other hand, Russia exports about 40% of the global supply of palladium, a metal that is used in certain chip components. Mukul (2022) suggests that the supply of semiconductors, which plummeted as a result of COVID-related disruptions but started picking up as manufacturing chains went back to normal, is once again threatened by the Ukraine crisis because of disruptions to the supply of two key raw materials (neon and palladium) that are at a risk of being constrained.

By the end of 2023, the global chip shortage had not fully dissipated, without a clear indication on when it would come to an end. Harris (2022) contends that even infusions of cash from the US and the European Union will not solve the problem. On the other hand, Kharpal (2023) expresses the view that the chip shortage arising at the height of the pandemic has turned into a chip glut, to the extent that some of the world's biggest chip makers are taking a hit. It is debatable whether or not the shortage has come to an end, will come to an end soon, or it will be around for some time (see, for example, Applied Energy Systems, 2023).

4.3   THE ENERGY CRISIS

Since 2021, the world has been immersed in a global energy crisis symbolised by rising prices of all energy sources. The prices of natural gas, electricity and coal have reached prices never seen before, while the price of oil reached its highest level since 2008. Energy markets began to tighten in 2021, as a result of the economic rebound from the pandemic. The situation of tight markets was aggravated to become a full-blown global energy crisis following Russia's invasion of Ukraine in February 2022.

In response to the invasion of Ukraine, European countries declared their intention to phase out Russian gas imports completely, while Russia curtailed or even turned off its export pipelines. Consequently, the price of natural gas reached record highs, and so did electricity, at least in some countries. Oil prices initially soared as international trade routes were reconfigured following the embargo of Russian oil. Some shippers started to refuse to carry Russian oil because of sanctions and insurance risk. Many large oil producers were unable to boost supply to meet rising demand. Major oil companies could not obtain energy supplies from Russia to distribute to European countries that depend on Russia's energy imports.

Other contributory factors, as identified by Ozili and Ozen (2023), are the global campaign to reduce carbon emission and the shortage in fossil fuel reserves due to divestment from fossil fuels. These are the consequences of international efforts and consultations to respond to the threat posed by climate change on the global economy, which have led to several international climate change meetings. Examples of these meetings are the COPs (Conference of the Parties), which are a series of United Nations climate change conferences that have been running since 1995. As a result of these meetings, calls have been made for deliberate reduction in carbon emissions and, more specifically, reduction in the use of fossil fuel globally.

Let us look at some facts and figures (obtained from FRED and the US Energy Information Administration) which are shown in Figure 4.1. The figure displays monthly data on (a) the Henry Hub natural gas spot price ($/million BTU), (b) the global price of natural gas ($/million BTU), (c) the WTI crude oil price ($/barrel), and (d) the price of propane ($/gallon). All of the prices reached their lowest levels between March and June 2020 as a result of the COVID restrictions. However, resumption of the upward trend in all four series happened before February 2022, which shows that the crisis was brewing before the Russian invasion of Ukraine. All of the prices peaked around mid-2022, which explains why the inflation rate has already peaked.

This energy crisis is more severe than the energy crisis of the 1970s for two reasons. The first is that the 1970s crisis was specific to crude oil, whereas the current crisis engulfs almost all fossil fuels. In a December 2022 interview with Bloomberg, oil historian Daniel Yergin said that the current energy crisis is "potentially worse" than the crisis of the 1970s, rippling across not just oil but natural gas and coal (Richards, 2022). The second reason is that the world economy is much more globalised now than in the 1970s, and this is why the current crisis is truly global. Other differences, as suggested by Richards (2022), are the following: (i) oil prices are unregulated now, (ii) the supply crisis pushing up prices is partly a political choice, and (iii) both interest and inflation rates are significantly lower than in the 1970s. An alternative view that is put forward by Kilgore (2021) is the following: "Anyone who lived

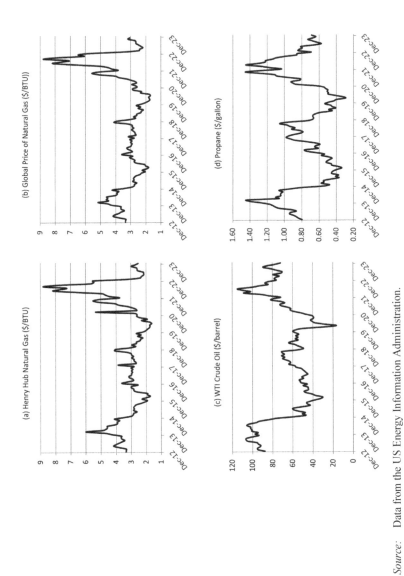

Source: Data from the US Energy Information Administration.

Figure 4.1 *Energy prices*

through the economic conditions of the late 1970s should laugh at the suggestion that we're in the same spot."

However, one important reason why the current energy crisis is worse than
the crisis of the 1970s is that neoliberalism was not the guiding philosophy
then. The role of neoliberalism in igniting the current cost of living crisis will
be discussed in Chapter 5, but what is important here is that in the 1970s the
government provided a cushion that helped reduce the pain inflicted by the
crisis, which is no longer the case. This point was made in Chapter 1 with
respect to the overall cost of living crisis. The arguments are equally valid for
the energy crisis.

4.4   THE FOOD CRISIS

The global food crisis, also known as the global hunger and malnutrition crisis,
is attributed by the World Food Programme (2023) to conflict, economic
shocks, climate extremes and soaring fertiliser prices. More frequent and
intense weather events destroy land, livestock and crops. The effect of conflict
is evident in the Ukraine war because Ukraine and Russia are big producers
of (among others) wheat, sunflower oil and fertilisers. According to the World
Food Programme (2023), high fertiliser prices could turn the current food
affordability crisis into a food availability crisis. Figure 4.2 shows that the
global fertiliser price index peaked in April 2022 and started to decline, and by
December 2023, it had declined by almost 60% relative to the peak.

The World Bank (2023) identifies a factor that has made the global food
crisis even worse, which is the surge in trade-related policies imposed by countries following Russia's invasion of Ukraine. These policies aim at increasing
domestic supply and restricting exports. According to the World Bank, 19
countries have implemented 27 food export bans, and nine have introduced 17
export-limiting measures (and that is only up to 11 December 2023).

Figure 4.3 shows the price indices reported by FAO for meat, dairy, cereals,
oils and sugar, as well as the overall price index for food. We can see that all of
these prices have peaked and started to decline. The overall price index peaked
in March 2022 and by December 2023 it was down by 26%. According to
Rother et al. (2023), this decline, which eased pressure on most international
food markets, was produced by strong harvests in large food producing countries, steep declines in shipping costs, and more affordable energy and fertiliser
prices.

4.5   THE GLOBAL SUPPLY CHAIN CRISIS

A supply chain is the process of producing and distributing products from
a supplier to a firm and then to the customer. A supply chain shortage occurs

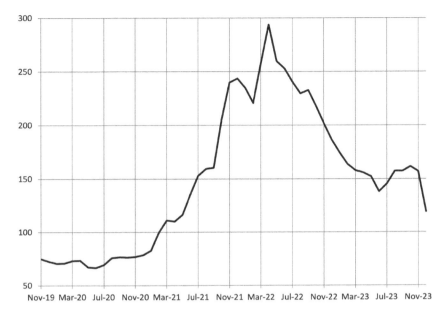

Figure 4.2   Global fertiliser price index

when one or more steps in this process are disrupted, which causes delays in the delivery of products to the customer or makes it impossible to meet consumer demand. A supply chain disruption is defined by Andriantomanga et al. (2023) as "a business' inability to receive, produce, ship, and sell their products".

Global supply chain disruptions, which are typically attributed to the COVID-19 pandemic and the Russian invasion of Ukraine, caused worldwide shortages of manufactured products. Logistics was one of the first industries to be hit hard at the early stages of the pandemic. As a result of lockdowns, quarantines and travel restrictions, the ability to store, move and distribute products became nearly impossible. Store shelves became empty, shipping containers piled up off the coast, and businesses struggled to find the supplies they needed to meet consumer demand. The effect of the pandemic stems from the increasing numbers of sick workers and the restrictions affecting the availability of staff. In cargo shipping, goods remained at port due to staffing shortages. As countries opened up, demand for goods began to outstrip supply, resulting in port congestions and higher shipping costs. In particular, the strict

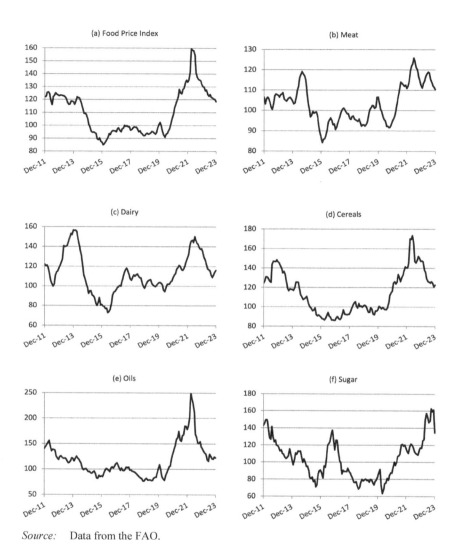

Source: Data from the FAO.

Figure 4.3   Food price indices

zero-case policy pursued by the Chinese government led to closures of Chinese firms providing parts and components to other countries.

The economic sanctions imposed on Russia have produced adverse effects on global supply chains. Many multinationals have suspended operations in Russia and hundreds of ships laden with wheat and corn have been stranded at Ukrainian ports, as the war restricted shipping in the Black Sea. Hamilton (2023) examines the effect of the Ukraine war on US supply chains, noting that the war has restricted the supply of key metals imported from Russia. For example, 30% of platinum group elements, 13% of titanium, and 11% of nickel imported into the US from Russia are no longer available. Since nickel is used as an input in many industries, these shortages have disrupted the production of important goods. Titanium shortages are also of significant concern, since it is one of the strongest metals used to manufacture a variety of industrial products (Hamilton, 2023).

Out of the several dimensions of supply chain disruptions, Andriantomanga et al. (2023) argue that two dimensions stand out: (i) disruptions in manufacturing production, and (ii) higher transportation costs. A newly developed indicator by the Federal Reserve Bank of New York, the global supply chain pressure index (GSCPI), captures both of these dimensions by combining several cross-border transportation cost indicators and global manufacturing data. The Federal Reserve Bank of New York (2023) notes that the motivation for coming up with the index was "to develop a parsimonious measure of global supply chain pressures that could be used to gauge the importance of supply constraints with respect to economic outcomes" and argues that "changes in the GSCPI are associated with goods and producer price inflation". The GSCPI indicates that disruptions in 2021 and 2022 were three to four standard deviations above the historical average, as shown in Figure 4.4. The index peaked in December 2021 and entered negative territory in February 2023.

By examining the GSCPI over time, Friesen (2023) concludes that the crisis is over because "every component in the global supply chain has seen improvement". These components include ocean freight shipping, the price of shipping containers, barge transportation, air cargo, trucking and warehouse capacity. Earlier, Friesen (2021) had said that there was no end in sight for the COVID-led global supply chain disruption. Then he described the situation as follows: "Massive dislocations are present in the container market, shipping routes, ports, air cargo, trucking lines, railways and even warehouses. This situation has produced shortages of key manufacturing components, order backlogs, delivery delays and a spike in transportation costs and consumer prices."

4.6   WAGE-PUSH INFLATION

The business-government complex is promoting the proposition that inflation is caused by rising wages and that the current inflationary episode is no exception. This argument has been repeatedly used to dismantle trade unions and allow for a bigger redistribution of income from labour to capital. It is also used to justify the introduction of policies and legislations that depress wages and boost corporate profitability. When they leave public service, government

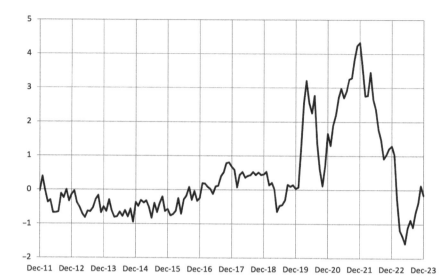

Source: Data from the Federal Reserve Bank of New York.

Figure 4.4   Global supply chain pressure index

officials (including cabinet ministers and central bank officials) who contribute to this effort are rewarded handsomely by the corporate sector. This is the
essence of the business-government complex.

   In Australia, the proposition that this is wage-push inflation is heard quite
frequently from business executives and their backers in government. The
opposite view is put forward by Richardson et al. (2022), who argue that
"labour costs have played an insignificant role in the recent increase in inflation". They present figures showing that labour costs account for just 15% of
economy-wide price increases while profits have played an overwhelming role,
accounting for about 60% of inflation. In the midst of the inflationary episode
of 2022, some statements were made by "business people" to blame rising
wages for inflation. Andrew Mackellar, CEO of the Australian Chamber of
Commerce and Industry, claimed that "aggressive wages growth will only spur
further inflation growth" (Marin-Guzman and Shapiro, 2022). Innes Willox,
CEO of the Australian Industry Group, expressed the view that "we are now
at risk of a wages and inflation and interest rates death spiral" (Indaily, 2022).
He also said the following: "In the current circumstances, there is a clear risk
that a high increase in wages without improved workplace productivity would
fuel inflation and increase the likelihood of a steeper rise in interest rates to the
detriment of growth and job creation" (Hannam, 2022). The fact of the matter

is that productivity gains are not passed on to labour in terms of higher wages but rather used to boost profit, and this is why real wages have been stagnant.

Richardson et al. (2022) dismiss these claims on the basis of two factual observations: (i) real wage growth is at historically low levels and has been for some time, and (ii) the share of wages in GDP is near its recent record low while the share of profit remains close to its recent record high. Hannam (2022) notes that "the recent spurt in inflation has little to do with workers being paid more" and describes the claim that wage increases could set off inflation as "over-the-top alarmism". Jones (2023) describes the claim that rising wages are driving inflation as a "dangerous rightwing myth" and argues that "a dangerous myth has been deliberately manufactured into an apparent piece of common sense: that wages must be suppressed if surging prices are to be contained". Jericho and Stanford (2023) examine the effect of minimum wages on inflation, suggesting that "rises in the minimum wage have almost no impact on inflation" and recommend a 7% increase as a "necessary recompense for Australia's lowest paid worker", given the collapse in the value of the minimum wage in real terms over the past two years. They further suggest that a 1% increase in the minimum wage (even if completely passed through into higher prices) would result in a virtually undetectable increase in economy-wide prices. This undetectable increase is "so small that a mere 0.2% fall in profits would be enough to cancel any impact on prices at all".

Highly paid government officials always argue against wage increases in defence of their corporate masters. For example, Jones (2023) notes that "British economic policymakers have opted to disregard the overwhelming evidence [on the role of wages and profits in igniting inflation] and deny reality rather than take on corporate power." In February 2023, Andrew Bailey, the governor of the Bank of England who earns £575,500 a year, demanded "quite clear restraint" from British workers. In May 2023, Bailey claimed that Britain was suffering a wage-price spiral, where rising labour income drives up the prices of goods and services. Huw Pill, the chief economist of the Bank, who earns £190,000 a year, demands that households "need to accept" that they are poorer and stop seeking pay increases. He also said: "And what we're facing now is that reluctance to accept that, yes, we're all worse off, and we all have to take our share" (Wearden, 2023). In an interview with BBC Radio 4, JP Morgan's Karen Ward, who sits on the Chancellor's economy advisory council, warned of a "price-wage spiral" and recommended the inducement of a recession to "get price rises under control" (Graham, 2023). The same goes for politicians. Elliott (2023) refers to "attempts by [British] ministers to finger workers for the persistence of the cost of living crisis", arguing that there is no real evidence that this is the case. Insensitive remarks made by government officials who are not affected by the crisis (because they earn inflation-proof salaries) are indicative of an omnipresent culture of blaming the victim.

Wage growth cannot be the cause of inflation when real wages fall. In its *Global Wage Report 2022–23*, the International Labour Organization (2023) notes that "the severe inflationary crisis combined with a global slowdown in economic growth … are causing a striking fall in real monthly wages in many countries". The results reported by the ILO show that real wages in the advanced G20 countries declined by 2.2% in the first half of 2022, whereas real wages in the emerging G20 countries grew by 0.8%, 2.6% less than in 2019, the year before the COVID-19 pandemic. The report states that "the cost-of-living crisis comes on top of significant wage losses for workers and their families during the COVID-19 crisis, which in many countries had the greatest impact on low-income groups". The report also shows that rising inflation has a greater cost-of-living impact on lower-income earners because they spend most of their disposable income on essential goods and services, which are subject to greater price increases than non-essential items.

Solid arguments against the proposition that wage growth is the cause of inflation are presented by Bivens (2022) who makes several interesting points on the wage–price nexus. The first is that the rise of inflation has unambiguously not been driven by tight labour markets pushing up wages. The second is that nominal wage growth has been fast over the previous year relative to the past few decades, but it has lagged far behind inflation, meaning that labour costs are dampening, rather than amplifying, price pressures. The third point is that if the only change in the economy over the previous year had been the acceleration of nominal wage growth relative to the recent past, inflation would be roughly 2.5–4.5%, instead of the 8.6% pace it ran through March 2022. The fourth point is that the claims that the Fed needs to shift into a much more hawkish mode to keep wages from amplifying inflation and to bring inflation back down to more normal levels are often greatly overstated and understate how much damage this strategy could cause. In short, non-wage factors are clearly the main drivers of inflation.

4.7   PROFIT-PUSH INFLATION

Profit-push inflation, which is sometimes known as "greed inflation" or "greedflation", is related to price gouging, a practice whereby the corporate sector takes advantage of an external crisis to charge excessive prices for basic necessities. That was the case during the COVID-19 pandemic as it is now under the cost of living crisis. If and when high inflation prevails, business firms with market power tend to raise their profit margins to boost their bottom lines. High inflation is conducive to price gouging for at least two reasons. The first reason is that if prices are rising rapidly, consumers will not be able to distinguish the rise due to inflationary pressures and the additional rise generated by higher profit margins. If consumers believe that inflation is generated by external cost-push factors, rather than higher profit margins, they will not complain, in which case agencies in charge of consumer protection will not be under pressure to do something about it, even though they do not do anything about it anyway. The second reason is that firms are likely to face menu costs when they are forced to change prices frequently. It follows that when prices start to rise, they take the opportunity to make big changes all at once, rather than several small changes. Elliott (2023) notes that even the IMF and the European Central Bank (ECB) support the idea that companies are gouging their customers when they can, suggesting that "the non-technical term for what is going on is greedflation".

Lapavitsas et al. (2023), who think that profit-push inflation is axiomatic, suggest that some economic phenomena, such as resurgent inflation, can have very simple explanations. This is how they explain the situation:

> If prices are rising rapidly, but most people's incomes – whether wages, pensions, or benefits – are not going up so quickly, someone must be taking the difference. It is not hard to work out who that is. The difference between much higher prices and incomes failing to keep up is taken as greatly increased profits, especially by big companies.

Profit-push inflation generates windfall profits for the companies that are capable of raising their profit margins, which requires the kind of economic power enjoyed by monopolists and oligopolists. In the UK, for example, Jung and Hayes (2022) show that "the profits of the largest non-financial companies were up 34 per cent at the end of 2021 compared to pre pandemic levels" and that "90 per cent of the increases in profits is accounted for by only 25 companies" (the companies that have enormous market power). Likewise, Lapavitsas et al. (2023) note that profits for the 350 biggest companies listed on the London Stock Exchange are 73% higher than they were in 2019, just before the pandemic. They also note that Shell and BP, between them, made £40 billion in profit on their global operations in 2022, which was more than twice the £19 billion increase in domestic energy prices. And in July 2022, British Gas announced an incredible five-fold increase in its half-yearly profits.

It is typical that those who dismiss the role of wage-push inflation argue that the culprit is corporate profit. For example, Jones (2023) argues that "corporate greed is the culprit", warning that "policymakers daren't take on big business". Jung and Hayes (2022) contend that while (current) inflation is primarily driven by global factors, surging profits could be a contributing factor to rising prices. Therefore, they question the arguments of the prime minister and the governor of the Bank of England that wage restraint is needed to keep inflation down, suggesting instead that that profit restraint is required. Another study, conducted by Unite the Union (2022), exposes "how corporate profiteering is driving inflation not workers' wages", attributing 60% of the inflation rise to corporate greed. The study reveals that profit margins for the biggest British companies were 73% higher in 2021 relative to 2019, even though sales had fallen. A similar point is made by Hansen et al. (2023) who estimate that rising corporate profits account for almost half of the increase in Europe's inflation over the past two years as companies put up prices by more than the increase in the costs of imported energy. They point out that "European workers suffered a real-terms wage drop of approximately 5% last year, while Europe's businesses have so far been shielded more than workers from the adverse cost shock."

In June 2023, the head of the ECB (not exactly a pro-working-class institution) said that corporate profits were the biggest factor driving up prices in 2022 and would be again in 2023 unless businesses were forced to absorb rising wage bills (Inman, 2023). In a 2022 speech, Isabel Schnabel, a member of the board of the ECB, said that "profits have recently been a key contributor to total domestic inflation" (Schnabel, 2022). She went on to say the following:

> Many firms have been able to expand their unit profits in an environment of global excess demand despite rising energy prices ... To put it more provocatively, many euro area firms, though by no means all, have gained from the recent surge in inflation. The fortunes of businesses and households have diverged outside of the euro area, too, with corporate profits in many advanced economies surging over the past few quarters. Poorer households are often hit particularly hard – not only do they suffer from historically high inflation reducing their real incomes, they also do not benefit from higher profits through stock holdings or other types of participation.

Schnabel was right in saying that not all euro area firms have gained from the surge in inflation, but that is not because they chose (for humanitarian reasons, of course) not to raise their prices. Most likely, the firms that have not raised their prices do not have the monopoly or oligopoly power to do that. The suppliers of goods with high elasticity of demand do not raise their prices to avoid the consequence of losing their customers. The euro area firms that benefited from inflation are most likely the suppliers of food and energy, the goods with low elasticity of demand.

Richardson et al. (2022) respond to the claim made by the executives of big firms that they have "no choice" but to raise prices, suggesting that those firms have the choice to accept lower profit. Commenting on the conditions in Australia, they suggest that since profits currently account for a record share of GDP, there is simply no truth behind the assertion that the corporate sector has no choice but to pass on cost increases in full in the form of higher prices. The rising profit share of GDP indicates that Australian firms have, for some time, been choosing to raise their prices by more than the rise in costs. The situation in the US is described by Konczal and Lusiani (2022) who note that "markups and profits skyrocketed in 2021 to their highest recorded level since the 1950s" and that business firms "increased their markups and profits in 2021 at the fastest annual pace since 1955". Elliott (2023) sums it up succinctly as follows: "This isn't wage-price inflation, it's greedflation – and big companies are to blame." By "big" Elliott means companies that have monopoly or oligopoly power in the provision of goods that have low elasticity of demand.

Jim Stanford, Director of the Australian Institute's Centre for Future Work, refers to the work published by the OECD (again, not a working-class supporting institution) showing that the contribution of unit labour costs to overall inflation was much smaller than in the 1970s, and that higher unit profits have been the leading component of recent inflation in several countries (including Australia, Canada and the euro zone). In the case of Australia, the OECD says that over the five quarters to the end of 2022, higher unit profits accounted for an average of 51% of the year-over-year increase in the GDP deflator, while higher unit labour costs accounted for only 21%. Based on this analysis and the analysis of the Australian Institute, Stanford makes the following observation (Australian Institute, 2023):

> Companies in Australia and many other industrial countries have taken advantage of the disruptions, shortages, and desperation of the pandemic to push up profit margins far beyond normal levels. In Australia, corporate profits reached their highest share of GDP ever in 2022, and that has been the leading cause of the current cost-of-living crisis.

Then he goes on to say:

> Workers are now struggling to catch up to prices and recover the loss in their real wages. However, the RBA [Reserve Bank of Australia] continues to ignore the role of profits in driving prices, while doubling down on its determination to suppress wage growth.

Stanford (2023) uses the concept of "profit-price spiral" as opposed to "wage-price spiral", arguing that "the pain experienced by workers through this inflationary episode contrasts sharply with an unprecedented upsurge in business profitability at the same time", attributing rising corporate profit to "businesses increasing prices for the goods and services they sell, above and beyond incremental expenses for their own purchases of inputs and supplies". He suggests that without the inclusion of excess profits in final prices for Australian-made goods and services, inflation since the pandemic would have been much slower than was experienced in practice and that inflation would have fallen within the RBA's target inflation band. A similar view is expressed by Lapavitsas et al. (2023) to describe the situation in the UK by suggesting that "there is no 'wage-price spiral' in the UK" – instead, there is a "relentless rise in profits that takes advantage of rising prices, boosting profit margins, and keeping prices high". They conclude that "growing profits are behind the persistence of inflation in 2022 and beyond, not wages that have failed to keep up with rising prices".

For Lapavitsas et al. (2023), profit-push inflation is a global phenomenon, indicated by the "extraordinary profits of big businesses in the UK and across the world in 2021–22". These extraordinary profits, they note, "are not in the slightest due to technological or managerial efficiency, much less resulting from risk taking or opening up new avenues of production, as mainstream economists usually like to think". Rising profits, they believe, are "purely the result of an income transfer directly out of workers' wages into capitalist profits".

Let us take a look at the fact and figures for the US as reported by FRED. In Figure 4.5 we find four time series of corporate profit and the share of labour compensation in GDP. These series are (a) corporate profit before tax (for non-financial firms), (b) corporate profit after tax, (c) profit (after tax) per unit of real gross value added of non-financial corporate business, and (d) share of labour compensation in GDP at current prices. We can see that while the first three series have been going up, the fourth one has been going down. The big jump in the before-tax and after-tax profit occurred in the second quarter of 2020, coinciding with the first round of price gouging during the pandemic. The same is true of profit per unit of gross value added.

Yet, politicians and policy makers ignore these facts and figures to avoid doing something about the malpractices committed by their partners in the business-government complex. A question that may arise here is the following: what can they do? For a start, consumer protection agencies can impose price controls, which is what they did during the pandemic. Yes, fixing prices may have unintended consequences, but desperate times require desperate measures. They can also impose tax on windfall profits and redistribute income from a small number of corporate monsters to the wider population. Boosting competitiveness by curbing monopoly power would go a long way in reducing the ability of firms with monopoly power to raise prices unjustifiably.

4.8   PRODUCTIVITY SLOWDOWN

The connection between productivity and inflation is that inflation accelerates when productivity growth falls below the growth rate of wages. In other words, stable inflation requires productivity growth to be higher than the growth rate of wages. Productivity growth has slowed across developed economies, following a period of strong growth in the 1990s and early 2000s. Figure 4.6 shows the growth rate of labour productivity in the US manufacturing sector. The superimposed trend shows some sort of rising productivity growth

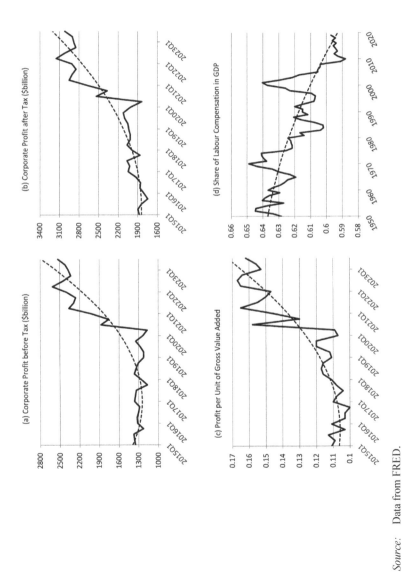

Source: Data from FRED.

Figure 4.5   *Indicators of corporate profitability*

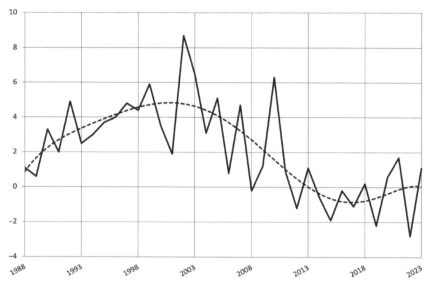

Source: Data from FRED.

Figure 4.6   Labour productivity growth rate in the US

between 1998 and 2002, followed by a decline in subsequent years. It is interesting to observe that productivity growth rose in the COVID years of 2020
and 2021, which can be attributed to a decline in the number of hours worked.

Weak productivity growth is attributed by Bruno et al. (2023) to slowdown
in "business dynamism, job mobility, global trade, and policy reform". They
note that "the global nature of the productivity slowdown suggests economies
must be dealing with common shocks, not only country-specific regulatory
developments". Accordingly, they warn that a continuation of high nominal
wage growth and subdued productivity growth would contribute to ongoing
inflationary pressures. Other causes of the slowdown in productivity growth
are a declining rate of technological diffusion, measurement issues and ageing
population structures (for example, Adler et al., 2017; Andrews et al., 2016;
Goldin et al., 2022). Hambur (2021) and Daley (2021) attribute the observed
slowdown in productivity growth to declining competition and slowing regulatory and economic reform. It is also believed that the global financial crisis
has led to persistent productivity losses, in part because capital investment
has diminished to very low levels, implying that workers have become less
productive because they have less capital to work with.

Weak productivity growth weakens the ability of the the economy to provide goods and services. For example, Lapavitsas et al. (2023) explain the "deep and persistent weakness of aggregate supply in the UK" in terms of the "the country's very poor investment record over a long time" and the "remarkably poor record in labour productivity", pointing out that "weak investment and weak productivity growth are closely related". Furthermore, they argue that "the most important source of productivity growth in an economy is manufacturing industry", which has all but been abandoned as financialisation took hold.

What we are interested in here is whether or not weak productivity growth in recent times is a contributory factor for the resurgence of inflation. Productivity growth rose during the initial stages of the pandemic when the number of hours worked fell faster than output. Improvement in productivity growth was driven by a significant compositional effect, as hours were cut in low-productivity sectors to a far greater extent than in higher productivity sectors. Movement restrictions and lockdowns led to a declining share of hours worked in the (lower productivity) high-contact services sectors, and an increase in the share of hours worked in the (higher productivity) business services sectors where working from home was feasible (Gordon and Sayed, 2022; Lopez-Garcia and Szörfi, 2021; Thwaites et al., 2021). These compositional changes were no longer effective following the end of the acute phase of the pandemic, and with it came a decline in productivity growth in 2022, propelled by significant shocks such as China's zero-COVID-19 policy and Russia's invasion of Ukraine, which undermined global supply chains and energy supply.

It is more plausible to suggest that productivity was adversely affected by the same factors that propelled inflation rather than being a cause of inflation in itself. The resurgence of inflation came many years after the slowdown that started in 2002. For the business-government complex, attributing the resurgence of inflation to slowdown in productivity growth is a convenient excuse for demanding a "wage restraint" and for shifting the blame to the working class rather than the corporate sector. Furthermore, the reasons for the slowdown in productivity growth that are found in the mainstream neoclassical literature and the neoliberal media seem to put the blame on lack of "economic freedom". For example, identifying deregulation and pro-competition policy "reforms" as causes of productivity slowdown means that to boost productivity, measures should be taken to dismantle all obstacles that prevent business firms from accumulating more power and wealth at the expense of the average person. The so-called "pro-competition policy reforms" have led to nothing but the rise of monopolistic and oligopolistic power. Slowdown in business dynamism (the rate at which firms enter the market, grow, shrink, and then leave the market) is also blamed on regulation, even on consumer protection. Chowdhury (2020) makes this point strongly by saying the following: "Rather

than dredging up the usual wish-list of the business community (more deregulation, more privatisation, and more deunionisation), it's time to look at the
deeper, structural factors behind stagnant productivity." For Chowdhury, the
real culprit is financialisation, as he argues that "one can trace the deeper cause
of the long-term declining trend in productivity growth since the 1970s to
financialisation". This is why he concludes as follows:

> No amount of corporate tax cuts or suppression of labour rights in the name of
> structural reform will solve the productivity conundrum. What is really required is
> the taming of finance.

Financialisation and deindustrialisation cause slowdown in productivity
growth. Since productivity depends crucially on the capital-labour ratio,
moving away from high-productivity sectors (such as manufacturing industry)
to parasitic financial services leads to a slowdown in overall productivity.
For example, Rowthorn and Ramaswamy (1997) believe that manufacturing
industry is "technologically more progressive than services", which explains
why deindustrialisation has an adverse effect on productivity growth. As deindustrialisation proceeds, because of deliberate policy actions, the growth of
overall productivity becomes increasingly dependent on the growth of productivity in services. In a financialised economy, non-financial firms spend less
on real capital accumulation because financialisation imposes short-termism
on management and curtails animal spirits with respect to investment in real
capital stock, the outcome being increasing preference for financial investment
to generate short-term profits from financial transactions. It also drains the
internal means of finance available for real investment purposes owing to
increasing dividend payments and stock buy-backs (for details, see Moosa,
2023a, and on the connection between financialisation and deindustrialisation,
see Moosa, 2023b).

   In short, resurgent inflation has not been caused by wages rising faster
than productivity, because this has not been the case as we are going to see in
Chapter 5. However, productivity slowdown is associated with financialisation
and deindustrialisation, which have undermined the productive capacity of the
economy, thereby contributing to the inability of the economy to accommodate
growth in aggregate demand and consequently inflation.

4.9   INFLATIONARY EXPECTATIONS

The term "inflationary expectations" is used to refer to the rate at which economic decision-making units (consumers and firms) expect prices to rise in the
future where the future can be any number of months ahead. The underlying

idea is that actual inflation depends on where we expect it to be. This is how Lee et al. (2020) describe the transmission mechanism:

> If everyone expects prices to rise, say, 3 percent over the next year, businesses will want to raise prices by (at least) 3 percent, and workers and their unions will want similar-sized raises. All else equal, if inflation expectations rise by one percentage point, actual inflation will tend to rise by one percentage point as well.

It sounds so neat, just like everything else in neoclassical economics. Papadimitriou and Wray (2021) argue that the Fed wandered fruitlessly in the wilderness for 40 years searching for a workable theory of inflation, finally settling on the "spurious" idea that inflation is caused by inflationary expectations. According to this proposition, managing inflation is a simple matter of managing expectations, because if economic decision-making units do not expect higher prices, then prices will not rise. This sounds like the proposition that people will not die if they expect not to die. It also means that any cost of living crisis can be avoided by convincing people not to expect a cost of living crisis. Then, is managing expectations simple? Do people make the same expectations and is it possible to make them make the same expectations? I doubt very much that those who believe in the inflationary expectations proposition are capable of giving simple answers to these legitimate questions.

According to the proposition that inflation is caused by inflationary expectations, failing to act decisively against inflation now (by crushing people with rapidly rising interest rates) would "unanchor" expectations. Lee et al. (2020) explain what is meant by "anchoring" as follows: "If everyone expects the Fed to achieve an inflation rate of 2 percent, then consumers and businesses are less likely to react when inflation climbs temporarily above that level (say, because of an oil price hike) or falls below it temporarily (say, because of a recession)." This is ivory tower theorising at its best, typically proved by using sophisticated mathematics, without any relevance to reality – that is, without going out and asking people if that is what they do in reality.

Let us look at the facts and figures. Figure 4.7 displays the one-year inflationary expectations and the actual CPI inflation rate in the US, as reported by FRED. We can see that correlation is high, but again correlation does not imply causation, neither does it tell us anything about the direction of causation. The inflationary expectations proposition implies that causation runs from inflationary expectations to actual inflation, when it is more plausible to suggest that causation runs from inflation to inflationary expectations. Papadimitriou and Wray (2021) argue that expectations do not drive inflation, but the opposite is true, and this is why they suggest that "the tail is truly wagging the dog".

The process whereby expectations are formed (the expectation formation mechanism) is studied extensively in economics because decision making

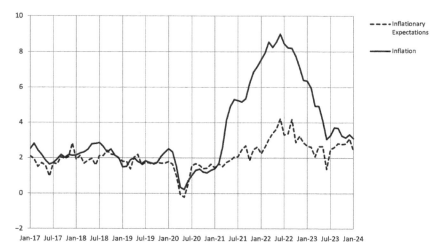

Source: Data from FRED.

Figure 4.7   *Inflationary expectations and actual inflation in the US*

depends on expectations. Several expectation formation mechanisms are
suggested by economic theory, including extrapolative, regressive, adaptive
and rational expectations (see, for example, Moosa and Shamsuddin, 2004).
Extrapolative expectations mean that when inflation is rising, people expect it
to rise further, and vice versa. Regressive expectations imply that when inflation is rising, people expect it to fall, and vice versa. Adaptive expectations
are formed by adjusting expectations by a fraction of the expectation error in
the previous period. The theory of rational expectations states that economic
decision makers collect and process all available information in such a way
as to produce expectations without making systematic errors. Irrespective of
which of these mechanisms is more realistic, they all imply that expected inflation depends on actual current and past inflation rates. This is the case even
for rational expectations, which is a pillar of neoclassical economics to which
central bankers subscribe. Under rational expectations, the expected inflation
rate is determined by all available information on the factors that are likely to
affect inflation as well as historical observations on the inflation rate itself.

The proposition that inflation is caused by inflationary expectations is
rejected by Lapavitsas et al. (2023) who argue that the evidence for such a causal
relation between expected and actual inflation is "close to non-existent". The
data displayed in Figure 4.7 show that correlation between inflationary expectations and lagged inflation is consistently stronger than correlation between
inflation and lagged inflationary expectations. This observation implies that

it is more likely that inflation determines inflationary expectations, not vice versa. We can also see the big gap between inflation and inflationary expectations in the recent period, implying that people underestimated inflation consistently, which provides evidence against the proposition that people do not make systematic errors under rational expectations. The current inflation was caused by rising energy and food prices, not by expectations. It is unfortunate, therefore, that central banks use this kind of ivory tower theorising in order to justify the use of a destructive interest rate policy, on the grounds that high interest rates suppress inflationary expectations and consequently actual inflation.

4.10 GLOBALISATION

Two questions typically arise in any discussion of the effect of globalisation on domestic inflation: (i) whether global factors are more or less important than domestic factors for domestic inflation; and (ii) whether globalisation has a positive or negative effect on domestic inflation – that is, whether globalisation aggravates or alleviates domestic inflation.

The effect of globalisation on inflation is ambiguous, and this is why there are two competing propositions. The first proposition is that the global component of inflation reflects price swings in energy and commodity markets, which means that globalisation-related factors have a negligible effect on domestic inflation. This proposition is inconsistent with the recent resurgence of inflation, caused by rising food and energy prices globally. Even though the world economy was not as globalised in the 1970s as it is now, the inflation of the 1970s was caused by rising commodity (specifically, crude oil) prices. The second proposition is that global factors do matter for domestic inflation – in other words, globalisation may have reduced the sensitivity of inflation to domestic slack (the amount of unused resources, such as unemployed labour). This is the globalisation of inflation hypothesis, which states that the determinants of inflation are becoming increasingly global or that the global determinants of domestic inflation are assuming increasing importance. Those who believe in the validity of this hypothesis have started to reassess the predictive power of standard inflation models by taking into account globalisation-related factors to explain low sensitivity of inflation to domestic determinants.

The increasing synchronisation of inflation rates across countries reflects the influence of common factors, as documented by Ciccarelli and Mojon (2010) who identify large co-movement in headline inflation rates in OECD countries and show that global inflation accounts for about 70% of the cross-country variance of inflation. They also demonstrate that the inclusion of global factors consistently improves domestic inflation forecasts. International inflation co-movements may be explained by common shocks, such as fluctuations in oil and non-oil commodity prices.

To determine if globalisation has a positive or negative effect on inflation, we have to understand the mechanisms whereby the former affects the latter. Globalisation has a direct and an indirect effect on inflation. The direct effect is produced by the increased availability of cheap consumer goods, which follows from lower trade barriers. According to Corrigan (2005), globalisation has made it virtually impossible for domestic firms to raise domestic or export prices, regardless of the pressure to do so emanating from rising costs of production. The indirect effect, on the other hand, works through changes in the price-setting behaviour of firms as a result of changes in the competitive environment, the availability of production inputs, and the impact on labour markets. Thus, it is not obvious whether globalisation aggravates or alleviates inflation. However, it seems that an accepted view is that at one time, globalisation kept the lid on inflation but not any longer, as evident in the global cost of living crisis.

Schnabel (2022) believes that the pandemic and the war in Ukraine provide tangible evidence in favour of the globalisation of inflation hypothesis. Her explanation is that large global excess savings and exceptionally strong global excess demand for many internationally traded goods have contributed to the rise in the pricing power of firms across developed countries. This has fed into price pressures even in countries where domestic slack remains present. The implication here is that globalisation has aggravated inflation in the recent period. Schnabel (2022) believes that things have changed in such a way that global factors may de-anchor inflationary expectations (that is, short-term price shocks may change long-term expectations). She concludes as follows:

> Before the pandemic, the integration of many large emerging market economies into global value chains led to an unprecedented rise in global production capacity, weighing on inflation. Today, global demand is exceeding global supply, putting persistent upward pressure on prices in countries all over the world. In the 2010s, global shocks were largely disinflationary, contributing to the secular decline in long-term inflation expectations. Today, global conditions give rise to the risk of a de-anchoring of inflation expectations to the upside.

According to Schnabel, therefore, globalisation has aggravated domestic inflation through global demand-pull factors, which may or may not be true because no measures of aggregate demand and aggregate supply are available. It is true, however, that global supply was affected adversely by the pandemic. It is more straightforward to contemplate the effect of global cost-push factors such as rising prices of food, energy and fertilisers, as well as the prices of numerous imported goods. A consensus view that has emerged is that the main drivers of current inflation are related to global variables, in particular disruptions in global supply chains, input shortages in key manufacturing sectors, and rising energy and food prices. The very trend towards deglobalisation and reshoring shows that disruption of supply chains leads to disruptions in production, which is inflationary.

4.11 CONCLUDING REMARKS

Out of the factors considered in this chapter as having caused current inflation, two have been found to be questionable: wage-push inflation and inflationary expectations. Wage-push inflation is the factor favoured by the business-government complex, which is convenient to justify refusal to raise minimum wages, the use of interest rates as an anti-inflationary tool and to hide profit-push inflation, thereby shifting the blame from the business sector to wage and salary earners. The inflationary expectations proposition is defunct, but it provides justification for using faulty policy and gives undue credit to central banks.

Resurgent inflation has been caused mostly by cost-push and profit-push factors, particularly the rise in food and energy prices. The situation was aggravated by "feedback loop pressures" because food production is highly energy-intensive. Lapavitsas et al. (2023) argue that inflation rose sharply in the UK in 2021, primarily because aggregate supply was unable to respond to the boost in aggregate demand represented by rising private consumption and government expenditure. This is how they explain the situation:

> The true cause of the cost-of-living crisis is to be found on the side of supply, which is unable efficiently to produce what we need to live and prosper. And yet, as prices began to rise rapidly in Britain in 2021, large enterprises were able to make enormous profits at the expense of workers and the rest of society.

This is why they conclude that "the problem is not too much money" and it is "not that wages are too high". The problem, they argue, is that "profits are too high". Inflation, as Lapavitsas et al. see it, represents a "struggle between workers and capitalists for the distribution of the value that is produced". Monetary policy conducted by the central bank cannot do anything about this kind of inflation. Regulation and consumer protection can.

5.   Causes of the crisis: wage stagnation and neoliberalism

5.1   WAGE STAGNATION: THE STYLISED FACTS

In Chapter 2, we saw how anaemic wage growth has been across the developed world. Wage stagnation, however, is not a recent phenomenon but rather it is a trend that has been around for some time. Mishel et al. (2015) suggest that "wage stagnation for the vast majority was not created by abstract economic trends" – rather, "wages were suppressed by policy choices made on behalf of those with the most income, wealth, and power". Wage stagnation has occurred as a result of the rise of neoliberal thinking, which glorifies the private sector and demonises the public sector. Consequently, wage earners have to deal with the price hikes of the necessary goods and services transferred to the private sector through a reverse-Robin Hood wealth redistribution process known as "privatisation". The stagnation of wages has occurred simultaneously with the destruction of the welfare state and deprivation from the basic services traditionally provided by the public sector.

Mishel et al. (2015) find that over the entire 34-year period between 1979 and 2013, the hourly wages of middle-wage American workers were stagnant, rising just 6%, which means less than 0.2% per year. They further show that wage growth has been decoupled from productivity growth, because the benefits of productivity growth have been realised for most part by capital rather than labour, meaning that the benefits of productivity growth have been used to boost corporate profit rather than wages. This trend has been quite conspicuous since neoliberalism took over as the guiding philosophy for policy makers and elected politicians.

In what follows, we look at the figures used by Mishel et al. (2015), updated by more recent observations from FRED. In this data series, wages are defined as compensation (wages and benefits) of production non-supervisory workers in the private sector. In Figure 5.1, we can see nominal wages, the general price level (CPI) and real wages calculated accordingly. We can see that the general price level has risen much more than wages, particularly in the latter period. As a result, real wages rose initially (until about 1964), then started to decline. Over the period 1948–2023, nominal wages grew at an average annual

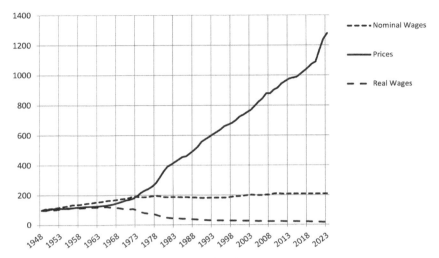

Source: Data from Mishel et al. (2015) and FRED.

Figure 5.1   Nominal wages, CPI and real wages in the US

compound rate of 1%, compared to 3.5% for prices. As a result, real wages declined at an average annual compound rate of 2.4%.

This may be an extreme case due to the use of the wages in the private sector only. While the use of another definition of wages gives a slightly improved picture, this picture is still gloomy. Figure 5.2 displays the movement of US real wages over the same period of time by using two different definitions of nominal wages: the cost of unskilled labour and production workers' hourly compensation (obtained from www.measuringworth.com). In this case we can see that real wages grew until about 1973, after which they remained largely flat on average. Over the initial 26 years (1948–73) real wages of unskilled labour went up a total of 86%. Over the following 50 years, real wages barely moved, rising by a minuscule 4.7% or 0.09% per year.

Mishel et al. (2015) compare wages with productivity over the period 1948–2013 and conclude that "slow and unequal wage growth in recent decades stems from a growing wedge between overall productivity – the improvements in the amount of goods and services produced per hour worked – and the pay (wages and benefits) received by a typical worker". Figure 5.3 is similar to their figure 2, except that it is updated until 2023. In Figure 5.3, wages are represented by compensation of production non-supervisory workers in the private sector whereas productivity is measured as output per hour in the non-farm business sector (obtained from FRED). The figure shows

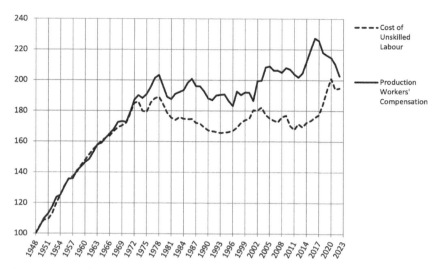

Source: Data from https://www.measuringworth.com/.

Figure 5.2   *US real wages for two types of nominal wages*

that wages grew in tandem with productivity until about 1973, but the gap between the two has been increasing ever since. During the period 1948–73, productivity grew at an average annual compound rate of 2.7% compared with 2.6% for wages. Contrast this with what has been happening since 1973: during the period 1973–2023, the average annual growth rates of productivity and wages were 1.8% and 0.18%, respectively.

Other depressing facts and figures are presented by Mishel et al. (2015):

- Over the period 1948–2013, earnings of the top 1% grew 138% while wages of the bottom 90% grew just 15%.
- Over the period 1979–2013, the wages of middle-wage workers were stagnant, rising just 6%, which is equivalent to less than 0.2% per year.
- Wage stagnation is not a problem of insufficiently skilled or educated workers. It is also a problem for university graduates.
- Employers have been depriving young workers, both university and high school graduates, from healthcare.

The stylised facts on wage stagnation seem to paint a grim picture, with no potential improvement in sight. In the following section we consider the causes of wage stagnation, bearing in mind that not all wages have been stagnant, certainly not the "wages" of corporate bosses.

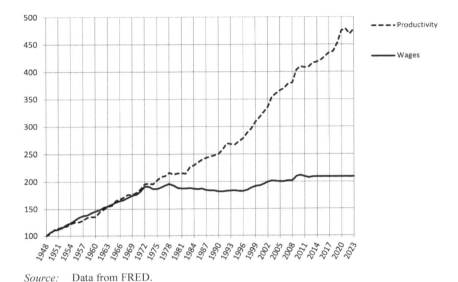

Source: Data from FRED.

Figure 5.3   *US productivity and wages*

5.2   CAUSES OF WAGE STAGNATION

One reason why wages have been stagnant is that CEOs have been grabbing an increasingly larger share of the wage "pot". Figure 5.4 shows some stylised facts. In the US, one company (ticker symbol, NUS) pays the CEO more than 9000 times the average worker. The number ten company in this respect pays the CEO more than 2000 times the average worker. In the US also, the average CEO pay went up from $11.7 million in 2013 to $16.7 million in 2022. In the US also, the CEO to worker pay ratio went up from just over 20 in 1965 to 344 in 2022. While the US has the highest CEO to worker pay ratio, other countries are not that far behind. In two countries with large numbers of impoverished people, India and South Africa, CEOs get paid 229 and 180 times the average worker, respectively. In a neoliberal world, this is the norm because somehow the market says that the CEO should be paid 1000 times the pay of the average worker. The market, we are told, has to be obeyed because it is "neutral" and "objective". It also has no morals, something that free marketeers are proud of.

When CEOs grab an increasingly larger share of the wage "pot", the wage of the average worker stagnates and may even decline. This proposition can be demonstrated with the help of some simulation results. For this purpose, we assume that the initial value (at time 0) of the wage pot is 100, growing at

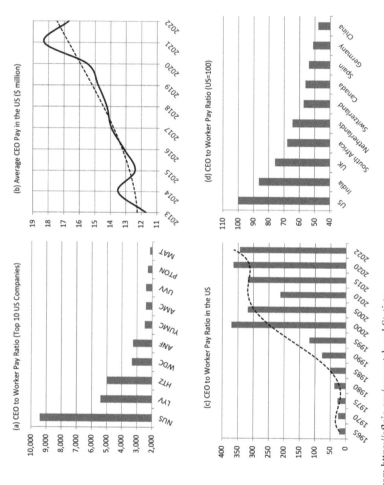

Source: Data from https://aflcio.org/paywatch and Statista.

Figure 5.4   *CEO pay relative to workers*

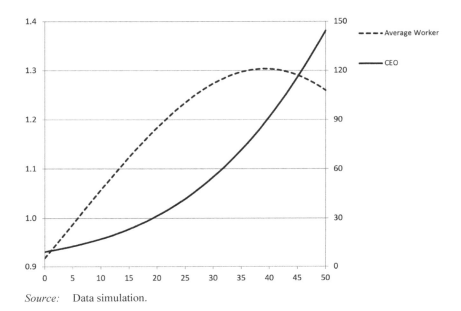

Source: Data simulation.

Figure 5.5   *Trajectory of worker and CEO pay (simulated data)*

2% per period. Another assumption is that 99% of those making claims on the wage pot are average workers and the remaining 1% are CEOs. At time zero, the ratio of CEO to worker pay is 10:1, rising at the rate of 5% per period. The trajectories for CEO and average workers' pay over 50 periods are shown in Figure 5.5, with startling results. While CEO pay grows at an increasing rate, average worker pay grows at a declining rate and eventually starts to fall. Over the entire period, workers' pay grows at an average compound rate of 0.6% per period, compared with 5.7% for CEO pay.

Other reasons for wage stagnation, as identified by Mishel et al. (2015), include reluctance to raise the minimum wage, which is more pronounced in the US, and the erosion of collective bargaining as a result of the decline in union membership. They show that the drop in the share of workers under collective bargaining contracts is the mirror image of the rise of incomes of the top 10%. This negative association stems from the observation that collective bargaining not only raises wages for union members but also compels employers to raise the wages and benefits of non-union workers to come closer to union wage standards. Figure 5.6 shows US union membership over the period 1973–2022 where we can see that union membership peaked in 1979, then started to decline in 1980 following the war launched by Ronald Reagan and Margaret Thatcher on trade unions for the benefit of corporate interests.

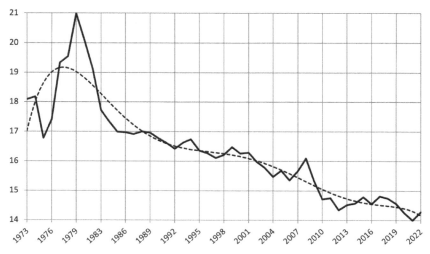

Source: Data from https://www.unionstats.com/.

Figure 5.6   Union membership in the US

Yet another reason for wage stagnation, as envisaged by Mishel (2015), is globalisation, which he thinks (correctly) "is deeply influenced by American policy decisions". Globalisation is conducive to wage stagnation because international trade agreements are designed in such a way as to protect employers without providing any protection for workers who, as a result, endure the consequences of a race to the bottom with respect to labour standards. Mishel argues that global integration with low-wage countries leads to a reduction in the wages of domestic low-paid workers while boosting profits and the incomes of the highest earners. Globalisation has all but wiped out US manufacturing industry, leading to diminishing manufacturing employment, with significant adverse spillover effects on the rest of the economy.

The same story goes for other countries, including Australia where wage growth is among the worst in OECD countries (Peetz, 2019). Like Mishel et al. (2015), Stewart et al. (2022) identify the erosion of collective bargaining as a cause of wage stagnation. They also identify two government-related factors, failure to raise the minimum wage relative to the median wage, and pursuing deliberate policies to restrain wage growth (allegedly to fight inflation). As far as business is concerned, they mention wage underpayment (also known as "wage theft"), which apparently is endemic. Another factor is fragmented business structures and organisational models whereby businesses avoid direct employment of workers through subcontracting, labour hire and franchising, all of which drive down wages. Sometimes business firms draft contracts that portray workers as being self-employed, just to save on superannuation and other employment costs. Last, but not least, businesses pay the casual wage rate to workers performing work that is not temporary by any means. In short, the business-government complex has been doing a good job to realise the objective of wage stagnation. Hutchens (2023b) attributes wage stagnation in Australia to "formidable employer power".

The UK is in the same boat as the US and Australia. Rawlinson (2023) describes wage stagnation in the UK as follows: "Workers in the UK are £11,000 worse off a year after 15 years of almost completely unprecedented wage stagnation that signals a failure of recent economic policy" (in reference to the neoliberal policy prescription of liberalise, privatise and deregulate). The situation is even worse as portrayed by the Trades Union Congress (TUC, 2022): "UK workers are suffering the longest and harshest pay squeeze in modern history." The analysis of the TUC shows that "working people lost nearly £20,000 in real earnings between 2008 and 2021 as a result of pay not keeping pace with inflation".

The problem of wage stagnation cannot be solved by payments that only provide short-term relief. Work insecurity as a result of automation and corporate greed makes the problem even worse, and so does the systematic dismantling of the welfare state under the pretext of private sector efficiency. Blakeley (2022) attributes the cost of living crisis to the "extraordinary power of corporate and financial elites over our economy", which would not be possible without the complicity of the government. This means that the business-government complex enables wage stagnation, and consequently the emergence of the cost of living crisis.

5.3   THE ROLE OF NEOLIBERALISM

Neoliberalism is a term that is used to refer to the 20th-century resurgence of 19th-century ideas associated with free-market capitalism that flourished in Victorian England. The term is generally associated with policy actions that involve privatisation, deregulation and liberalisation, as well as a drastic reduction in government spending for the purpose of boosting the role of the private sector in the economy. To put it mildly, neoliberalism is associated with austerity, profit-push inflation, redistribution of income the wrong way, a twisted tax code, deindustrialisation, financialisation, and the erosion of public services and the welfare state in general. On an international level, neoliberalism is associated with globalisation, the Washington Consensus and IMF conditionality. Neoliberalism is even associated with militarism and imperialism. There is no wonder, then, that neoliberalism has contributed to the two dimensions of the cost of living crisis all around the world: rising inflation and stagnant wages. Monbiot (2016) argues that neoliberalism has played a major role in the advent of the global financial crisis, the offshoring of wealth and power, the slow collapse of public health and education, and resurgent child poverty.

The idea of neoliberalism was born in the 1940s as an alternative to the laissez-faire economic consensus that had collapsed as a result of the great depression. The "midwives" included the usual suspects (Friedrich Hayek, Milton Friedman, Karl Popper, George Stigler and Ludwig von Mises) who opposed the ideas implicit in the 1930s New Deal, which was introduced by the administration of Franklin Roosevelt in response to the devastation inflicted by the laissez-faire-driven great depression. Those pundits saw the New Deal and the gradual development of Britain's welfare state as "manifestations of a collectivism that occupied the same spectrum as Nazism and communism" (Monbiot, 2016). The "usual suspects" also opposed any collectivist trends that, according to them, posed a threat to individual freedom, the freedom of entrepreneurs individually and collectively to rape the nation, and enrich themselves in the process, with total impunity.

For the proponents and the beneficiaries of neoliberalism (the oligarchy) individual freedom does not include the freedom of ordinary people from illiteracy, disease and poverty. For them, individual freedom is threatened by the welfare state, universal healthcare, environmental regulation, progressive taxation, anything that undermines the freedom of the oligarchy to accumulate wealth, anything that is conducive to the common good, and anything that is done to help the poor and vulnerable. For example, universal healthcare is a threat because it deprives the oligarchy from lucrative business opportunities (for example, selling a pill for $1000, even though it costs 50 cents to produce). The freedoms they advocate are the freedoms that provide privileges to the oligarchy and enhance their ability to accumulate wealth and power at the expense of the majority. Freedom from trade unions and collective bargaining means freedom to suppress wages. Freedom from regulation means freedom to poison rivers, endanger workers and sell toxic financial assets. Freedom from tax means freedom from the obligation to contribute to the society for the purpose of providing a social safety net that lifts people out of poverty. Selfishness is the name of the game whereas compassion and altruism are rejected because somehow they are conducive to economic inefficiency that undermines the ability of the oligarchy to rape the society and control the economy.

For decades after the advent of neoliberalism, the notion was largely confined to a small number of think tanks and universities that received generous grants from the oligarchy. However, the stagflation of the 1970s paved the way for neoliberal policy proposals to be taken seriously, even though there was nothing in the neoliberal policy prescriptions that would allow policy makers to avert or alleviate the effects of a major crisis. The stagflation of the 1970s was a convenient excuse to put in place a neoliberal agenda that progressively made the rich richer and the poor poorer. Beginning in the early 1980s, the Reagan administration and Thatcher government implemented a series of neoliberal policy prescriptions that involved wholesale deregulation and the privatisation of everything under the sun. Margret Thatcher and her Tory government embarked on a mission to dismantle manufacturing industry, mining and any meaningful productive activity in preference for parasitic activities involving transactions in financial assets and real estate. The Thatcher-Reagan package also involved massive tax cuts for the rich, the crushing of trade unions, outsourcing and competition in public services.

Neoliberalism has since become the dominant paradigm on a global scale. Through the IMF, the World Bank, the Maastricht Treaty and the World Trade Organization, neoliberal policies have been imposed (typically without democratic consent) on much of the world. Monbiot (2016) argues that when neoliberal policies cannot be imposed domestically, they are imposed internationally, through trade treaties incorporating "investor-state dispute settlement": offshore tribunals in which corporations can press for the removal of social and environmental protections. Whenever parliaments vote to restrict sales of cigarettes, protect water supplies from mining companies, freeze energy bills or prevent pharmaceutical firms from ripping off the state, corporations sue, often successfully.

The neoliberal recipe for a sustainable state of affairs rests on a self-regulating market and management of the money supply by an independent central bank, which means that the power of the public sector should be curtailed significantly through privatisation and budgetary constraints, in what amounts to a policy that is intended to "starve the beast". Every element of this recipe is wrong. A self-regulating market means an unregulated market that puts no limit on the insatiable appetite of the oligarchy to accumulate wealth. An independent central bank is immune from public scrutiny because it is not accountable to elected politicians.

Starving the beast implies a rejection of the welfare state and the notion of income redistribution through taxes and subsidies. Personal taxation is regarded as evil, even for the wealthiest, on the grounds that personal income is nothing but the result of personal success stories, which means that taxing the rich is an illegitimate confiscation mechanism. Effectively, "starving the beast" boils down to starving the masses. It is interesting to note that those calling for starving the beast do not mind feeding the beast as long as the feeding is financed by middle- and lower middle-class wage and salary earners, and as long as the beast engages in military adventurism to boost the wealth of the wealthy. Taxing the rich is unfair but taxing the poor and middle class to finance wars of aggression is fine, even necessary to "defend the nation".

In a neoliberal world, redistribution of wealth is common but it goes in the wrong direction, from the poor and middle class to the rich and super-rich. A twisted tax code encourages the accumulation of debt for the benefit of the financial oligarchy and allows the rich and super-rich to get away with minimal tax payments. As a public policy tool, neoliberalism is used to justify the privatisation of public sector entities and services, the deregulation of economic activity, and the attainment of a balanced budget (with minimal taxation) by imposing austerity. For these reasons and others, the term "neoliberalism" is used as a pejorative by the critics. In *The Handbook of Neoliberalism*, for instance, it is suggested that the term has "become a means of identifying a seemingly ubiquitous set of market-oriented policies as being largely responsible for a wide range of social, political, ecological and economic problems" (Springer et al., 2016). Likewise, Stedman-Jones (2012) notes that the term "is too often used as a catch-all shorthand for the horrors associated with globalisation and recurring financial crises". Bittman (2014) identifies the neoliberal principles as "anti-unionism, deregulation, market fundamentalism and intensified, unconscionable greed". However, no one describes neoliberalism better than Monbiot (2016) who opines:

> Neoliberalism sees competition as the defining characteristic of human relations. It redefines citizens as consumers, whose democratic choices are best exercised by buying and selling, a process that rewards merit and punishes inefficiency … . Attempts to limit competition are treated as inimical to liberty. Tax and regulation should be minimised, public services should be privatised. The organisation of labour and collective bargaining by trade unions are portrayed as market distortions … . Inequality is recast as virtuous: a reward for utility and a generator of wealth, which trickles down to enrich everyone. Efforts to create a more equal society are both counterproductive and morally corrosive … . The rich persuade themselves that they acquired their wealth through merit … . The poor begin to blame themselves for their failures, even when they can do little to change their circumstances.

Neoliberalism as a doctrine creates an economic system that is exposed to economic and financial crises and weakens the ability of policy makers to deal with any crisis. With respect to the cost of living crisis, Lapavitsas et al. (2023) identify "a range of major long-term weaknesses", including "deskilling of the labour force, low levels of investment, very weak productivity growth, persistent current account deficits, chronically low spending on infrastructure and health, education, and care, escalating inequality, entrenched imbalances between the regions of the country, and the domination of financial institutions over the lives of households". They call for abandoning neoliberalism without calling it so by saying the following:

> The route ahead for the UK ought to be the reverse of that taken over the past forty years, initiated by Margaret Thatcher. Britain's extreme unleashing of market forces

involved the unprecedented privatisation and selling of public assets, wholesale deindustrialisation, and deregulation of the financial sector. It included the systematic introduction of anti-union legislation, the break-up of collective bargaining, and the erosion of the value of pensions as well as continual downward pressure on wages.

This is exactly what neoliberalism has done since the destructive "reforms" introduced by Thatcher and Reagan on both sides of the Atlantic and followed by the rest of the "West" and the "international community", all the countries in which the average person is enduring financial difficulties unseen before, while a minority has never been exposed to a cost of living crisis.

Neoliberalism is a destructive and an immoral doctrine designed to benefit the rich and powerful. This doctrine has enabled the commodification of everything under the sun and the privatisation of schools, hospitals, prisons, natural resources, utilities, childcare, and even war, for the benefit of corporate interests. Macfarlane (2022) suggests that to tackle the cost of living crisis, we must end the "Great British Rip Off" (that is, neoliberal policies). According to him, the cost of living crisis is not new, suggesting that the crisis "is not simply the result of rising gas prices". For decades, he argues, British households have been squeezed by a pincer movement of persistently low incomes, on the one hand, and extractive business models, on the other. This pincer movement is what neoliberalism delivers.

5.4 THE ROLE OF FINANCIALISATION

Financialisation, the increasing power and dominance of the financial oligarchy, is a product of neoliberalism as suggested by many scholars. For example, Radzievska (2016) argues that "the term 'financialization' grew out of the ideology of liberalism in the 1920s and was widespread in the 1990s based on the establishment in the late 1970s–early 1980s of the ideology of neoliberalism". The two pillars of neoliberalism identified by Ostry et al. (2016) are conducive to financialisation. The first is deregulation-enhanced competition and the drive to open up domestic markets, including financial markets, to foreign competition. The second is using privatisation to undermine the role of the public sector and put limits on the ability of the government to run fiscal deficits and accumulate debt. By opening up financial markets to foreign competition, the size of the financial sector grows by more than what can be achieved in the absence of foreign financial institutions. Deregulation itself is a primary driving force of financialisation (see, for example, Moosa, 2023a). Privatisation produces a smaller public sector and constitutes a significant source of revenue for investment banks that arrange the IPOs whereby a publicly owned firm is handed over to the private sector. It also boosts the capitalisation of the stock market (that is, the aggregate value of all traded stocks).

In general, it has been found that financialisation has adverse effects on living standards, capital accumulation, consumption, productivity, aggregate demand, value added, income distribution, employment, wages, tax revenue, asset price inflation, financial stability, and the opacity and complexity of the financial sector. The contribution of the financial sector to employment is disproportional to the share of corporate profit that the sector commands. According to Tomaskovic-Devey (2015), financialisation has led to lower living standards through four channels: diminishing employment, lower wages for the employed, reduced capital investment in new production and declining tax revenue. Financialisation has changed the relations between social classes with the emergence of an elitist group of highly paid employees of the financial sector. On the receiving end are new categories of first-time home buyers, new segments of the working poor suffering foreclosure for unpaid debt and those whose pensions or health insurance has been financialised, and new social movements protesting the financial sector.

Financialisation has changed the way governments provide public services (in countries where they still do that) even though some of those services, such as healthcare and education, are seen as human rights. In a financialised economy, financial markets play a major role in the provision and financing of public services. At one time, the public sector provided utilities (such as water and gas) at reasonable prices, and free services like healthcare and education. In a financialised economy, the provision of public services is executed by a system of indirect public provision, where the government enters a partnership with a private, profit-maximising firm. The partnership between private finance and public services has also affected the provision of social housing, which once upon a time was the responsibility of the public sector. The total or partial withdrawal of the public sector from the provision of social services (in the name of efficiency, of course) has led to a situation where the responsibility and burden have been shifted to the individual. The impact of speculative trading on food prices has been particularly severe. As a by-product of neoliberalism, financialisation is divorced from morality and conducive to greed.

The economic effects of financialisation are highly relevant to the cost of living crisis. An adverse effect on capital accumulation leads to diminishing productive capacity and declining productivity, both of which are inflationary. The adverse effect on income distribution produces more poor people who are less able to cope with a cost of living crisis than the minority of rich people. The adverse effect on wages aggravates the effect of the crisis by its direct impact on the second dimension of the crisis. Lower tax revenue reduces the ability and willingness of the public sector to provide public services that reduce the intensity of a crisis. Financial crises, which are more frequent in a highly financialised economy, are typically followed by recessions, which deprive people of their incomes and hamper wage growth.

5.5   THE WASHINGTON CONSENSUS AND IMF CONDITIONALITY

The neoliberal agenda has been reinforced and spread worldwide by international organisations such as the IMF, World Bank and the OECD. These organisations are guided by the principles of the Washington Consensus, which can be summarised in three words: privatise, liberalise and deregulate. The ten commandments of the Washington Consensus, as specified by Williamson (1990), can be classified under four pillars: fiscal reform, interest and exchange rate policies, liberalisation, and privatisation/deregulation (for a detailed description, see Moosa, 2021).

A quick look at the ten commandments of the Consensus reveals the hypocrisy behind them. The intention behind fiscal discipline, as preached to developing countries, is a deliberate reduction in the size of the public sector, allegedly to enhance efficiency. Redirecting public expenditure to pro-poor, health and education sounds noble but it is ludicrous because ample evidence exists to suggest that IMF operations are detrimental to social expenditure as available financial resources are used to pay off debt. Competitive exchange rates (implying an undervalued domestic currency) make cheap public assets, as a result of privatisation, even cheaper for foreign investors (primarily multinationals). The rest of the commandments are designed to benefit foreign investors and the local oligarchy. Developing countries are told by the preachers and enforcers of the Washington Consensus that it is in their own interest to cut tax for the rich and corporations, open up their financial systems, remove any trade protection so that foreign corporations have access to new markets, and secure the rights of foreign investors to buy (or loot) public assets. That was exactly what China was told to do in the 19th century by the preachers of free trade. When China refused to allow British "entrepreneurs" to sell Indian-grown opium on its territory, Royal Navy ships travelled all the way from Portsmouth to the Chinese coast line and started a relentless campaign of bombardment that lasted until the end of the Opium War and the financialisation of a part of China that is known as Hong Kong.

IMF conditionality is a set of conditions that any country seeking financial assistance from the IMF must abide by. Typically, these conditions are based on laissez-faire free-market economics and the ideology of neoliberalism, in the spirit of the ten commandments of the Washington Consensus or variants thereof. Compliance with conditionality is enforced by disbursing funds in instalments that are linked to demonstrable policy actions (effectively an act of brutal blackmail). The IMF assesses the underlying situation periodically to

determine whether or not modifications are necessary for achieving the underlying objectives (for example, the removal of subsidies to boost "efficiency").
The conditions typically include (among others) the following: currency devaluation, austerity, restructuring of foreign debt, free-market pricing, enhancing
the rights of foreign investors vis-à-vis national law, and financialisation.

While IMF conditionality is supposed to prevent and resolve crises, the
exact opposite is true: it is conducive to cost of living crises in developing
countries. Conditionality is intended to allow plunder via privatisation and
currency devaluation, thereby weakening the ability of the public sector to
provide public services. Free-market pricing in the absence of government
support means rising prices and rapid erosion of real incomes. Austerity
means that those suffering from the erosion of real incomes will not get any
help. Every element of the Washington Consensus and IMF conditionality is
actually conducive to cost of living crises. This is why developing countries
"blessed" with financial help from the IMF have been in a perpetual cost of
living crisis.

5.6   CONCLUDING REMARKS

In this chapter we discussed wage stagnation, as the second dimension of the
cost of living crisis, and neoliberalism (and its offshoots) as a contributory
factor to both of the dimensions of the crisis. In this concluding section we
want to recap on the aspects of neoliberalism and its offshoots that have contributed to the two dimensions of the crisis.

The erosion of the welfare state has forced people to allocate increasingly
larger portions of stagnant wages to pay for services that once upon a time
were provided by the public sector, most notably health and education.
Likewise, the privatisation of utilities has forced people to allocate larger
portions of tighter budgets to the payment of utility bills. For example, since
the water sector was privatised in England in 1989, bills have risen by 40%
above inflation. Households in England are paying £2.3 billion more a year
for their water and sewerage bills under the current privatised system than if
the water companies had remained in public ownership. The same goes for
the privatisation of transport. Since rail services in the UK were privatised in
1994, rail fares have increased by a fifth in real terms. The same goes for the
privatisation of social care. In the UK, the cost of care in residential homes has
risen by almost 30% since 2012 (from £27,000 to £35,000 a year).

Neoliberalism is the reason why a twisted tax code puts most of the burden
on wage and salary earners. It is the reason why the public purse is inadequate
except for financing wars to "defend the nation and save lives" and also to
enrich arms manufacturers and those in public service who get rewarded by
arms manufacturers. Neoliberalism is the reason why minimum wages are

stagnant, given that they are not market-determined, which means (according to free marketeers) that they represent some sort of economic inefficiency. Financialisation and deindustrialisation, two offshoots of neoliberalism and two sides of the same coin, have led to diminishing productive capacity and the decline of manufacturing industry, making the economy unable to accommodate a demand shock. Neoliberalism is the reason why central banks should be independent, which means that they can, with impunity, pursue policies that hurt people. It is the reason why collective bargaining is a thing of the past, which has reduced the ability of workers to preserve their real wages and allowed businesses to channel productivity gains to profit rather than wages. Last, but not least, neoliberalism is the reason why natural resources are owned by a few oligarchs rather than the public sector, which is deprived of the financial resources that can be provided by ownership of natural resources. It is, therefore, unfair to blame Putin for the cost of living crisis, because the occurrence of cost of living crises is endemic to an economic system that is run according to neoliberal thinking.

6. Implications for economic theory: inflation as a monetary problem

6.1 THE MONETARY THEORY OF INFLATION

Milton Friedman, who was the high priest of monetarism and the most out-spoken advocate of the monetary theory of inflation, is known to have said that "inflation is always and everywhere a monetary phenomenon" (Friedman, 1963). In Chapter 4, several reasons were listed for the resurgence of inflation as the first dimension of the cost of living crisis, including the universally agreed upon factors of semiconductor chip shortage, the energy crisis, the food crisis, and disruption to the global supply chain. Other causes, which are debatable or not specific to this crisis, are rising wages and profits, diminishing productivity, inflationary expectations and globalisation. So far, there has been no mention of the money supply as a causing factor, but some economists and observers believe that monetary factors, represented by the monetary expansion that came in response to the pandemic, is the (or a) cause of resurgent inflation.

The monetary theory of inflation is based on the quantity theory of money, where money is defined as the stock of assets that perform the functions of money: medium of exchange, measure of value and store of value. Therefore, the money supply is the sum of currency in circulation and deposits with various degrees of liquidity. It follows that money is created by the central bank (the currency part) and commercial banks (the deposits part). In practice, the money supply is represented by a number of monetary aggregates, ranging from the narrow money supply, M1, to broader measures such as M2, M3 and M4. These aggregates are obtained by adding less liquid assets to M1, which contains demand deposits and other liquid deposits only. While central banks create money by issuing currency, commercial banks create money by granting credit and opening bank accounts (deposits) against them. This is why inflation is also linked to the availability of credit.

The quantity theory of money explains how monetary growth leads to inflation. The idea behind the monetary theory of inflation is simple: if more money is created (by the central bank and/or commercial banks) than what is required to buy the available stock of goods and services, prices will rise – that is, the value of money in terms of goods and services (or the purchasing power of money) will decline. Inflation, in other words, arises when too much money chases too few goods. In the 19th century, the relation between the money supply and inflation was articulated by Joplin (1826) as follows: "There is no opinion better established, though it is seldom consistently maintained, than that the general scale of prices existing in every country, is determined by the amount of money which circulates in it."

The quantity theory of money, also called the quantity equation of money, is based on the simple idea that the amount of money required to settle trans-actions depends on the value of transactions – hence, on the volume of output and prices (that is, nominal output). It is represented by the identity $MV = PY$, where M is the money supply, V is the velocity of circulation of money, P is the general price level and Y is real output (real GDP) – hence, PY is nominal output. The velocity of circulation is the number of times each dollar is spent or changes hands. The quantity theory of money can be used to state the fol-lowing propositions:

1. A proportional relation between P and M exists if the ratio V/Y is constant or stable. This means that when the money supply rises by 10%, the general price level rises by 10%. In other words, the inflation rate is equal to the monetary growth rate (the percentage change in the money supply).
2. If the velocity of circulation is stable, the inflation rate is the difference between the monetary growth rate and the growth rate of real output. This means that inflation arises only if the monetary growth rate is higher than the growth rate of real output.
3. If velocity changes, inflation could arise even without monetary growth. Furthermore, monetary growth in excess of output growth does not cause inflation if it is offset by a proportional drop in the velocity of circulation.

Those who believe in the quantity theory as providing an explanation for inflation argue that the velocity of circulation is stable and predictable and that money is neutral with respect to real output (that is, changes in the money supply do not affect real output). These are, however, testable hypotheses, not undisputed facts of life as portrayed by the "true believers" who think that inflation is entirely a monetary phenomenon, caused by monetary-driven excess aggregate demand.

Take, for example, Mehra (2000) who criticises the cost-push view of infla-tion on the grounds that it does not recognise the role of monetary policy in determining the causal influence of wage growth on inflation. He argues that if a non-accommodative monetary policy is pursued to keep inflation under control, firms may not be able to pass on excessive wage gains in the form of higher product prices. This issue of accommodative versus non-accommodative monetary policy will be considered in Chapter 7. However, it suffices for the time being to say that the implication of Mehra's argument is that the central bank can prevent inflation if it wishes, which is bizarre.

Some economists think that the relation between money and inflation depends on whether inflation is high or low. For example, Borio et al. (2023) argue that "the strength of the link between money growth and inflation depends on the inflation regime", such that "it is one-to-one when inflation is high and virtually non-existent when it is low". The validity of this statement depends on how high inflation is: moderately high or extremely high. As we shall see later, the link between monetary growth and inflation is conspicuous under hyperinflation, but not otherwise.

6.2   A STATEMENT OF FRIEDMAN'S PROPOSITION

The full version of Friedman's proposition on the monetary nature of inflation is that "inflation is always and everywhere a monetary phenomenon, in the sense that it is and can be produced only by a more rapid increase in the quantity of money than in output" (Heritage Foundation, 2021). This is exactly the prediction of the quantity theory of money as described in the previous section under the assumption that the velocity of circulation is constant, which may or may not be the case as we are going to see.

Friedman was also a free marketeer and (like Friedrich Hayek, Karl Popper, George Stigler and Ludwig von Mises) a founding member of the Mont Pelerin Society in 1947, which was financed by some self-serving millionaires for the purpose of proposing a neoliberal alternative to the laissez-faire economic consensus that had collapsed as a result of the great depression. He also supported the violent 1973 *coup d'état* in Chile and provided the "intellectual" rationale for Thatcher and Reagan to go ahead with their destructive "reforms". Believing that the public sector is the source of all mishaps, Friedman blamed inflation squarely on the government by suggesting that inflation is driven by government spending, which is financed by monetary expansion, assuming that the government can control the money supply. The following is the reasoning as stated by Friedman (Hayward, 2022):

> Inflation is always and everywhere a monetary phenomenon. It's always and everywhere, a result of too much money, of a more rapid increase in the quantity of money than in output. Moreover, in the modern era, the important next step is to recognize that today, governments control the quantity of money. So that as a result, inflation in the United States is made in Washington and nowhere else.

Perhaps the government can control the quantity of money in Washington (which is not the case), but how did Friedman know that this is also the case for every country and every continent and every island nation in every ocean? He could not have had the time to study the working of every monetary system in the 200 plus countries on this planet. This cannot be the case when countries have different degrees of central bank independence, which Friedman's followers brag about, even though it means less control by the government over the money supply. Furthermore, Friedman discarded the role of cost-push and profit-push factors, which can be readily used to explain the recent resurgence of inflation, a prime (though not the only) cause of the cost of living crisis. Friedman went on to say:

> If you listen to people in Washington talk, they will tell you that inflation is produced by greedy businessmen or it's produced by grasping unions or it's produced by spendthrift consumers, or maybe, it's those terrible Arab Sheikhs who are producing it. Now, of course, businessmen are greedy. Who of us isn't? Trade unions are grasping. Who of us isn't? And there's no doubt that the consumer is a spendthrift. At least every man knows that about his wife.

The generalisations are astounding: everyone living on this planet is greedy and grasping. Surely, one exception to this rule is Charles Feeney who donated almost all of his wealth to charity before he died, only to live a modest life (and there are thousands like him). Every consumer on this planet is spendthrift, but surely the typical consumer is not as extravagant as Michael Jackson and Omar Sharif.

Here, Friedman identifies and rejects cost-push, profit-push and demand-pull factors, apart from the demand-pull arising from government fiscal expansion financed by monetary expansion. According to him, greedy businessmen do not raise profit margins and cause profit-push inflation (which is counterfactual), wage-push is not inflationary, even though greedy businessmen tend to pass on higher wages to consumers by raising prices, and the 1970s quadrupling of oil prices was not inflationary. It follows that rising energy, food and housing prices did not contribute to the latest resurgence of inflation. By implication, he did not believe in "imported inflation" resulting from changes in prices at the origin or from a depreciating domestic currency.

Some Friedmanites acknowledge the inflationary effect of cost-push and demand-pull factors but they present one or two twists. They may argue that rising wages and energy prices are not inflationary, in the sense that they do not contribute to "sustained" inflation – that is, they are one-off events that lead to a temporary rise in the inflation rate. Otherwise, they argue that the effects of demand-pull and cost-push factors will not materialise unless they are accommodated by a monetary expansion. This is exactly the point made by Mehra (2000) and referred to earlier. Expressed differently, (aggregate) demand and supply shocks do not cause inflation unless they are accommodated by a deliberate monetary expansion (these points will be discussed in detail in Chapter

7). The silver lining (at least for Vladimir Putin) is that had Friedman lived to witness the current cost of living crisis, he would have exonerated Putin from the charge that he (Putin) is responsible for igniting inflation, even though I doubt very much that Friedman would have refrained from accusing Putin of being responsible for every other mishap.

Friedman went on to explain why greedy businessmen, grasping unions, spendthrift consumers and Arab Sheikhs do not produce inflation as follows:

> But none of them produce inflation for the very simple reason that neither the businessman, nor the trade union, nor the housewife has a printing press in their basement on which they can turn out those green pieces of paper we call money.

The assumption here is that governments control the printing press, meaning that governments can expand spending as they wish and finance the fiscal expansion by using the printing press to produce cash. This might have been true in the Weimar Republic of Germany in the 1920s where high-speed printing presses were operated round the clock to print banknotes that the government used to pay its bills. And even then, it is plausible to suggest that the Germans did that intentionally so that the resulting hyperinflation would reduce the real value of the reparations they were paying Britain and France.

This is not exactly the case in modern America or Britain, not only because they are not paying war reparations but also because governments do not own the printing presses that produce banknotes. The printing press is owned by the central bank, which in theory at least is independent of the government. In accordance with the principles of neoliberalism, which have been embraced by the governments of Western countries, central bank independence is conducive to controlling inflation and boosting welfare.

As a matter of fact, countries brag about having a high degree of central bank independence. In 2023, the Australian government introduced legislation to Parliament to "reform, strengthen and modernise the Reserve Bank of Australia (RBA)". The motivation was to boost the independence of the RBA by making it less accountable to elected politicians, giving it a free hand to crush people with high interest rates. In a case like this, whoever happens to be in charge of the RBA can inflict enormous damage on ordinary people and transfer big chunks of their incomes to commercial banks via mushrooming interest payments. Politicians who are elected to represent ordinary people will not be in a position to object to, let alone veto, any action deemed appropriate by the governor of the central bank and her/his lieutenants. The moral of the story is that if the central bank is independent of the government, then the government does not own or operate the printing press, just like it cannot influence the interest rate decisions taken by the central bank.

In the US, the central bank (Federal Reserve) is not only independent, it is a shareholding company owned by commercial banks. This has been the case since the establishment of the Federal Reserve in a 1913 stealth operation – surely Friedman would have been aware of this fact when he claimed that the government owned and operated the printing press. But then the printing press produces cash only, and cash is a small part of the money supply in a modern economy. The government (or rather the central bank) has even less control over the money supply – this is a point that will be discussed in detail in Chapter 7.

Friedman defined inflation in such a way to be consistent with the narrative that it is a monetary phenomenon. He defined it as a "steady and sustained rise in prices", which means that a rise in prices that is not steady or sustained does not represent inflation. According to Henderson (2021), this is why "one could not find inflation anywhere in the world that was not caused by a prior increase in the supply of money or in the growth rate of the supply of money". The emphasis here is on the words "steady" and "sustained" because one-off rises in energy or food prices, for example, are not inflationary (even though sometimes they are called "inflationary bursts"). This is interesting: the Friedmanites claim that inflation is a monetary phenomenon, so if you argue that the inflation of the 1970s was caused, amongst other factors, by a signif-icant rise in oil prices, they would say that it was not inflation because it was neither "steady" nor "sustained", just a one-off jump in the CPI.

Henderson (2021) suggests that Friedman's statement was "an empirical one, not a logically necessary one". I am not sure what this means, but my first impression (and I could be wrong) is that Friedman's proposition is based on an empirical regularity rather than sound theory or at least sound intuition. The theoretical weakness stems from the absence of a plausible transmission mechanism whereby changes in the money supply affect the general price level and consequently inflation. Furthermore, Henderson argues that the followers of John Maynard Keynes did not agree with Friedman initially, but "within a decade, the evidence from the United States and other countries had convinced most economists that Friedman was right". Which decade was that? Who are the followers of Keynes who eventually surrendered to the "intellectual" arguments pinpointing Friedman's proposition? And what was the evidence that apparently covered Planet Earth? I doubt very much if any economist who does not believe in the monetarist dogma (a follower of Keynes or otherwise) would defect to the monetarist school just on the basis of manufactured empirical evidence. In any case, the evidence from the US and other countries is not overwhelmingly supportive of Friedman's proposition, as claimed by Henderson. In Chapter 7 we will find out that the evidence is at best mixed.

Henderson is one of many die-hard Friedmanites who make unsubstantiated statements in support of the leader of the school of monetarism. For example, Sumner (2022) notes that "Friedman was right that persistent inflation is almost 100% a monetary phenomenon." I am not sure about the meaning of the word "almost" here. Does this mean that the money supply explains 97% of inflationary episodes and only 3% are explained by cost-push and other factors? What is the evidence that justifies the use of the word "almost"? It is possible for any Friedmanite to use the con art of econometrics to prove that Friedman was right, particularly because what matters, according to Henderson (2021), is the empirical evidence, not logic (this is at least my interpretation of Henderson's argument that Friedman's statement is "an empirical one, not a logically necessary one").

Once I used the con art of econometrics to prove that divorce is caused by the consumption of margarine, that people die by becoming tangled in bed sheets because of increasing revenue generated by skiing facilities, that motorcycle deaths are caused by the consumption of sour cream, and that suicide is caused by spending on science and technology (Moosa, 2016, 2017). However, I am unable, even with the help of the con art of econometrics, to prove that these are universal cases. For example, the divorce–margarine nexus can be proved by using data from the state of Maine and the suicide–science spending nexus was proved by using US data. While these findings represent spurious correlation, there is no guarantee that using data from the British county of South Yorkshire and data on UK spending on science and technology will produce even spurious correlation. Likewise, no Friedmanite, not even with the help of the con art of econometrics, can prove the validity of the money–inflation nexus for every country and all the time.

6.3   THE STYLISED FACTS

Sometimes the Friedmanites argue that the relation between monetary growth and inflation only appears in the long run. For example, Lucas (1980) used US data covering the years 1955–77 to show that M1 growth and CPI inflation moved together when short-run movements had been reasonably filtered out. Following Lucas, many other researchers hold the view that the central prediction of the quantity theory is that, in the long run, monetary growth should affect the inflation rate on a one-for-one basis. In his Nobel lecture, Lucas (1996) viewed the evidence on the relation between monetary growth and inflation as a "great success of QTM and Monetary Economics". One cannot blame Thompson et al. (2006) for thinking that the (economics) Nobel Prize is awarded for nonsense. Talking about the "great success of QTM and Monetary Economics" is rather far-fetched when we move from one crisis to another that is even worse. This is a case of indulgence in self-glorification.

On the other hand, Ryczkowski (2021) attributes the deterioration of the relationship between monetary growth and inflation to new monetary policy regimes, changes in the velocity of money, globalisation and other factors. Kaushal (2017) argues that time and again the quantity theory of money has been proved wrong, citing in evidence the observation that "central bankers in the US, the eurozone, Japan and China have been pumping their economies with money without inciting inflation". Likewise, Neely (2023) suggests that monetarism largely fell out of favour because "it was nearly impossible to find strong and consistent relations between monetary aggregates and variables of interest, such as prices and output". He attributes the "falling out of favour" to "technological and legal financial innovations", which have contributed to instability in such relations.

Yet, there are still those who attribute the rise and fall of the inflation rate during the period 2021–23 to monetary factors, when the recent inflation was propelled primarily by cost-push factors (the rise and fall of food and energy prices). In Figure 6.1 we can see the rise and fall in the money supply in five OECD countries and the euro zone. Some economists believe that the latest inflation was caused by monetary expansion during the COVID years whereas the lower inflation rate in 2023 was caused by the decline in the money supply. For example, Neely (2023) has the following to say about the case of the US:

> Recent inflation behavior has been consistent with a lagged effect of M2 on personal consumption expenditures (PCE) inflation. That is, PCE inflation … began to rise in February 2021, at the peak of M2 growth rates and a year after M2 growth began soaring in February 2020 … . Just as inflation followed M2 growth up, it followed it coming back down. Headline PCE inflation peaked in June 2022, almost 18 months after the peak of M2 growth, at a time when M2 growth had finally fallen back to historically unremarkable levels.

However, Neely does not discount the effect of the cost-push factors, suggesting that "non-monetary factors affected short-run inflation in 2022". Likewise, Curry (2023) notes that "reducing the money supply to mute the effects of inflation became a strategic focus of the Federal Reserve in 2022 and 2023". A report published by S&P Global (2023) uses the word "possibly" in describing the effect of US monetary contraction on cooling inflation.

Figure 6.2 displays monetary growth and inflation in the US and UK over the period 2018–23. We can see strong positive correlation between the inflation rate and the monetary growth rate lagged 15 months. Correlation between the two rates is 0.82 in the US and 0.57 in the UK, which may be taken in support of the proposition that the recent inflation was caused by monetary expansion during the COVID years and that the 2023 decline in the inflation rate was due shrinking money supply. However, correlation does not necessarily imply causation.

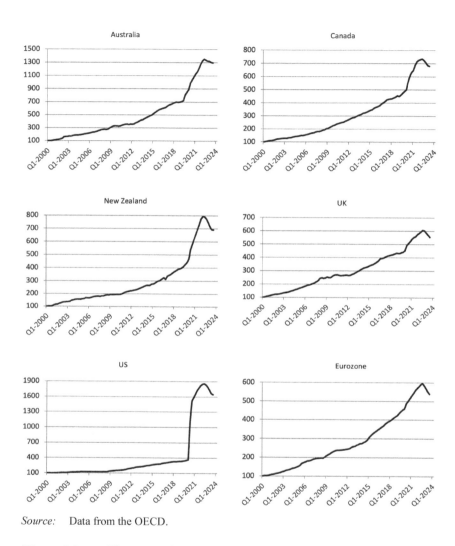

Source: Data from the OECD.

Figure 6.1   The rise and fall of the money supply (M1)

For a causal relation between the monetary growth and inflation, the rise and
fall in the money supply must be the product of a deliberate policy action to
affect an exogenous money supply. The money supply, however, is endogenous, determined by the collective action of the central bank, commercial
banks and the public. The money supply consists of currency in circulation
and deposits which can be created by credit expansion. Therefore, the money

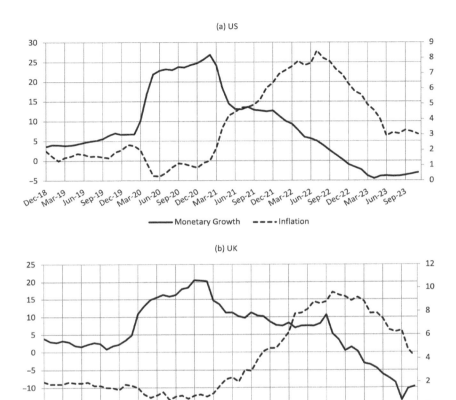

Source: Data from FRED.

Figure 6.2   *Monetary growth and inflation (US and UK)*

supply can shrink without any policy action if banks are less able or less willing to expand credit and if the public behave in such a way as to raise the currency to deposits ratio. Some of these non-policy factors are mentioned even by those who think that the money supply was the reason for the rise and fall in the inflation rate. For example, Goldman Sachs (2023) mentions the decline in deposits as a contributory factor, S&P Global (2023) identifies a decline in credit availability as a contributing factor, and Curry (2023) sees some association between a shrinking money supply and three non-policy factors: (i) diminished deposit inflows into banks, (ii) a rising incidence of deposit withdrawal, and (iii) difficulty in lending. The *Financial Times* (2023) attributes the decline of the euro zone money supply to a stalling private sector lending and deposits decline, not to deliberate action taken by the European Central Bank.

In order to verify these observations we look at Figure 6.3, which shows monthly data, over the period since July 2022, on monetary aggregates, deposits, currency and reserves in the US, as reported by the Federal Reserve Board. To start with, we can see that both M1 and M2 have been declining, but this decline cannot be attributed to central bank action because the monetary base (B) has been rising. The rise in commercial banks' reserves (R) indicates their unwillingness to expand credit and preference for reserve accumulation. We can see that the demand for currency has been rising, even though interest rates are rising. This may be due to apprehension of the public about the possibility of bailing in failed banks by confiscating deposits. We can also see that the demand for liquid deposits (demand deposits, DD, and other liquid deposits, OLD) has been declining while the demand for less liquid deposits, such as time deposits and money market funds (MMF), has been rising.

In a nutshell, the rise and fall of the inflation rate is not due to monetary expansion followed by contraction because the latest inflationary episode is the product of cost-push and profit-push factors. The rise and fall of the inflation rate are due to the rise and fall of energy and food prices. Neither are they the result of changes in interest rates, as we shall find out in Chapter 8.

6.4   CONCLUDING REMARKS

Einstein is known to have said the following: "everything should be made as simple as possible, but no simpler" (Robinson, 2018). This means that a simple plausible explanation for an observed phenomenon should be preferred to an implausible complex explanation that requires theories and models involving a set of unrealistic assumptions. The rise and fall of the inflation rate in 2021–23 is such a phenomenon. The simple plausible explanation is that inflation is measured as the percentage change in the CPI, which is calculated as a weighted average of the prices of the components of the CPI, including energy, food and housing. We know that the cost of living crisis of the 2020s is characterised by rising prices of energy, food and housing, which can be blamed on Vladimir Putin or otherwise. Therefore, explaining this inflation as a cost-push phenomenon is straightforward. Just as important is the profit-push factor, and perhaps there is a role for the pent-up demand caused by the COVID pandemic.

The complex implausible explanation is that the rise and fall of inflation is caused by monetary expansion and contraction, respectively, which is a prediction of the quantity theory of money. This explanation gives the central

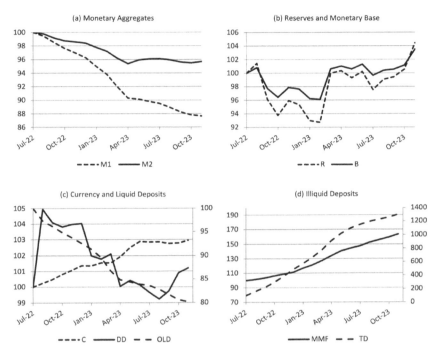

Source: Data from the Federal Reserve Board.

Figure 6.3   US monetary indicators

bank undue credit for having the power to cause and put an end to inflation at will, simply by turning the tap of the money supply on and off. When the economy is in recession, inflation can be tolerated, in which case the central bank turns on the tap, igniting inflation in the process. When inflation is high, the central bank turns off the tap and puts an end to inflation. For this process to work, a set of counterfactual assumptions must be satisfied. The first is that the central bank can control the money supply, which it cannot because the money supply is endogenous. The second is that the velocity of circulation is constant, which is not what is observed in reality. The third assumption is that a monetary expansion (contraction) leads to a rise (fall) in interest rates, which may or may not happen. The fourth assumption is that the level of interest rates (on its own) determines the ability and willingness of banks to lend, and the willingness of people to finance their purchases by borrowing from banks. The fifth assumption is that monetary expansions and contractions do not affect real output. Only if all of these assumptions are satisfied will the transmission mechanism work and the predictions of the quantity theory of money come true. These assumptions will be discussed in Chapter 7, in the process of debunking the myth implied by Friedman's proposition that inflation is always and everywhere a monetary problem.

Just before moving to Chapter 7, I thought that I would mention Margaret Thatcher once more because she was not only a believer in Milton Friedman's laissez-faire economics, but also the monetary theory of inflation. Once I came across a YouTube clip (https://www.youtube.com/shorts/autB8S1V8bA) in which Margaret Thatcher praised Enoch Powell, a controversial British politician who in 1968 called for the repatriation of immigrants in an inflammatory "rivers of blood" speech. This is what she said in praise of Powell:

> Enoch was the best parliamentarian I ever knew. Everything in Enoch's speeches had to be worked out in reason from first principles. He was of course the very first person to realise that inflation had nothing to do with prices and incomes. It was to do with the money supply, and if you put the money supply up then up would go the prices and incomes, but it was the money supply therefore the interest rate you had to look at and he was the first person to realise that.

This heroic statement, which represents Thatcherism-Powellism at its best, is worthy of a big "wow". I did not know that Powell talked economics, but here we go – he was the first to comprehend the monetary theory of inflation. I wonder if this means that Powell realised that only money causes inflation before Friedman himself, or perhaps Powell formulated the theory independently of Friedman. Maggie (God bless her soul) was wrong on several counts, apparently because she had no clue what inflation was, even though she subscribed fully to anything that came from Friedman (and Powell). Inflation has everything to do with prices and incomes: inflation is rising prices leading to declining real incomes. Look at the contradiction between "inflation had nothing to do with prices and incomes" and "if you put the money supply up then up would go the prices and incomes". Incomes do not necessarily rise with rising prices, which is why real incomes decline as a result of inflation (which is the essence of the cost of living crisis). The implication of what she said was that the best way to boost incomes was to expand the money supply, but she obviously did not know the difference between nominal income and real income. I am not sure about "the first person to realise that": is that the first British parliamentarian, or was he a pioneering monetary economist in disguise? Well, Powell himself was more modest in describing his knowledge of inflation: in a speech given on 20 November 1971, he claimed that he was "one of the few politicians to have some understanding of the cause of inflation" (Buick, 2017). Needless to say, Powell's understanding of inflation was based on Friedman's proposition, which will be dismantled systematically in Chapter 7.

7. Implications for economic theory: debunking the Friedmanite myth

7.1 INTRODUCTION

Economics is the science of puzzles and myths. Myths are perceived as such by some economists while others consider them to be undisputed facts of life. They arise primarily in normative economics where value judgement plays an important role in determining how the state of affairs ought to be. Myths can be found in various areas of economics, and this is why we have, amongst others, the myths of econometrics, the myths of laissez-faire, the myths of financial economics, and the myths of macroeconomics. For example, the myths of laissez-faire include the propositions that the private sector is always more efficient than the public sector and that privatisation boosts growth.

Whether a myth is truly a myth or otherwise depends on the strength of arguments and evidence for one claim or another. For example, an argument can be easily presented for the proposition that the private sector is not necessarily more efficient than the public sector, which debunks the myth that the private sector is always more efficient than the public sector. For this author, the superiority of the private sector is a myth – for free marketeers, on the other hand, it is the truth, the whole truth, and nothing but the truth. For most of the profession, econometrics provides useful tools for empirical research, but for a minority (including this author) econometrics is a con art that can be used to prove anything – hence, it is useless at best and dangerous at worst.

Some acclaimed puzzles in economics are based on myths. Consider, for example, the myths that under all conditions free-market "reforms" are conducive to growth, that an oversized public sector retards growth, that "systemic transformation" (meaning moving towards laissez-faire, I assume) boosts growth, and that capitalist countries should grow faster than communist countries. In a publication of the World Bank entitled *Puzzles of Economic Growth*, several questions are raised and portrayed (at least implicitly) as being puzzles pertaining to observed cross-country differences in economic growth (Balcerowicz and Rzońca, 2015). For example, an alleged puzzle is the observation that Australia is so much ahead of New Zealand, in spite of the latter being held up as a paragon of free-market reform. Another alleged puzzle is the observation that Mexico is so much poorer than Spain, despite having been wealthier all the way into the 1960s. Yet another puzzle is the observation that "communist" China has outstripped "capitalist" India (and every other capitalist country). And there is more where these came from. The fact of the matter is that the alleged puzzles are not puzzles, because plausible explanations are available, and that myths can be debunked by using factual observations and common sense (for details, see Moosa, 2020).

In this chapter we consider a puzzle that is based on a myth, which is no different from the puzzle that "communist" China has been growing more rapidly than "capitalist" India. Even if we accept the myth, the puzzle can be solved by observing that, in terms of their economies, India is as "communist" as China and China is as "capitalist" as India, because both have mixed economies where the public sector plays a major role in the economy. The myth is that economies driven by laissez-faire grow more rapidly, which is inconsistent with the rapid industrialisation and growth of the Soviet economy following the October 1917 revolution. Intuitively, economies should grow more rapidly when the public sector plays a bigger role in economic activity, at least by putting in place the kind of regulation that helps avoid crises that interrupt growth. Once the myth is debunked, the puzzle disappears.

The myth considered in this chapter is that inflation is always and everywhere a monetary problem. The corresponding puzzle is that if this is the case, why is it that quantitative easing has not produced inflation, and why is it that there is a big gap between monetary growth and inflation? In the rest of this chapter, the myth implied by Friedman's proposition (the Friedmanite myth) is debunked systematically. Once the myth is debunked, the puzzle disappears.

7.2   PRELIMINARY REMARKS ON FRIEDMAN'S PROPOSITION

Friedman was (and his disciples are) so obsessed with the money supply that they reject intuitively simple causes of inflation and choose to explain it in terms of a complex cause-and-effect relationship that sounds bogus, even though it is intended to sound "sophisticated" and "scientific". This is why Robert Solow, the founder of the exogenous growth model and a Nobel laureate, noted that "everything reminds Milton of the money supply", then he went on to say the following: "everything reminds me of sex, but I keep it out of the paper" (Fix, 2021).

Inflation is measured as the rate of change of the CPI, which is a weighted average of the prices of goods and services such as food, energy, housing and healthcare. These items represent the components of the CPI. It follows that if the price of one or more of these components goes up, the CPI goes up by a percentage (the inflation rate) that reflects changes in the prices of the components and the weights assigned to each component. This is intuitive and does not need a theory or a model, sophisticated or otherwise. If wages go up, business firms raise prices to maintain their profit margins, leading to a rise in the CPI and hence inflation. If (and when) business firms decide to raise profit margins, prices of the components of the CPI rise, leading to a rise in the CPI and hence inflation. Again, this does not need a theory or a model, sophisticated or otherwise. Hence, the effect of cost-push factors on inflation is easy to comprehend without the need for a theory or a model, sophisticated or otherwise. This reasoning is valid for demand-pull factors, in the sense that when, for some reason, the demand for energy rises, the price of energy (which is a component of the CPI) rises, leading to a rise in the CPI and hence inflation.

Simulation can be used to demonstrate how cost-push factors affect the prices of the components of the CPI, leading to rising and falling inflation rates. We can even simulate the rise and fall in the inflation rate in 2022–23 as a result of the moderation or decline in the prices of food and energy. Let us assume that the CPI is calculated as a weighted average of the prices of energy, housing, food, consumer durables and services. The weights assigned to these components of the CPI are respectively 0.2, 0.3, 0.3, 0.1 and 0.1. In Figure 7.1, we can see how the components of the CPI, and the CPI itself, behave over time under certain assumptions. It is assumed that initially the prices of energy, housing and food rise rapidly, reach a peak and start to decline, whereas the prices of services and consumer durables keep on rising at diminishing rates. It can be seen that the CPI rises rapidly at first, then moderates, reaches a peak and then starts to decline. This means that the inflation rate, which is the percentage change in the CPI, rises first, reaches a peak, then it starts to decline. At one stage it becomes negative, implying a period of deflation. Figure 7.2 shows the inflation rates of the prices of the components of the CPI and the CPI itself. Apart from the deflation represented by negative rates of change, this behaviour resembles the rise and fall of inflation in 2022 and 2023, as shown in Figure 2.1.

The effect of profit-push factors can be simulated in a similar manner, given that profit-push implies action taken by the corporate sector to raise profit margins and consequently the prices of the components of the CPI. Let us assume that the CPI is calculated in the same way as in Figure 7.1 and consider three scenarios: under scenario 1, profit margins are constant, under scenario 2, profit margins are rising, and under scenario 3, profit margins are rising at a higher rate than under scenario 2. Figure 7.3 shows what happens to the CPI under the three scenarios. At any point in time, the CPI is higher under scenario 3 than under scenario 2, which in turn is higher than under scenario 1. Under scenario 1, the CPI reaches a peak and starts to decline, implying disinflation. Under scenario 2, the CPI reaches a peak and drops very slowly. Under sce-

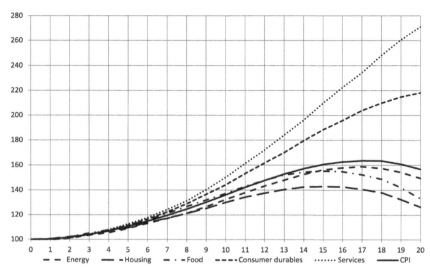

Source: Data simulation.

Figure 7.1   *Simulated behaviour of the CPI and its components*

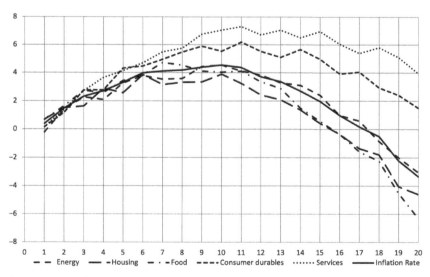

Source: Data simulation.

Figure 7.2   *Simulated behaviour CPI inflation and its components*

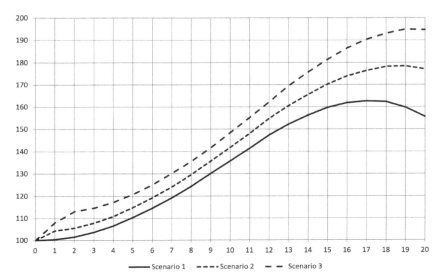

Figure 7.3   *Simulated CPI with constant and rising profit margins*

nario 3, the CPI stabilises but does not decline, meaning that the inflation rate does not turn negative in this case.

The transmission mechanism from cost-push factors to inflation is straight-forward – it is represented by the formula used to calculate the CPI from the prices of its components. Like cost-push factors, the transmission mechanism from rising profit margins to inflation is straightforward because rising margins lead to rising prices of the components of the CPI, hence rising CPI and inflation.

One cannot say that about the effect of the money supply on inflation, which is normally explained in terms of the quantity theory of money. Unlike the effect of cost-push factors, the effect of the money supply needs an elaborate transmission mechanism, which can be dubious (in fact there is no agreement on the transmission mechanism). Unlike the effect of cost-push factors, the effect of the money supply on inflation needs some assumptions that may be unrealistic such as the neutrality of money, the constancy of the velocity of circulation, and the assumption that real output is at the long-run permanent level, whatever that is. For example, Wang (2017) refers to assumptions about the way in which output is determined, how velocity moves over time, and whether or not it is affected by output and the money supply. This is what Fix (2021) refers to as "dubious assumptions about human behaviour".

It is ludicrous to claim that cost-push factors do not affect inflation, which is implicit in the proposition that inflation is always and everywhere a monetary phenomenon. This is why some Friedmanites add some twists to the quantity theory of money by claiming that cost-push factors have a role to play in the inflation generation process. Consider, for example, the following twist, which can be found on the Market Monetarist website that promotes the slogans "markets matter" and "money matters" (Market Monetarist, 2023). While emphasising the words "ALWAYS" and "EVERYWHERE", intentionally written in upper-case letters, the twist is based on the quantity theory of money, which tells us that the inflation rate is equal to the monetary growth rate adjusted for changes in the velocity of circulation and the growth of real output. Consider, for example, a rise in energy prices, which is a component of the CPI and the price of a production input that affects output. If the price of energy rises, then the inflation rate will rise, as shown in Figure 7.2. However, the Friedmanites argue that this will happen only if the central bank allows it, as if the central bank has a control room from which it can keep the economy on leash, which is preposterous. It follows that if the central bank does not like to see a rise in the inflation rate resulting from a rise in energy price, it can prevent that and avoid a rise in the inflation rate by reducing the money supply. One can only say "Hallelujah", even better while playing Leonard Cohen's song that bears that title.

This is once more the unrealistic assumption that the money supply (and not only the printing press) is under the control of the central bank. By using this twisted analysis, the Friedmanites firmly believe that the central bank is in a position to reduce the money supply correspondingly, which produces proportional declines in the price level and inflation. This means that shocks are manageable. By "correspondingly", it is meant that to prevent the general price level from rising by 3%, the central bank cuts the money supply by 3%. Naturally, the Friedmanites do not consider seriously the question whether or not the central bank can do that in a modern economy where most of the money supply consists of bank deposits held by households and the corporate sector. They just assume, and present as an undisputed fact of life, that the central bank has the power to do that. Even if the central bank can change the money supply, it is doubtful that it can change it by a precise percentage to satisfy the condition implied by "correspondingly". The fact of the matter is that the central bank has no control over the money supply, let alone that it is capable of reducing it by an amount or a percentage that satisfies the condition implied by "correspondingly".

Let us try to simulate this process of rising CPI because of cost-push and profit-push factors while the central bank takes "evasive action" by reducing the money supply correspondingly. We assume that the central bank takes evasive action when the CPI is announced at the end of each period. In response, the central bank reduces the money supply by exactly the same percentage as the rise in the CPI, such that the reduction of the money supply takes effect gradually over three periods of time. The effect is gradual because of various policy lags, including the inside lag (the time for gathering information, processing information and making decisions) and the outside lag (the time for policy dissemination, implementation and for the policy to take effect).

We also assume, as the Friedmanites believe, that the relation between the CPI and the money supply is proportional – that is, a 3% reduction in the money supply leads to a three percentage point reduction in inflation. The simulation results are displayed in Figure 7.4. It is assumed that without supply shocks, a situation of price stability exists such that the CPI moves randomly within a narrow range, as shown in Figure 7.4(a). When cost-push shocks are introduced at points in time 10, 20, 30 and 40, the behaviour of the CPI changes, as can be seen in Figure 7.4(b). If the central bank reduces the money supply proportionately to the rise in the CPI caused by the shock, the CPI will behave as in Figure 7.4(c). Figure 7.4(d) describes the behaviour of the inflation rate with central bank action, assuming that it can change the money supply and that a reduction in the money supply brings about a gradual decline of the CPI to the pre-shock level. We never see anything like this in the real world, either because the central bank does not try to offset the effect of a supply shock or because it cannot do that. Actually, it is both.

As stated earlier, the Friedmanites may ignore temporary shocks on the grounds that the inflation resulting from the shock is temporary because the inflation rate will go back to the pre-shock level. This is why it is common these days for central bankers and politicians to claim that the worst is behind because the inflation rate has peaked out. However, a declining inflation rate does not mean that real income, which is what matters, stops declining (as long as the inflation rate is positive), putting people in progressively more severe hardship. In Figure 7.5 we can see what happens to the real income corresponding to a constant nominal income as a result of the shocks described in Figure 7.4. It declines in a discrete rather than continuous manner, but this does not matter. Getting poorer in a discrete manner is still getting poorer.

The claims made by the Friedmanites fall in the realm of voodoo economics at its best. Suppose that the price of energy rises by 5%. As a component of the CPI, it will cause a rise in the CPI by 1.5% if the weight of energy in the CPI is 0.3. Energy is also a production input, which means that a rise in the price of energy will lead to a rise in the prices of other components of the CPI such as food and housing. Let us assume that the overall rise in the CPI is 3%. If the central bank does not like this, it will react by reducing the money supply. But how does this work? Will people, as a result of the reduction in the money supply, start spending less on energy because they cannot borrow

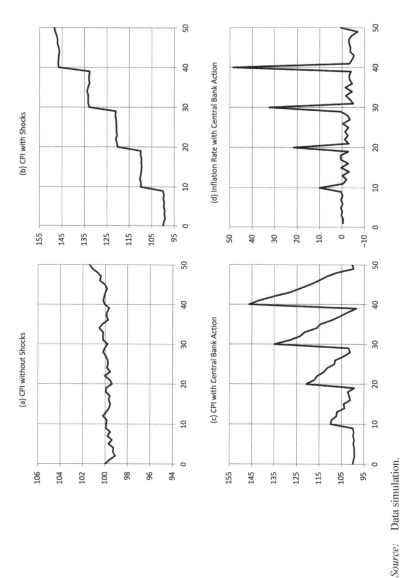

Source: Data simulation.

Figure 7.4   Simulated CPI and inflation with and without supply shocks

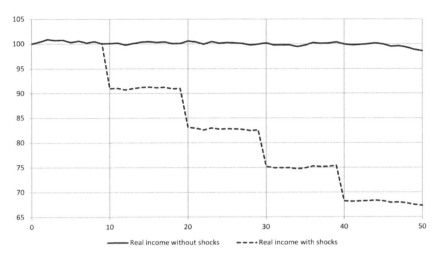

Source: Data simulation.

Figure 7.5   Simulated real income with and without supply shocks

money cheaply (assuming that a reduction in the money supply leads to a rise in interest rates, thereby depressing the demand for credit). And how long will that take? Presumably, the central bank wizards wait for the CPI figures, and if they do not like what they see (for example, a 3% rise) they reduce the money supply, somehow, by an amount that offsets exactly the 3% rise in the CPI. Having done that, they wait to realise this effect and when they do, they give each other high fives (or tens) on a job well done (and demand bonuses for saving the economy).

Even if the central bank is in a position to do that, which is far-fetched, inflation will appear because it takes time for central bank action to produce the desired results. This is where the other twist comes in: when monetarists talk about inflation, they do not mean individual months or quarters in which prices rise, but rather a continuous increase in the general price level. Thus they define inflation to suit their defunct theory.

7.3   FRIEDMAN'S LAW

The proposition that inflation is always and everywhere a monetary problem sounds as if Friedman had discovered an undisputed fact of life, something like a law of physics. We should actually call this proposition "Friedman's law" because, like Boyle's law, it holds across time and space, or so they tell us. Why not, since economists are notorious for talking about laws in economics when there are no laws in economics. For example, Baltagi (2002) describes as "the exciting thing about econometrics" the concern "for verifying or refuting economic laws, such as purchasing power parity, the life cycle hypothesis, the quantity theory of money, etc.". Then he says that "economic laws or hypotheses are testable with economic data". Baltagi, it seems, cannot tell the difference between laws and hypotheses, which are different. Laws, which are universal, are proposed before and during validation by experiment and observation. Hypotheses are not laws because they have not been verified to the same degree, but they may lead to the formulation of laws.

Boyle's law is a law because an inverse relation can be observed between the volume of gas and the pressure exerted on it, subject to constant temperature. A verification of Boyle's law requires the conduct of an experiment whereby the pressure exerted on a gas is raised progressively while taking observations on volume. When a data set containing matched observations on volume and pressure is available, it can be plotted on a graph, which will be a perfect rectangular hyperbola, meaning that the product of pressure and volume, at any level of either, is constant. This result will be obtained, provided that temperature is held constant, no matter where the experiment is conducted, in the North Pole or the South Pole, in Somalia or Fiji, in Asia or Africa, in an island or a land-locked country, in a kingdom or a republic – that is, wherever the experiment is conducted. This is the universality of the laws of physics, which is also valid for propositions in geometry and trigonometry that are called theories or identities (an example is the Pythagorean Theorem).

Laws must satisfy the following conditions: (i) validity, in the sense of no repeatable contradicting observations; (ii) universality, in the sense that it holds everywhere; (iii) simplicity, in the sense that a law is typically expressed in terms of a single mathematical equation; and (iv) stability, in the sense of staying unchanged since discovery. Like Boyle's law, the quantity theory is expressed in terms of a single mathematical equation, which means that the quantity theory satisfies condition (iii). However, it does not satisfy condition (i) because the empirical results of testing the theory empirically are inconsistent and contradictory. It does not satisfy condition (ii) because the results of empirical testing are not universal, in the sense that the theory works well for some countries but not for others. It does not satisfy condition (iv) because the results change over time. Moosa (2017) presents a comparison between the credentials of the quantity theory and Boyle's law.

Is the universality associated with the laws of physics applicable to the quantity theory of money, upon which Friedman's law rests? If the answer is in the affirmative, then testing the theory for any data set covering any country over any period of time should produce results that support the underlying hypothesis of a positive (and proportional) relation between money and prices. This is not the case, as noted by Moosa (2017), who argues that the quantity theory does not "command overwhelming support when it is subject to empirical testing" because "the results are highly supportive only under the extreme conditions of hyperinflation, and even then the relation does not necessarily turn out to be proportional". Let us therefore look at the empirical evidence on the quantity theory.

If the quantity theory is universal, then it should hold for Nigeria, like any other country. On the basis of their empirical results for Nigeria, Salami and Kelikume (2013) state explicitly that "inflation is not always and everywhere a monetary phenomenon", which raises "serious doubt on the continuous use of monetary policy tool to achieve price stability in Nigeria". Their reasoning is simple:

> The effective prediction of the relationships between inflation and money supply depends largely on the existence of a stable and predictable relationship between monetary aggregates, inflation and the output in the economy. If the money market is largely underdeveloped and the relationship between the chosen monetary aggregates and the ultimate policy objective are weak, monetary targeting becomes a very weak instrument.

Well, we cannot discredit the empirical validity of the quantity theory of money just because it does not work in Nigeria, even though this is a requirement for universality as implied by the word "always" which is always used by the Friedmanites. Can we, then, say that the quantity theory works everywhere in the world, except Nigeria? Not really, according to the evidence on 160 countries provided by De Grauwe and Polan (2014). While they find a "strong positive relation between long-run inflation and the money growth rate", the relation is not proportional. Furthermore, they find that "the strong link between inflation and money growth is almost wholly due to the presence of high- (or hyper-) inflation countries in the sample". They also find a weak relation between inflation and monetary growth for low-inflation countries (on average less than 10% per annum over 30 years).

The quantity theory is not universal across space, neither is it universal across time. Wang (2017) re-examines the contention of Lucas (1980) that "a simple formulation of the Quantity Theory of Money did surprisingly well at capturing the long-run co-movements of consumer price inflation and a certain measure of money supply". No one would say that Boyle's law does "surprisingly" well in catching co-movements of the volume of gas and the pressure exerted on it. By using the same statistical and economic criteria, but a much larger data set (covering both a longer period and many more countries), Wang (2017) shows that Lucas's results are "extremely fragile". This is what he concludes:

It appears that the period 1955–1980 is the only period during which QTM fits data well in most of our sample countries. It starts to break down when we go beyond this period. Furthermore, the recent breaking down of QTM is global, even though different countries have different breaking dates. Fragility is robust.

Like everything else in economics, some studies find supportive evidence while others do not, and in both cases the results may be engineered by cherry picking or otherwise (even fabrication) to confirm prior beliefs, such as belief in Friedman's law. While abundant research has established support for the quantity theory of money, abundant research has also found contrasting (negative) results (see, for example, Abate, 2020; Akinboade et al., 2004; Kiganda, 2014; Nelson, 2008; Rasool and Tarique, 2017; Roshan, 2014). A recent study by Ryczkowski (2021) concludes that "the one-for-one long-run association of money growth and inflation is confirmed by data from different countries, centuries, and monetary policy regimes", but "since 1990, this famous relationship seems to have disappeared from simple scatterplots in low-inflation countries". Last, but not least, Teles et al. (2016) find that "for countries with low inflation, the raw relationship between average inflation and the growth rate of money is tenuous at best" and that "the sample after 1990 shows considerably less inflation variability, worsening the fit of a one-for-one relationship between money growth and inflation".

The fact of the matter is that the Friedmanites make claims that are inconsistent with the available evidence. Recall Sumner (2022) who notes that "Friedman was right that persistent inflation is almost 100% a monetary phenomenon" and Henderson (2021) who opines that "one could not find inflation anywhere in the world that was not caused by a prior increase in the supply of money or in the growth rate of the supply of money". This is not what the empirical evidence tells us. Even casual empiricism does not support Friedman's proposition, particularly the strong version of it that the relation between money and prices is positive and proportional.

Let us see if casual empiricism supports Friedman's proposition for the US. Figure 7.6 shows the growth of the money supply and the CPI for the US on a monthly basis between 1959 and 2023. The most striking observation is the widening gap between the CPI and the money supply, which means that the evidence precludes the presence of a proportional relation between the two variables. The divergence accelerated dramatically after the initiation of quantitative easing in 2008. The quantity theory of money tells us that if inflation is lower than the growth rate of the money supply, then this may be because real output has been growing. This means that the gap between inflation and monetary growth may be due to real output growing at an increasing rate, which is counterfactual. So, why is it that inflation has not picked up as predicted by the

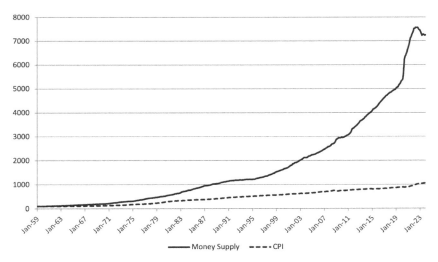

Figure 7.6   Money supply and CPI in the US

quantity theory of money? This is a puzzle based on a myth, as was stated at the very beginning of this chapter.

Several explanations have been put forward for the growing gap between the money supply and the general price level, proxied by the CPI. The first is that the gap is accounted for by changes in the velocity of circulation, because a declining velocity offsets the effect of monetary growth on the general price level. Recall that one of the assumptions required to produce a proportional relation between money and prices is a constant velocity (we will come back to this point later). Another explanation is that a significant portion of the US money supply, particularly currency, is held abroad. This explanation is not valid because the money supply is more than currency – it is mostly deposits. This means that the bulk of the US money supply is held within the US. In November 2023, currency in circulation was 13% of the narrow money supply (M1) and 11% of the broad monetary supply (M2). Borio et al. (2023) argue that "monetary aggregates have gradually lost relevance since the heyday of monetary targeting in the 1970s and 1980s as their link with inflation has weakened considerably".

Perhaps a more valid explanation for the gap is that inflation is reflected more in asset prices than the prices of goods and services, which makes sense because investors use borrowed funds to buy financial assets more than consumers use borrowed funds to finance purchases of goods and services. In

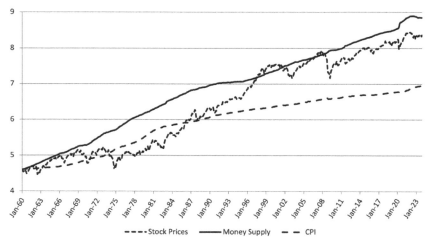

Source: Data from FRED.

Figure 7.7   *Money supply, CPI and stock prices in the US (logarithmic values)*

Figure 7.7, which displays the logarithmic values of the three variables, we can see that the gap between stock prices and the money supply is narrower than the gap between the money supply and the CPI.

Figure 7.6 shows that a proportional relation between the money supply and the CPI is out of the question. The Friedmanites like to show a graph in which the growth rate of the money supply moves in tandem with the inflation rate. Moving together means positive correlation, unlike equality, which implies proportionality. Figure 7.8 is a scatter plot of the US inflation rate on the monetary growth rate, both of which are calculated as the percentage change relative to the same month of the previous year over a period going back to January 1960. A correlation ellipse that contains all of the observations is close to being a circle, where a perfect circle indicates zero correlation. When the extreme values (the outliers) are excluded, the correlation ellipse becomes almost a perfect circle.

The Friedmanites may argue that the lack of correlation in Figure 7.8 may be due to the use of contemporaneous values when the relation between monetary growth and inflation is lagged. This means that inflation is not a function of the contemporaneous but the lagged monetary growth rate, as we saw in Chapter 6. Figure 7.9 shows scatter plots of the monetary growth rate lagged 6, 12, 18 and 24 months. No matter what the lag length is, the lagged relation is not as

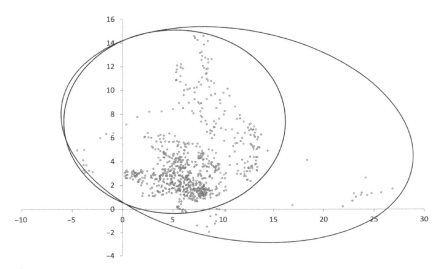

Source: Data from FRED.

Figure 7.8   A scatter plot of monetary growth on CPI inflation

strong as envisaged by the Friedmanites. There is in particular no indication whatsoever that the relation is proportional.

7.4   THE ABILITY OF THE CENTRAL BANK TO CONTROL THE MONEY SUPPLY

The central bank has very little power to control the money supply because the money supply is endogenous (determined by the workings of the economy) as opposed to being exogenous (determined by the central bank). Money is believed to be endogenous because most of it is supplied by commercial banks in the form of bank deposits according to a process whereby they respond to the demand for loans or preferences regarding the form of money that people want to hold (for example, demand deposits versus saving deposits). Those believing in the exogeneity of the money supply argue that this is so because central banks have a monopoly on the issue of currency, which gives them the ability to control the money supply. This argument may have been valid for the Weimer Republic of Germany and other classical cases of hyperinflation, but not for a modern economy where deposits, which are not created by central banks, form the bulk of the total money supply. The exogenous money supply proposition has been challenged by, among others, Kaldor (1970), Chick (1973) and Moore (1989).

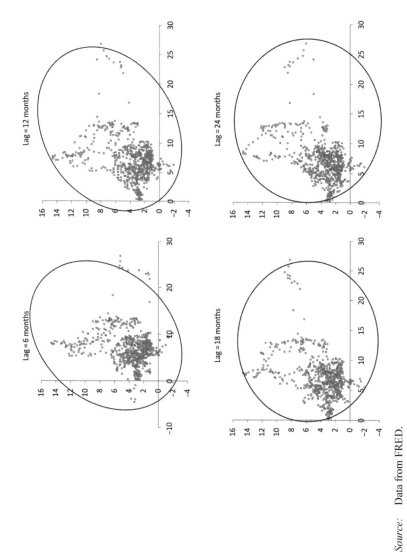

Source: Data from FRED.

Figure 7.9   *Inflation as a function of lagged monetary growth*

The money multiplier model can be used to get a feel of the power (or lack thereof) of the central bank to control the money supply. In this model, the monetary base (total currency issued by the central bank) is the sum of currency held by the public (currency in circulation) and banks' reserves. The money supply is defined, as usual, as the sum of currency and bank deposits. According to the money multiplier model, the money supply expands by a multiple of any increase in the monetary base, which means that if the central bank wishes to expand the money supply, it will boost the monetary base by issuing more currency. The money supply will increase by some multiple of the increase in the monetary base. Conversely, a reduction in the monetary base is required to reduce the money supply. In other words, the central bank can control the money supply by turning the monetary base tap on and off.

While the monetary base is under the control of the central bank, the money multiplier is not. Rather, it is determined by two behavioural ratios: the currency to deposits ratio, as determined by public preferences, and banks' reserves to deposits ratio, which is determined by their preferences as well as the reserve requirements imposed on them by the central bank (which is typically ineffective because banks tend to hold more reserves than what is implied by the required reserve ratio). When people prefer to hold cash as opposed to deposits and banks prefer to hold reserves as opposed to grant loans, the value of the multiplier will be low, which means that the expansion in the money supply corresponding to a given expansion in the monetary base will be small. The money supply expands when banks decide to lend and consequently create fresh deposits in a process that represents the connection between credit and money. However, this can only happen if households and the corporate sector want to borrow. It follows that the money supply is determined jointly by the central bank, through its control of the monetary base, by commercial banks in determining the reserve ratio, and by households that determine the currency to deposits ratio.

In the 1960s, Philip Cagan, a monetary economist who was famous for his writings on hyperinflation, used the money multiplier model to demonstrate that all big, sustained changes in the money supply were due to policy-driven changes in the monetary base. This is how he described the money multiplier model (Cagan, 1965):

> Given the quantity of high-powered [base] money, the public and the commercial banks jointly determine its division between public holdings [of cash] and bank reserves. The public determines the fraction of total money balances it wants to hold in the form of high-powered money … . The banking system determines the volume of monetary liabilities it is willing to create, through loans and investment, per unit of high-powered money it holds (that is, its reserves).

Cagan went on to describe the money multiplier model as expressing the money supply in terms of high-powered money, the currency to deposits ratio and the reserves to deposits ratio, which he called the "determinants of the money stock". By analysing movements of the money supply and its determinants over the period 1875–1960, he concluded that "the secular growth in the money stock has depended primarily on additions to high-powered money".

Despite the implication of Cagan's analysis that the money supply can be controlled by the central bank, because of its ability to create high-powered money, he admitted that "the contribution of the two ratios to variations about the growth trend of the money stock has at certain times been substantial". If the ratios are unstable, the relation between the monetary base and the money supply becomes loose. In Figure 7.10, we can see that the behaviour of the money supply (M2) in the US does not resemble the behaviour of the monetary base as implied by the money multiplier model. In Figure 7.10(a), where the money supply and the monetary base are measured as indices, the monetary base has been both more volatile and growing faster than the money supply, particularly since the beginning of quantitative easing in 2008. The lack of correspondence between the two variables can be attributed to the instability of the reserve and currency ratios, and consequently the multiplier.

The view expressed by Cagan is challenged even by central bankers themselves. In a study published in the *Bank of England Quarterly Bulletin*, McLeay et al. (2014) state the following:

> Another common misconception is that the central bank determines the quantity of loans and deposits in the economy by controlling the quantity of central bank money – the so-called "money multiplier" approach. In that view, central banks implement monetary policy by choosing a quantity of reserves. And, because there is assumed to be a constant ratio of broad money to base money, these reserves are then "multiplied up" to a much greater change in bank loans and deposits. For the theory to hold, the amount of reserves must be a binding constraint on lending, and the central bank must directly determine the amount of reserves.

The money multiplier model predicts that the central bank can control the money supply, by controlling the monetary base, only if the money multiplier is stable or constant, and this is why they refer to the assumption of a "constant ratio of broad money to base money", which means a constant multiplier. McLeay et al. go on to explain the money creation process as follows:

> Commercial banks create money, in the form of bank deposits, by making new loans. When a bank makes a loan, for example to someone taking out a mortgage to buy a house, it does not typically do so by giving them thousands of pounds worth of banknotes. Instead, it credits their bank account with a bank deposit of the size of the mortgage. At that moment, new money is created … . Money creation in practice differs from some popular misconceptions – banks do not act simply as intermediar-

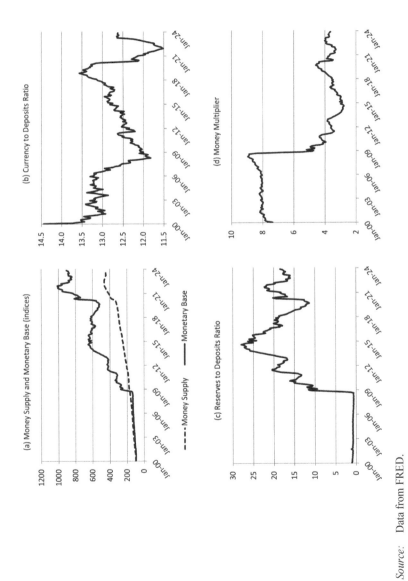

Source: Data from FRED.

Figure 7.10   Monetary base, money supply and the multiplier (US data)

ies, lending out deposits that savers place with them, and nor do they "multiply up" Central Bank money to create new loans and deposits.

A similar view is held by Benes and Kumhof (2012) who argue that "private banks are almost fully in control of the money creation process". The fundamental implication of the credit creation theory is that commercial banks, rather than the central bank, determine the money supply. The central bank is obliged to support the lending decisions of banks by providing sufficient reserves to ensure that all payments are settled at the end of the day. Holtemoller (2002) suggests that "the money stock and the monetary base are determined endogenously by the optimizing behaviour of commercial banks and private agents like households and firms".

The view that the central bank has a limited ability to control the money supply is also expressed by Sigurjonsson (2015) who points out that capital requirements, reserve requirements and interest rates are inadequate for the purpose of controlling the money supply. Starting with capital requirements as a tool, the underlying idea is that if the capital ratio (the ratio of capital to assets) falls below a certain level, banks would be unable to extend credit without boosting equity. In practice, however, capital requirements do not fully constrain bank lending for various reasons. The first reason stems from the fact that retained earnings are a component of equity, implying that a bank can expand credit by retaining part of its earnings (which are generated by credit expansion). If lending is profitable, banks extend credit and create money, which produces retained earnings and boosts their ability to extend credit. The second reason is that banks can raise capital by issuing new stock. When the economy is booming, banks' profits tend to be high and consequently stock prices rise as return on equity goes up. Under these conditions, banks find it easy to raise capital and consequently expand credit and the money supply. The third reason is that banks can free up capital via securitisation. The fourth reason is that the Basel rules allow banks to calculate regulatory capital requirements by using internal models, which means that they are in a position to manipulate their models and change regulatory capital in such a way as to be able to lend more (see, for example, Moosa, 2007, 2008). Banks can also use creative (read fraudulent) accounting to minimise regulatory capital.

Banks make loans and look for reserves later, as suggested by Sigurjonsson (2015). In accordance with its function of a lender of last resort, the central bank provides reserves on demand – otherwise, a liquidity crisis may be triggered or interest rates rise to high levels. If the central bank refused to provide more reserves, the commercial bank needing reserves would be unable to make payments to other banks, forcing it to sell some of its assets to obtain the reserves it needs. This means that a liquidity problem may become a solvency problem, which may cause a cascade of bankruptcies throughout the entire banking system. If this course of events materialises, the central bank would be accused of putting financial stability in jeopardy. Central bankers do not allow this to happen because they would risk losing highly paid and privileged jobs.

Another reason why reserves may not constrain bank lending is that if payments are made between customers of the same bank, no extra reserves will be required. This is because payment by one customer (reduction of reserves) will be offset by the deposit made by the receiver of the payment. Naturally, payments are not made exclusively by the customers of one bank, but this also means that if the banking system is dominated by a few large banks, a big fraction of the payments will be offset by deposits placed by the receivers without any need for central bank reserves. Furthermore, if credit expansion by various banks runs at similar rates and the flows of deposits are fairly balanced, banks can expand lending activity considerably without needing a significant amount of reserves. Last, but not least, window dressing can be used to satisfy reserve requirements by borrowing overnight funds.

Controlling the money supply by using interest rate policy is an issue that will be dealt with in detail in Chapter 8. For the time being, it suffices to say that higher rates may not be effective in curbing lending, particularly when the economy is booming and asset price bubbles are present. For example, Pilkington (2014) suggests that the demand for credit can be driven by speculative excesses in the property or stock market, inflationary wage-price spirals, and economic growth. Furthermore, higher deposit rates attract more deposits, perhaps even from foreigners.

In a nutshell, the central bank cannot control the money supply, by controlling the monetary base or otherwise, because the money supply is endogenous, determined collectively by the actions of the central bank, commercial banks and their customers. Even though the money multiplier model tells us that banks cannot expand the money supply by expanding credit unless they have excess reserves, this is inadequate for enabling the central bank to control the money supply. The central bank may wish to expand the money supply by increasing the monetary base (using the printing press) but this will not happen if banks do not want to lend and customers do not want to borrow while tending to hold currency as opposed to deposits.

7.5   THE ASSUMPTION OF CONSTANT OR STABLE VELOCITY

For a proportional relation between monetary growth and inflation, velocity (the average number of times a single unit of money changes hands in an economy) must be constant or stable. The quantity theory of money tells us that if velocity rises, inflation will rise even with no change in the money supply. It also tells us that if velocity rises, reducing the money supply will not

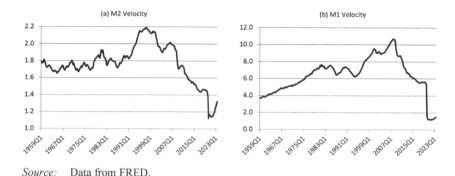

Source: Data from FRED.

Figure 7.11   *Velocity of circulation in the US*

bring about a reduction in the inflation rate. It is easy to check whether or not velocity has been stable by looking at Figure 7.11, which shows the velocity of circulation for M1 and M2 in the US economy since 1959. We can see that the velocity of M2 has been falling since 1997, whereas the velocity of M1 has been falling since 2007.

Several reasons have been presented for the instability of velocity. For example, Nunes et al. (2018) attribute instability to the emergence of new institutions and the behaviour of macroeconomic variables, whereas Berentsen et al. (2015) attribute it to improved access to money markets. Other reasons include the change in the pattern of asset holding by individuals because of deregulation, financial innovation, common access to ATMs, increasing role of money substitutes, new production technology, changes in operational management, and financial intermediation increasing in complexity (Fanta, 2013; Itaya and Mino, 2007). Wen and Arias (2014) attribute the decline in velocity in the aftermath of the global financial crisis to (i) a bearish economic outlook, and (ii) the dramatic decline in interest rates that forced investors to readjust their portfolios towards liquid money and away from interest-bearing assets such as government bonds. What matters for the present discussion is that velocity is not stable. As a matter of fact, Wen and Arias (2014) note that velocity "has never been constant", which is one reason why inflation did not arise as a result of quantitative easing triggered by the global financial crisis and reinforced by the COVID-19 pandemic.

7.6   THE DIRECTION OF CAUSATION

While the quantity theory of money tells us that the money supply and the general price level (hence monetary growth and inflation) are related, it is not obvious what the direction of causation is. In his critique of Friedman, Fix (2021) argues that the quantity theory, like so much of neoclassical economics, is based on an accounting identity that makes the theory look good. He also refers to Friedman's "F-twist", whereby he (Friedman) argued that a theory's assumptions are irrelevant because all that matters is that the theory makes accurate predictions. Musgrave (1981) notes that the essence of Friedman's F-twist is that "the more significant the theory, the more unrealistic the assumptions", arguing that "Friedman's position … stems from his failure to distinguish three different types of assumption": negligibility assumptions (some factor has a negligible effect upon the phenomenon under investigation), domain assumptions (to specify the domain of applicability of the theory), and heuristic assumptions as a means of simplifying the logical development of the theory. Musgrave suggests that "Friedman's dictum is false of all three types of assumption."

To ensure that the theory is consistent with the evidence, Fix argues, neo-classical economists (including Friedman) frame the theory in terms of an accounting identity (such as $MV = PY$). Since the identity is true by definition, any test of the theory should produce supportive results. This proposition is not valid because supportive results are rarely obtained, and never for the notion of proportionality. However, even if we assume that Fix's proposition on using identities to produce supportive results is valid, the identity tells us nothing about the direction of causation. Is it that too much money causes prices to rise, or is it that rising prices make it necessary to create more money to settle transactions? During any hyperinflationary episode, causation goes both ways: too much money pushes prices upwards, making the available stock of money inadequate for financing transactions, which forces the monetary authority to boost the money stock in a process that resembles a vicious circle. Hence, causation goes from money to prices and then from prices to money.

While monetarists like to think that causation runs from money to prices, Hoover (1991) argued long ago that "surprisingly little evidence has been brought to bear directly on this claim". By examining the causal direction between prices and money in the US, he found that the balance of evidence supports the view that money does not cause prices and that prices do cause money. Most of the empirical evidence provided by the Friedmanites is based on Granger causality, a dubious econometric test that can be used to prove almost anything (see, for example, Moosa, 2017). Instead of looking for empirical evidence derived from a dubious test, it is better to seek a plausible theoretical reasoning for why causation runs from money to prices as the Friedmanites claim. This can be found in the literature on the transmission mechanism of monetary policy, which explains how the central bank, by changing the money supply, can control inflation (assuming that the central bank can control the money supply, which is not the case).

An analysis of the relation between monetary growth and inflation is presented by Borio et al. (2023) who suggest that inflation is a two-regime process because inflation behaves very differently in the two regimes. The difference between the two regimes, they argue, carries over to the link between monetary growth and inflation. By using this proposition, they explain the recent surge in inflation, suggesting that the evidence indicates that "money growth and inflation have been closely linked recently". For example, they find that "across countries, there is a statistically and economically significant positive correlation between excess money growth in 2020 and average inflation in 2021 and 2022". However, they admit that their evidence says little about causality. This is what they have to say:

> The debate about the direction of causality in the link between money and inflation has not been fully settled. The observation that money growth today helps to predict inflation tomorrow does not, in and of itself, imply causality.

Anna Schwartz, Friedman's co-author of *A Monetary History of the United States*, describes the transmission mechanism on the Econlib website (https://www.econlib.org/) as follows:

> Because money is used in virtually all economic transactions, it has a powerful effect on economic activity. An increase in the supply of money works both through lowering interest rates, which spurs investment, and through putting more money in the hands of consumers, making them feel wealthier, and thus stimulating spending. Business firms respond to increased sales by ordering more raw materials and increasing production ... . If the money supply continues to expand, prices begin to rise, especially if output growth reaches capacity limits.

A monetary expansion is supposed to work its way to prices directly or indirectly: directly through demand for goods and services, and indirectly through demand for financial assets. The latter leads to higher asset prices, lower interest rates, more borrowing and less saving – hence more consumption (and inflation). I am not sure how the direct effect works, because I cannot imagine how the central bank puts more money in the hands of consumers and makes them feel wealthier. If what is meant here is that it becomes easier to borrow, this hardly makes people feel wealthy, knowing that they will have to repay debt with interest. It could be that this is a reference to the "helicopter money" that was suggested once by Friedman himself in his book on the optimum quantity of money (Friedman, 1969). The closest thing to a helicopter drop in recent times is the financial aid provided to citizens across the world during the COVID-19 pandemic and the cost of living crisis. However, it is not clear whether that was financed by an increase in the money supply or by other means. In any case, this kind of action does not represent a standard policy prescription, in which case we will concentrate on the indirect effect. Furthermore, it is unlikely that anyone felt wealthy after receiving government aid when they lost their jobs during the pandemic.

Consider a situation in which the central bank tries to control inflation by reducing the money supply. When the central bank reduces the monetary base, interest rates rise, making it more expensive to borrow money and spend. Simultaneously, banks become less capable of expanding credit as a result of the decline in excess reserves. Monetary contraction leads to falling asset prices, giving rise to adverse income and wealth effects. Consequently, spending falls, reducing pressure on the general price level. And this is not all, because higher interest rates lead to appreciation of the domestic currency, which brings down the domestic currency prices of imported goods. As inflationary pressures fall, inflationary expectations dissipate, which means that workers will be less inclined to ask for a pay rise, thereby easing inflationary pressures. Therefore, inflation dissipates as a result of a combination of falling demand, owing to the unavailability of cheap credit, lower import prices, and the taming of the wage-price spiral.

Well, this is fantasy that matches in excellence *Alice in Wonderland* and *Ali Baba and the Forty Thieves*. The story deserves to be included in the *One Thousand and One Nights* collection of fantasy stories. It is as if the economy is a machine that can be controlled through switches and levers. This highly hypothetical and implausible process is unlikely to work because the economy is not a machine. Reducing the money supply may or may not push interest rates up because of a combination of liquidity effect, inflation effect and inflationary expectations effect, which work in opposite directions. This means that interest rates are as likely to go up as to go down. If interest rates go up, there is no guarantee that the demand for credit will fall because it depends on more factors than the interest rate (for example, profitability and expectations). There is no guarantee that the manipulation of the reserve ratio and open market operations will affect the ability of commercial banks to grant credit because, as we have seen before, commercial banks tend to grant credit and look for reserves later. A higher interest rate may or may not lead to domestic currency appreciation because the exchange rate is affected by more than interest rates (which explains why the Turkish lira remains weak despite high levels of interest rates). Furthermore, the exchange rate becomes irrelevant unless the foreign currency is the currency of invoicing. If the prescribed scenario does not materialise, workers may not demand higher wages. Inflation could also be aggravated by steadily increasing profit margins.

Apart from viewing the economy as a machine and overblowing the ability of the central bank to control the money supply, two problems are associated with this kind of analysis. The first is that a modern economy is so complex that two-variable cause and effect relations do not work smoothly, since everything moves at the same time (like, for example, the determinants of exchange rates). The second is that in a modern economy, causation tends to be bidirectional (for example, the relation between interest and exchange rates). The third is that this analysis ignores real-world complications (for example, the simple and unrealistic assumption that currency appreciation necessarily leads to lower domestic currency price of imports).

7.7   INFLATIONARY BURSTS VERSUS SUSTAINED INFLATION

The Friedmanites define inflation in such a way as to offer support for the plausibility of their theory that inflation is only caused by monetary expansion. Thus, they use words like "steady", "sustained", "continuous" and "persistent" to describe a rise in prices that can be considered inflation. They claim that a rise in the general price level in a particular time period as a result of a shock does not represent inflation because the shock is a one-off event. Because the shock does not persist, the inflation rate returns to its pre-shock level, which is determined purely by monetary factors. What the Friedmanites choose to ignore is that a big supply shock that does not persist (such as a one-off big rise in energy prices) pushes the general price level (hence the cost of living) upwards and reduces real incomes. A decline in the inflation rate to its pre-shock level does not lead to a reversal of the erosion of real income as a result of the shock. While an event like this may be called an "inflationary burst", the Friedmanites do not consider it as inflation, implying that it is benign, in which case it can be safely ignored. Well, an inflationary burst may be temporary but it is more harmful (in terms of the erosion of real income) than gradual inflation.

The main reason why economists are interested in inflation is its adverse effect on the economy, the most important of which is the erosion of the purchasing power of income. Whether that erosion comes in one go or gradually does not matter because a rising price level erodes the purchasing power of income, either gradually or in one go. As a matter of fact, an abrupt loss of purchasing power is more harmful than a gradual loss. This proposition can be demonstrated with the help of simulated data, as shown in Figure 7.12 where the outcomes of two scenarios are plotted over ten time periods. Under scenario 1 of an inflationary burst, the general price level rises by 10% in period 1 and stays at the same level until period 10. This means that the inflation rate is 10% in period 1 and 0% thereafter (apparently the zero inflation thereafter is the source of comfort for the Friedmanites). Correspondingly, real income declines in period 1 and remains constant thereafter. Under scenario 2, the general price level rises by 0.96% per period, so that by the end of period 10, it will have risen by 10%. Correspondingly, real income declines gradually,

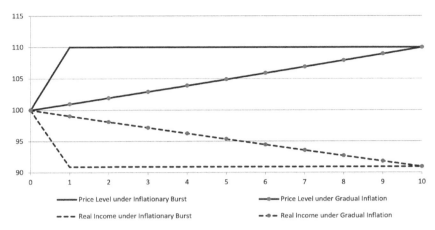

Source: Data simulation.

Figure 7.12 *The price level under gradual inflation and inflationary bursts*

reaching the same level as real income in period 1 (and 10) as under scenario 1. The damage inflicted by the erosion of real income is the same under both scenarios, or is it? It is actually worse under scenario 1, for two reasons. The first is that the accumulated loss of real income is faster under scenario 1 than scenario 2. The second is that gradual inflation is less harmful because it gives people the chance to adjust gradually. Disregarding inflationary bursts because they are not caused by monetary factors does not sound wise.

7.8 ACCOMMODATION OF SUPPLY SHOCKS

The Friedmanites believe that a supply shock does not cause a rise in the price level unless it is accommodated by monetary expansion. This means that the recent rise in the prices of housing, energy and food would not have materialised had central banks chosen not to indulge in monetary expansion to accommodate the increase in the value of transactions resulting from price rises. In general, this means that a sudden increase in energy price does not cause inflation unless it is accompanied by an increase in the money supply. We have already seen something similar, but the opposite situation – that the central bank can neutralise the effect of a supply shock by reducing the money supply.

The idea here is that an increase in energy prices leads to an increase in the value of transactions in the economy, which requires an increase in the money supply. If the central bank does not accommodate the increase in the value of transactions by boosting the money supply, interest rates will rise and bank reserves will not be adequate to provide the credit needed to finance the extra volume of transactions. Hence, the argument goes, in the absence of monetary expansion, demand will decline and inflation will be averted. The central bank, however, may accommodate the supply shock for fear of pushing the economy into recession. This course of events is implausible because commercial banks may be able to expand credit by using their excess reserves and because consumers may use their savings to finance extra purchases. People do not ordinarily borrow to finance the purchase of necessities, and this is why interest rates cannot be used to curb cost-push inflation, an issue that will be discussed in Chapter 8.

Then there is the issue of timing. When does the central bank decide whether or not to accommodate an increase in energy prices? Is the decision taken immediately following the rise in energy prices, or does the central bank wait until the inflation figures come out? Under what circumstances does the central bank decide to accommodate or otherwise? If the central bank always accommodates, then the money supply should rise and interest rates fall after any increase in energy prices or once it has been reflected in the CPI. I have not seen these questions asked because of the tyranny of the status quo. After all, it is heresy to question the wisdom of Milton Friedman.

Under the assumption that the central bank accommodates the supply shock by expanding the money supply, the cause and effect process goes as follows: higher energy prices lead to higher inflation, prompting the central bank to expand the money supply, which leads to a fall in interest rates. Table 7.1 shows the predicted correlation signs between any pair of the two variables when the shock is accommodated

Let us see if these predictions are consistent with the facts on the ground, using the oil price shock of the 1970s as an example. In Figure 7.13, we observe quarterly figures (obtained from FRED) on the three variables listed

Table 7.1   Predicted correlation signs under accommodation

Variable 1	Variable 2	Correlation Sign
Energy Price	Money Supply	+
Energy Price	Interest Rate	−
Energy Price	Inflation	+
Money Supply	Interest Rate	−
Money Supply	Inflation	+
Interest Rate	Inflation	−

Source: Author's own.

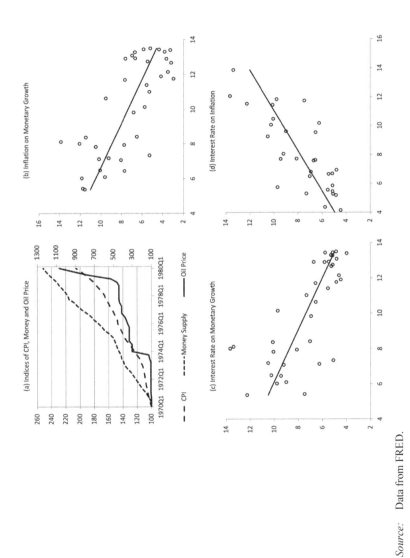

Source: Data from FRED.

Figure 7.13   Inflation and related variables in the 1970s (US data)

Table 7.2   Changes in variables over the 1970s

	Oil Price	CPI	Interest Rate	Money Supply
70Q1–73Q1	6.3	11.3	−3.7	33.5
73Q2–74Q1	184.0	9.6	3.2	6.1
75Q1–78Q3	33.1	25.2	0.6	46.1
78Q4–80Q1	141.3	16.2	4.0	9.6

Source: Author's own.

in Table 7.1 over the period between the first quarter of 1970 and the first quarter of 1980. During that period, the money supply grew much more rapidly than the CPI, which means that the inflation rate should have been much higher than what it was. The scatter plots show negative correlation between inflation and monetary growth, which is contrary to the prediction of the quantity theory, and the opposite of what should happen when a supply shock is accommodated. We can also see positive correlation between interest rate and inflation, which is again the opposite of what is supposed to happen under accommodation.

Table 7.2 reports the percentage changes in oil price, the CPI and the money supply as well as the absolute change in interest rate in four periods during the 1970s, including two periods that witnessed big jumps in the price of oil. We can see that the two big oil price jumps were not accompanied by big jumps in the money supply to accommodate oil price shocks. Monetary growth was weaker in periods of big jumps in oil prices, casting doubt on the proposition of accommodation. The money supply and interest rate are supposed to move in opposite directions, but that did not happen when the central bank was supposed to accommodate shocks. Perhaps the central bank did not accommodate the shock, but if this is the case, why did inflation go up when it is not supposed to go up without accommodation?

7.9   DOES THE MONEY SUPPLY MATTER?

The absence of a close causal relation between monetary growth and inflation, as predicted by the quantity theory of money, does not mean that money does not matter. The money supply matters for asset prices, but it is better if we look at the effect on asset prices in terms of credit. Low interest rates encourage people to obtain heavy mortgages to buy homes, creating a house price bubble. The availability of cheap borrowing also leads to stock price bubbles as companies borrow cheap funds to indulge in stock buy-backs. We have already seen that stock prices are more closely related to the money supply than the prices of goods and services (Figure 7.7). This point is made by Lapavitsas et al. (2023) who reject the idea that money causes inflation. Commenting on the expansionary monetary policy used by the Bank of England, they say:

> By creating new money and handing it to major financial institutions, the Bank of England has helped push up the price of financial and property assets. This happened because those financial institutions took the newly created money and used it to trade in financial assets (such as shares) and real estate. As a result, share prices and, especially, property prices in Britain were consistently pushed up.

Money is all that matters under hyperinflation when monetary growth is the only factor causing inflation, as can be seen in Figure 7.14, which depicts the money supply (in this case currency in circulation) and the cost of living index during the German hyperinflation of the 1920s. Figure 7.14(a) shows the situation in 1920–22, whereas Figure 7.14(b) shows what happened in 1923 when inflation accelerated dramatically. The correspondence between money and prices is very close, particularly in 1923. We have already come across the evidence presented by De Grauwe and Polan (2014) who attribute the strong link between inflation and monetary growth almost completely to the presence of high- (or hyper-) inflation countries in the sample. When inflation is moderate or low, there is hardly any link between the two variables, and inflation is predominantly a cost-push and profit-push phenomenon.

The proposition that hyperinflation is a monetary phenomenon but normal inflation is not is supported by Lira (2010) who attributed moderate inflation to demand-pull and cost-push factors, while describing hyperinflation as a monetary phenomenon. Moderate inflation, he argued, occurs when the economy overheats, forcing a rise in the price of labour and commodities, leading to a rise in the prices of goods and services, so that producers can keep up with costs. It is essentially a demand-driven phenomenon. Hyperinflation, on the other hand, is "the loss of faith in the currency", a condition under which prices rise "not because people want more money for their labor or for commodities, but because people are trying to get out of the currency". It follows that Friedman's proposition is valid for hyperinflationary conditions, but not for moderate inflation. It also follows that Friedman's proposition is not a law of physics that holds anywhere, any time.

Money matters in a third sense – that is, the money supply and general price level (or monetary growth and inflation) are more closely related in the long run (over a very long period of time). We have seen that when we compare inflation and monetary growth rates, measured relative to the same month of the previous year, we do not see any correspondence between the two rates (Figures 7.8 and 7.9). However, if we compare long moving averages of the two growth rates, we will find that the moving averages are highly correlated. In Figure 7.15, we observe moving averages ranging between 12 months and

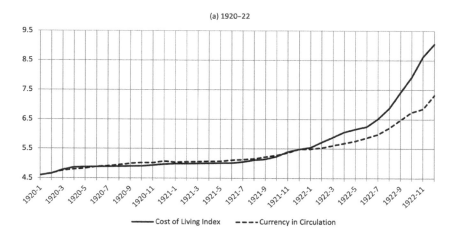

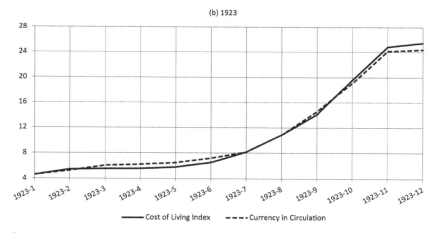

Source: Data from Holtfrerich (1986).

Figure 7.14   *Money and prices in the German hyperinflation (1920–23)*

770 months over the period between 1960 and 2023. The moving averages
of the monetary growth and inflation rate are plotted against the length of the
moving average on the horizontal axis. We can see that the moving averages
exhibit strong positive correlation. This means that average growth rates over
a very long period of time are correlated, but they are not equal, which means
that the envisaged proportionality between monetary growth and inflation is
not observed even in the long run.

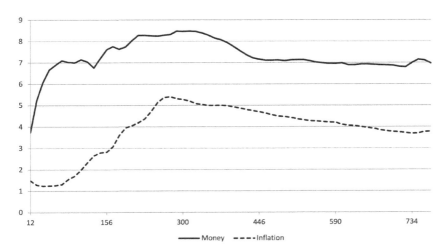

Source: Data from FRED.

Figure 7.15   *Moving averages of monetary growth and inflation*

Leaving proportionality aside, it seems that the positive correlation between monetary growth and inflation is supportive of the prediction of the quantity theory of money, or is it? Correlation, as shown in Figure 7.15, is very strong but correlation does not necessarily imply causation, particularly in the absence of sound theoretical reasoning. For all we know, real output tends to grow over time because of growth in factors of production (and consequently the productive capacity of the economy), which requires a larger amount of money. As incomes rise, and aggregate demand grows, the prices of goods and services rise. Prices rise over time for another reason, which is improvement in quality. As output, incomes and prices rise, money follows – it does not cause anything. Even the quantity theory of money tells us that money is needed to settle transactions, which means that an increase in the volume and value of transactions, as proxied by nominal output (PY), needs an increase in the money supply. Hence, the money supply is endogenous – it is caused by expanding economic activity, not the other way round.

7.10   CONCLUDING REMARKS

A discussion of Occam's razor as applied to the work of Milton Friedman is presented by Becchio (2020) who distinguishes between simplicity and parsimony by arguing that simplicity is related to the capacity of a model to describe a complex phenomenon in a "sophisticatedly simple way" whereas parsimony is "a proper subset of simplicity". Accordingly, he defines Occam's razor as follows: "the widely held principle of science that the simplest (often shortest) explanation that is adequate in number and type of assumptions (simplicity) and in technique (elegance) to explain the observed facts is the criterion by which to prefer explanations". Given this definition, Becchio (2020) argues that Milton Friedman gave precedence to simplicity in economic modelling. He further argues that Friedman and neoclassical economists in general have reduced economics (the science that describes economic individual and social behaviour) to physics (the science that describes nature). On the other hand, Ernst Nagel accuses Friedman of anti-realism by failing to distinguish among three kinds of "unrealism": the lack of an "exhaustive" description; the possible accordance between an unrealistic assumption and a correct theory; and the instrumental use of unrealistic assumptions when they reveal discrepancies between pure theory and described phenomena (Nagel, 1963). These are all characteristics of Friedman's proposition on the monetary explanation of inflation.

8. Macroeconomic policy implications: rethinking the role of interest rates

8.1   INTRODUCTION

Central banks are using interest rate hikes to curb inflation and claim that the inflation rate has come down as a result of this policy. The argument presented in this chapter is that interest rate policy is not an appropriate or effective anti-inflationary tool and that inflation is merely a reflection of rising energy and food prices. This reasoning is valid at least on this occasion, given that inflation is caused primarily by cost-push and profit-push factors. Consumers do not go to a bank and ask for a loan to buy food and energy – rather, they respond by spending an increasing proportion of their incomes on these essential items. Hence, raising the cost of borrowing will not force people to cut the consumption of food and energy. They may pay for food and energy by using a credit card and pay in instalments, but this is unsustainable. In any case, the interest rate charged on credit card balances is so outrageously high that two or three more percentage points of interest on a limited balance will not make much difference.

Higher interest rates add to the misery of those who allocate a big portion of income to mortgage payments. A critique will be presented in this chapter of the interest rate policy, adopted by the Fed and followed by other central banks, of taking interest rates to low and even negative territory, only to push them up rapidly. The claim that the crisis is under control because the inflation rate is going down in response to higher interest rates is false for two reasons. The first is that the decline in inflation is natural following a one-off shock, and has nothing to do with interest rates. This means that the inflation rate would have come down in 2023 even without the fall in the prices of food and energy, unless the general price level rises exponentially, which is a characteristic of hyperinflation. The second reason is that a declining inflation rate does not mean a containment of the crisis, because as long as the price level rises, real incomes decline and consumers find it increasingly more difficult to pay for what they need. An argument will be presented that interest rate policy is not only inadequate to curb inflation but also to boost the economy when it is in a recession.

8.2   THE INTEREST RATE–INFLATION NEXUS

Economists seem to be ambivalent on the relation between interest rate and inflation, because the former has two roles to play in the economy. As the return on investment, we are told that inflation and interest rate are positively related because as inflation goes up, depositors and investors demand and obtain higher nominal interest rates to maintain real returns. Financial institutions respond by raising deposit rates – otherwise, they will not be able to attract deposits. This causal relation is implied by the Fisher equation, named after the American economist Irving Fisher (1907). It tells us that the nominal interest rate is equal to the real rate plus the inflation rate, where the latter is the expected inflation rate if the equation is viewed from an *ex ante* perspective and the actual or realised inflation rate from an *ex post* perspective.

The underlying assumption is that the real interest rate is unaffected by monetary policy and hence unaffected by the expected inflation rate. It follows that, with a fixed real interest rate, a given change in the expected inflation rate will, according to the Fisher hypothesis, necessarily be met with an equal change in the nominal interest rate in the same direction. In this sense, the direction of causation runs from inflation to interest rates. In terms of casual empiricism, the Fisher equation seems to be supported by time series and cross-sectional data, as can be seen in Figure 8.1 and Figure 8.2, respectively. In Figure 8.1 we can see the inflation rate and interest rate (federal funds rate) in the US, going back to July 1954. Figure 8.2 is a scatter plot of interest rate on the inflation rate using 2022 data on 83 countries. In this sample of countries, Zimbabwe and Turkey have the inflation rates of 104% and 72%, respectively and they also have the highest interest (deposit) rates of 35% and 27%, respectively. In both Figures 8.1 and 8.2, inflation and interest rates are positively correlated, but the Fisher hypothesis tells us that causation runs from inflation to interest rate. On the other hand, the use of interest rate policy as an anti-inflationary tool implies that causation runs from interest rate to inflation. One cannot possibly envisage a situation where over a period of 70 years the Fed was so precise in using interest rate policy successfully to bring inflation down as shown in Figure 8.1. After all, the Fed has repeatedly switched from interest rate targeting to money supply targeting, and vice versa. Therefore, the positive correlation seen in Figure 8.1 cannot be attributed to policy action.

The rationale for using interest rate policy as an anti-inflationary tool is based on the observation that interest rate represents the cost of borrowing, in which case interest rate policy can be used to cool off demand and bring inflation down. When inflationary pressures appear in the economy, the central bank raises its official rate, which leads to rising market lending and borrowing rates. Borrowing becomes expensive, in which case people find it

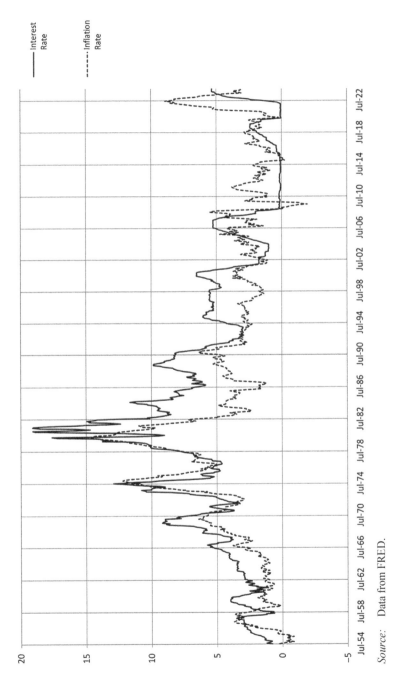

Source: Data from FRED.

Figure 8.1   Inflation and interest rates in the US

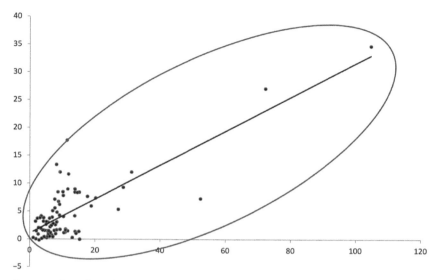

Source: Data from the World Bank.

*Figure 8.2   A scatter plot of inflation on interest rates (cross-sectional
               data)*

less attractive to borrow and spend. This cause and effect relation is also valid
when the interest rate is looked upon as the return on investment. In this case,
when interest rates are high, those who have the money (investible funds) find
it more attractive to save, consequently they reduce spending (but certainly
not on essentials such as food, energy and housing). In this sense, therefore,
interest rate as an inflationary tool works only if inflation is caused by demand
factors (that is, when demand-pull inflation prevails). However, even if inflation is predominantly demand-pull, interest rate policy is unlikely to work and
it has severe negative consequences.

   As an anti-inflationary tool, the quantitative link between interest rate and
inflation is prescribed by the Taylor rule (named after the American economist
John B. Taylor). It is a monetary policy targeting rule that can be used (by
central banks) to set the official interest rate at a level determined by inflation
and economic growth (Taylor, 1993). According to the rule, the optimal level
of the policy interest rate depends on the gap between the desired (targeted)
inflation rate and the actual inflation rate, as well as the output gap between
the actual and natural output levels. Cochrane (2021) describes the Taylor rule
as follows:

The Taylor rule recommends that interest rates rise one-and-a-half times as much as inflation. So if inflation rises from 2 percent to 5 percent, interest rates should rise by 4.5 percentage points. Add a baseline of 2 percent for the inflation target and 1 percent for the long-run real rate of interest, and the rule recommends a central-bank rate of 7.5 percent. If inflation accelerates further before central banks act, reining it in could require the 15 percent interest rates of the early 1980s.

In essence, the Taylor rule calls for a more aggressive monetary policy than what is observed in reality because it prescribes higher levels of interest rates than what central bankers like them to be. For example, Hofmann and Bogdanova (2012) argue that in some major advanced economies, policy rates were below the level implied by the Taylor rule, which means that monetary policy was too accommodative, from the perspective of this benchmark, during the "Great Inflation" of the 1970s. In contrast, policy rates were broadly consistent with the Taylor rule during the "Great Moderation" between the mid-1980s and early 2000s, a period characterised by low inflation and low macroeconomic volatility.

8.3   THE STYLISED FACTS

In this section we examine the behaviour of the federal funds rate, inflation and the general price level in the US over the period December 2019–December 2023 to find out if the act of raising of interest rates was the reason why inflation went down in 2023. In Figure 8.3, we can see that the Fed started raising interest rates in February 2022, perhaps to blame the resurgence of inflation on Putin's invasion of Ukraine, but it is obvious that inflation had started to pick up in May 2020 as a result of the supply chain chaos and other supply issues brought about by the pandemic. Four months later, inflation peaked at 9.1%, presumably in response to rising interest rate from 0.08% to 1.21%, which is implausible. Thereafter, interest rate was pushed up while the inflation rate went down. As the interest rate stabilised at 5.33%, the inflation rate picked up slightly. This kind of behaviour seems to provide some evidence that interest rate policy works, in the sense that a higher interest rate is associated with falling inflation. When the upward movement of the inflation rate was reversed, presumably as demand was restrained by the power of high interest rate, central bankers claimed victory over inflation and congratulated themselves on a job well done, even implying that the worst was behind.

Claiming victory over inflation made by triumphant central bankers and politicians seems to be accepted by the media. For example, Duggan (2023) comments on the decline in the US inflation rate from 3.2% in October 2023 to 3.1% in November 2023 by saying that "the Federal Reserve is making progress in its ongoing battle against inflation". In early December 2023, the

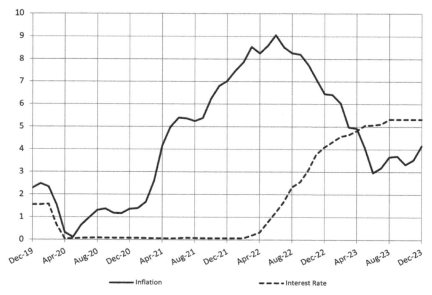

Source: Data from FRED.

Figure 8.3   *Inflation and interest rate in the US (recent data)*

Fed Chair, Jerome Powell, acknowledged that "inflation is moving in the right direction", but he insisted that the Fed plans on "keeping policy restrictive" until policy makers are convinced that inflation is headed back to 2%. By the time policy makers are convinced that inflation is under control as a result of their heroic endeavours, a large number of mortgage holders will lose their homes, and a big transfer of wealth from ordinary people to bankers will have occurred, not to mention the adverse effect on progress towards sorting out supply-side bottlenecks. Central bankers seem to have some illusion about the power of interest rate policy as an anti-inflationary device. After all, Powell (Jerome, not Enoch) has allegedly managed to bring the inflation rate down by raising the interest rate, and this is why he is leading the charge against inflation (holding a black flag with a white arrow pointing upwards) until it is down to a level he likes. Even an eminent economist like John Cochrane seems to believe in the power of interest rate policy, as he notes: "should inflation continue to surge, central banks' main tool is to raise interest rates sharply, and keep them high for several years, even if that causes a painful recession, as it did in the early 1980s" (Cochrane, 2021).

Even worse is the implication that the reversal of the direction of the infla-tion rate in 2023 indicates that the cost of living crisis has been contained and

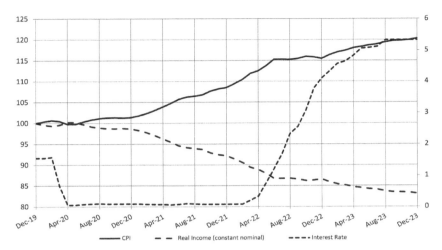

Source: Data from FRED.

Figure 8.4 *CPI, interest rate and real income in the US*

that the worst is behind. This is nonsense because a decline in the inflation rate does not mean that the cost of living has stopped rising, which is what containment of the crisis is all about. In Figure 8.4 we can see that the CPI was still on the rise following the fall of the inflation rate. With no change in nominal income, this means declining real income, hence a continuation of the crisis. Central bankers and politicians show an incredible degree of dishonesty when they talk about the inflation rate rather than the cost of living. They also show insensitivity by claiming, accordingly, that the crisis has been contained and that the worst is behind. The cost of living crisis is caused by declining real income, which happens even if the inflation rate is declining.

On the other hand, the 2023 decline in the inflation rate is not necessarily due to rising interest rates, because correlation does not necessarily imply causation. Furthermore, the process takes time. For example, the governor of the Central Bank of Ireland notes that "historical evidence, along with survey data, suggests that these effects start to kick-in around 12 months from the start of a rate-increase cycle, and permeate through economic activity for several years" (Makhlouf, 2023). Therefore, it is implausible to suggest that the direction of the inflation rate was reversed four months after the initiation of the high interest rate policy.

If interest rate hikes did not bring down the inflation rate, what did? A simple answer is that the reversal of the inflation rate was caused by (or accounted for, to use a better expression) declining prices of goods and services, which are unlikely to be related to interest rate hikes. Figure 8.5 shows the percentage changes in the prices of goods and services that constitute the components of the CPI in the US, as well as the prices of all items (the inflation rate), which declined in 2023. It is, however, a formidable task to prove that these declines were caused by higher interest rates as opposed to, for example, improvement in the supply chain situation and the availability of semiconductor chips – in other words, improvements in the structural supply-side factors that led to the resurgence of inflation in the first place. The price of food at home and away from home is not sensitive to changes in interest rates. I am yet to hear about someone who was planning to take a bank loan to invite some friends to a restaurant, only to send an apology saying that the interest rate charged on the loan has gone up from 1% to 4%. The demand for food at home is not sensitive to changes in interest rate because the consumption of food at home is not financed by a bank loan. The same goes for electricity. The same goes for recreation. The same goes for energy. Perhaps the only item in Figure 8.5 that is sensitive to changes in interest rates is new vehicles, but this is a very small component of the CPI and, unlike the consumption of food and energy, people do not buy new vehicles on a daily basis.

Consider now the situation in Australia. Between January 2022 and August 2023, the inflation rate went up from 3.5% to 5.2% while the interest rate went up from 0.1% to 4.1%, which made some economists sceptical about the effectiveness of using interest policy to fight inflation. In his comments on the failure of the RBA to curb spending by Australian households, David Bassanese, the chief economist at BetaShares, says the following (Hutchens, 2023a):

> The resilience of consumer spending (so far at least) reflects the tight labour market, a still substantial household saving buffer built up during the pandemic – and perhaps more controversially – the fact that rising interest rates have less direct effect on the two-thirds of households that don't have a mortgage. The incidence of tighter monetary policy is narrowly directed to a subset of households with heavy debt burdens … . For a broader effort in slowing economic growth, more heavy lifting would need to come from fiscal policy, though so far it's been missing in action.

For interest rate policy to be effective as an anti-inflationary tool, it must be able to deal with the causes of inflation. Ritchie (2023) wonders about how raising interest rates curbs inflation in Australia, starting correctly by identifying the causes of inflation. The first is higher food prices, resulting from the impact of the Queensland floods on transport and supply, as well as higher input costs. The second is record-level fuel prices, resulting from the oil price shock caused by the war in Ukraine, and the easing of pandemic restrictions. The third is higher construction costs caused by shortages of materials and

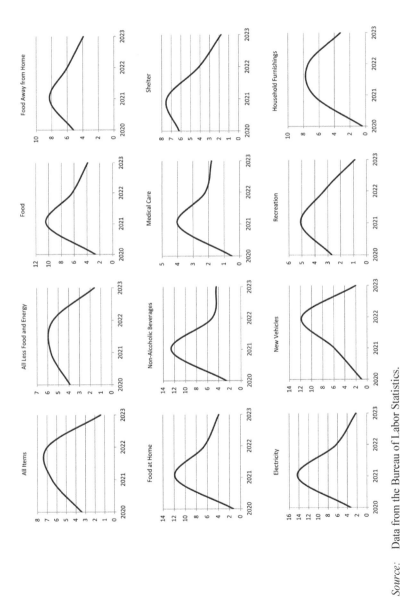

Source: Data from the Bureau of Labor Statistics.

Figure 8.5 *Percentage changes in the prices of goods and services in the US*

labour. Obviously, these are supply-side issues that cannot be resolved by raising interest rates. On the contrary, raising interest rates aggravates all of the factors that have led to the resurgence of inflation. The RBA justifies the lifting of interest rates aggressively in terms of a "potential wage-price spiral", meaning greedy workers demanding pay rise and putting pressure on the general price level, thereby aggravating inflation, by squandering the extra income on things they do not need. Therefore, to relieve the pressure put on the general price level, the RBA transfers big chunks of the incomes earned by workers to commercial banks via higher mortgage and borrowing rates (see, for example, Remeikis, 2023). This is the culture of blaming the victim at its worst. Commenting on the situation in Australia, Stanford (2023) says the following:

> Workers in Australia have suffered considerable economic losses as a result of accelerating inflation since the onset of the COVID pandemic. Reaching a year-over-year rate of 7.8% by end-2022, inflation has rapidly eroded the real purchasing power of workers' incomes … . Now, severe monetary tightening by the Reserve Bank of Australia (through higher interest rates) is imposing additional pain on millions of workers. Tens of billions of dollars of household disposable income are being diverted away from consumer spending, into extra interest payments made to banks and other lenders.

In November 2023, Rishi Sunak claimed credit for reducing the inflation rate in the UK, promising that he would single-handedly halve the rate (Baker, 2023; Hatton, 2023). In reality, even if the prices of food and energy had not gone down or moderated, the inflation rate would have reversed direction, simply because a continuously rising inflation rate requires explosive growth in the CPI, which is only observed under hyperinflation. Except under hyperinflation, the inflation rate is described by economists as a stationary, mean-reverting process, which means that it has the tendency to revert back to its mean value. In Figure 8.6 we can see simulated time series for the behaviour of the CPI over a period of 30 months under three scenarios: (i) a stable inflation rate, (ii) a rising inflation rate, and (iii) a falling inflation rate. For comparison, the actual CPI of the US is shown for the period April 2021–October 2023. We can see, first of all, that the behaviour under scenarios (ii) and (iii) is not typically observed and that in practice a typical CPI series under normal conditions resembles the behaviour under scenario (i) of a stable inflation rate. We can also see that the actual behaviour of the CPI in the US resembles the simulated behaviour under scenario (i).

The proposition that the inflation rate does not keep going up for an extended period of time is supported by data on the CPI in the US, going back to the 1940s. In Figure 8.7 we can see the movement of the CPI under six inflation episodes. The record for the number of consecutive months during which

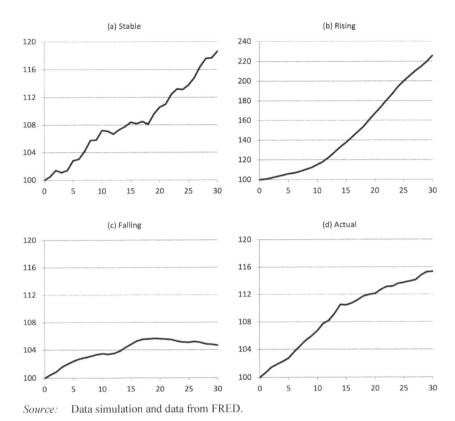

Source: Data simulation and data from FRED.

Figure 8.6   Simulated and actual CPI in the US

the inflation rate rose was 16 (December 1978 to March 1980). On another occasion, the inflation rate rose in 15 consecutive months between February 1950 and April 1951. In the most recent episodes, the inflation rate rose for seven months between December 2020 and June 2021, then for another seven months between September 2021 and March 2022. In all of these episodes, the inflation rate reversed direction, with or without the use of interest rate policy.

According to Rouse et al. (2021), the period right after World War II witnessed an inflationary episode that is the closest to the current one because the rapid post-war inflationary episode was caused by the elimination of price controls, supply shortages and pent-up demand. What happened then resembles what happened in 2021–23, in that the prices of the components of the CPI went up rapidly during the period February 1946–August 1948, subsequently either declined or rose slowly during the period August 1948–February 1950.

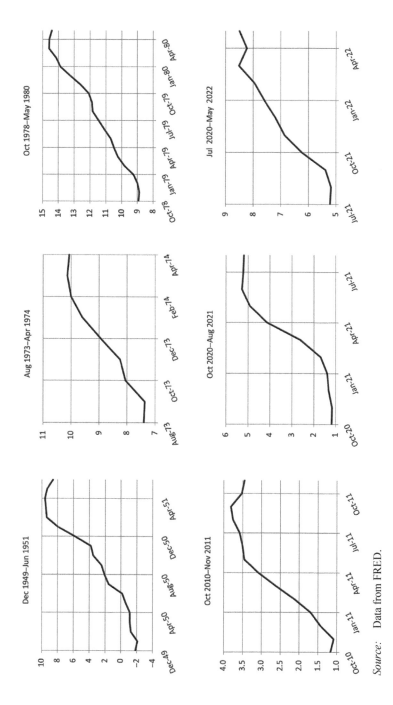

Source: Data from FRED.

Figure 8.7   *Inflationary episodes in the US*

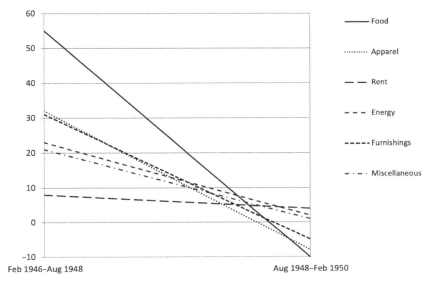

Source: Data from Rouse et al. (2021).

Figure 8.8 *Changes in prices (US, 1946–50)*

We can see that in Figure 8.8, where the price of food rose by 55% then declined by 10% while the price of apparel went up by 32% then declined by 8%. As a result, the inflation rate fell from 12.8% in the first period to −2.8% in the second period (Bureau of Labor Statistics, 2014). Rouse et al. (2021) point out that "the inflationary period after World War II is likely a better comparison for the current economic situation than the 1970s and suggests that inflation could quickly decline once supply chains are fully online and pent-up demand levels off". Nothing is said about monetary factors or the role of interest rates.

8.4 DEMAND-PULL VERSUS COST-PUSH INFLATION

High interest rates are supposed to restrain demand and ease pressure on prices. This may be the case, but only if inflation is generated by demand-pull rather than cost-push factors – that is, only if inflation is caused by rising demand as opposed to supply constraints. Interest rates can do little to ease supply constraints. In 2022, Fed Chair Jerome Powell stated the following in an interview: "What we [the Fed] can control is demand, we can't really affect supply with our policies … so the question whether we can execute a soft landing or not, it may actually depend on factors that we don't control" (Ryssdal, 2022). So, the question is whether resurgent inflation has been caused by supply or demand factors (whether it is cost-push or demand-pull inflation). If resurgent inflation is caused by supply-side (predominantly global) factors, interest rates become irrelevant.

Makhlouf (2023) describes current inflation as "a global phenomenon that was driven first by supply shortages coming out of the pandemic and then continued with the onset of Russia's war". Stiglitz (2023) subscribes to this view by opining as follows:

> There is overwhelming evidence that the main source of inflation was pandemic-related supply shocks and shifts in the pattern of demand, not excess aggregate demand, and certainly not any additional demand created by pandemic spending. Anyone with any faith in the market economy knew that the supply issues would be resolved eventually; but no one could possibly know when.

Some economists believe that demand-side factors have also contributed to resurgent inflation, which is plausible. The economic shutdown brought about by the COVID-19 pandemic led to a situation of pent-up demand, but as restrictions were relaxed, consumers came back with vengeance, armed with forced savings. As a result, a supply-demand imbalance emerged, forcing prices upwards. The question then becomes how much of the current inflation is attributed to demand and supply factors.

Economic models can be used to estimate how much supply-side and demand-side factors have added to inflation, although the results depend on the model used for this purpose. One approach, developed by Shapiro (2022), is to attribute changes in prices to shifts in demand if quantities move in the same direction in that period, and to shifts in supply if quantities move in the opposite direction (price changes are defined as "ambiguous" if the change in price or quantity is relatively small). His analysis for the US economy shows that both supply and demand factors have contributed to the resurgence of inflation. Specifically, he finds the following: (i) supply factors explain about half of the difference between current 12-month personal consumption expenditure (PCE) inflation and pre-pandemic inflation levels, and the effects appear to be rising more recently; (ii) demand factors are responsible for about a third of the difference, and those effects appear to be diminishing more recently; and (iii) the remainder is due to factors that cannot be definitively labelled as supply or demand. Cerrato and Gitti (2023) find that demand factors explain around 1.4 out of the 5.6 percentage point increase in CPI inflation in the US from March 2021 to September 2022. Konczal (2023) finds that the majority of the 2023 disinflation has been driven by expanding supply rather than diminishing demand. This conclusion is based on the finding that for the majority of items, prices fell while quantities went up, which is a sign of expanding supply.

The view that excess demand for goods and services is the primary driver of inflation is described by Madrick (2022) as "excess-demand tunnel vision". He goes on to say:

> There is ample evidence, however, that supply-side bottlenecks are driving inflation in America significantly more than demand, from manufacturing shortages to transportation blockages to explosively excessive profits due to corporate power to raise prices unjustifiably and to buy back stocks with the proceeds rather than invest. Excess profits are especially obvious in oil and gas, due to the cuts in supply by energy producers, including notably Russia, and lately the Arab oil nations.

Thus, Madrick brings about the role of profit-push inflation, which is a supply-side factor. To support his view on the role played by profit-push inflation, he gives the following example: The two largest American oil companies, ExxonMobil and Chevron, earned by far the highest profits in their history in the second calendar quarter of 2022, some $23 billion and $15.6 billion, respectively. He concludes by saying that "the way to get America back on track is to focus on the supply-side drivers of inflation, not simply raise interest rates to cause unemployment". While he mentions that both Joe Stiglitz and Paul Krugman are sceptical of the view that demand is the main driver of inflation, he also argues that Milton Friedman would have been happy about a policy that "won't solve America's economic problems rapidly or without causing a lot of pain", which is using high interest rates to create unemployment. I would go even further by saying that interest rate policy will not solve the inflation problem, even slowly and with a lot of pain.

The effect of demand is usually portrayed as originating from sustained reduction in consumption and the accumulation of savings that ended up with an explosion of spending and rapid drawdown of savings following the end of the critical part of the pandemic as more and more people got vaccinated. This is the pent-up demand hypothesis. For example, Remes et al. (2021) refer to a collapse of consumer spending when (all of a sudden) consumers were forced to accumulate savings. This is true, except that it did not last for long, and therefore accumulated savings did not represent pent-up demand. Those who lost their jobs naturally did not contribute to the accumulation of savings. This point is made by Lapavitsas et al. (2023) who argue that only "the layers of the population with higher incomes were able to accumulate savings at the peak of the restrictions as consumption was forcibly reduced". Figure 8.9 shows US consumer spending on a monthly basis. We can see that consumer spending dropped by almost 18% in March and April 2020, but the direction of change was reversed very quickly, and by September 2020, consumer spending had

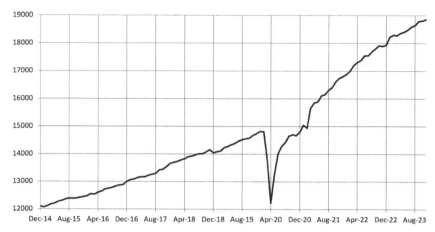

Source: Data from FRED.

Figure 8.9   *Personal consumption expenditure in the US ($ billion)*

risen by 18% compared to the April level. All that happened while the pandemic was wreaking havoc, way before the advent of the vaccine.

8.5   INTEREST SENSITIVITY OF DEMAND

Even if inflation is caused by demand-pull factors, interest rate policy is unlikely to work because a necessary condition for this policy to work is that consumer spending is interest sensitive, moving up and down as interest rates are pushed downwards and upwards, respectively. The rationale behind attempts to curb inflation by raising interest rates is that people find it expensive to borrow and spend, in which case they respond by borrowing less and spending less, relieving pressure on the prices of goods and services that comprise the CPI basket – consequently inflation goes down. This may be true for spending on consumer durables and luxuries (such as travelling for pleasure), but it is not true for necessities such as food, energy and housing, the core of the current crisis. Faced with more expensive food, energy and housing, people allocate more of their tight budgets to these necessities and cut down on other, less necessary items. Some people may borrow small amounts of money on a temporary basis to pay for necessities but borrowing is not a sustainable means of financing the purchase of necessities. People may also resort to savings, if they have any, or to crime if they are exceptionally desperate.

We have seen that the US inflation rate declined in 2023 because of declining or decelerating prices of the goods and services that people typically consume and which comprise the components of the CPI. For interest rate to be an effective anti-inflationary tool, the following implausible propositions must be valid.

- People borrow to eat in restaurants or order take-away food. When interest rates rise, they stop eating in restaurants and ordering take-away food. What happens in reality is that when people face inflation, they either stop or reduce the incidence of eating in restaurants and ordering take-away food. They opt instead to eat at home, because no one dies or suffers deprivation by not eating at MacDonald's, drinking coffee at Starbucks, or having an expensive steak in one of Gordon Ramsay's restaurants.
- People borrow to eat at home, which means that when interest rates rise, they starve. In reality, when people face rising food prices, they allocate more of their incomes to food, they eat less, they eat cheaper food, they resort to savings, or they line up at food banks.
- People borrow to pay their electricity and gas bills, which means that when interest rates rise, they stop using electricity and gas. What happens in reality is that people allocate more of their incomes to energy bills while reducing wasteful consumption. I have read a story about a pensioner living in England who reduced her consumption of gas and electricity by spending most of the day on fixed-fare buses.
- People borrow to go to the theatre or watch movies, implying that when interest rates rise, they stop doing that. In reality, no one borrows to go to the movies because they can live without it. Neither do people borrow to pay for a $1000 ticket to experience the extravaganza of a Taylor Swift concert, again because they can live without seeing Taylor Swift in action.
- People borrow to drink Pepsi and Coke, which means that when interest rates rise, they stop drinking Pepsi and Coke. In reality, people do not have to drink Pepsi and Coke and can choose the more healthy option of drinking water.

For the cause and effect process to work, people must be willing and able to borrow and banks must be willing and able to lend. People may not want to borrow at any interest rate because they hate debt or because they cannot afford to repay the debt. In this case, higher interest rates do not change anything. Banks, on the other hand, are more willing to lend at high rather than low interest rates. This means that high interest rates do not suppress the ability of banks to lend more.

The last point to be made here is that corporate spending is not interest sensitive. If companies can pass the increase in the cost of borrowing to their customers, they will borrow at any interest rate. Thus, if corporate borrowing and spending is not interest sensitive, and if most of personal spending is not financed by borrowing, then demand cannot be restrained by raising interest rates, particularly the demand for necessities such as food, energy and housing.

8.6   THE INFLATIONARY EFFECT OF RISING INTEREST RATES

Raising the level of interest rates to suppress demand and reduce inflation may be counterproductive because high rates tend to aggravate inflation. Interest rates are instrumental for the housing sector, which means that raising interest rates while rents are rising is like pouring fuel on fire. This is because landlords, who use the proceeds from rents to make mortgage payments, will pass on the increase in mortgage payments to their tenants. Commenting on the situation in Australia, Leggatt (2023) notes that "landlords simply pass on the higher mortgage costs to renters, creating a negative feedback loop". Furthermore, interest payments by business firms represent a cost of production. Therefore, an interest rate hike represents an increase in the costs of production, to which business firms respond by raising prices to preserve their profit margins. They may go even further by raising their prices more proportionately than the increase in the costs of production to boost their profit margins.

Stiglitz (2023) points out that raising interest rates could do more harm than good, by making it more expensive for firms to invest in solutions to the current supply constraints and argues that "the US Federal Reserve's monetary-policy tightening has already curtailed housing construction, even though more supply is precisely what is needed to bring down one of the biggest sources of inflation: housing costs". He adds:

> Moreover, many price-setters in the housing market may now pass the higher costs of doing business on to renters. And in retail and other markets more broadly, higher interest rates can actually induce price increases as the higher interest rates induce businesses to write down the future value of lost customers relative to the benefits today of higher prices.

Stiglitz is very sceptical about the ability of the central bank to fight inflation. He rejects the view that the inflation rate has been brought down precisely because central banks have signalled such resolve in fighting it, which is what central bankers brag about and claim bonuses for.

8.7   A CHAOTIC INTEREST RATE POLICY

The interest rate is a double-edged sword because it is the rate of return for investors and the cost of borrowing for borrowers. This is why interest rates should be neither too high nor too low. Therefore, the worst possible interest

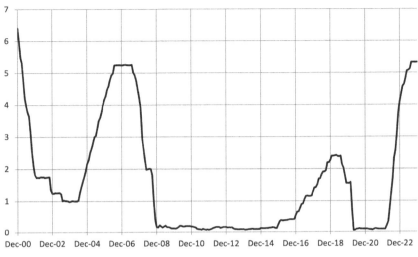

Figure 8.10 *Federal funds rate*

rate policy is to take interest rates to a low level very fast, then to a high level just as fast. This is exactly how central bankers have been turning people's lives into one tragedy after another. Figure 8.10 displays the movement of the federal funds rate in the US between December 2000 and December 2023. When interest rates are low, people are enticed to take mortgages they cannot afford, only to find themselves in a position where they cannot meet their mortgage payments when interest rates rise. As a result of bank foreclosure, they find themselves homeless. By looking at Figure 8.10, people who took mortgages in 2004 got into trouble in 2006, those who took mortgages between 2008 and 2015 got into trouble in 2019, and those who took mortgages during the COVID years are in trouble now.

Central bankers justify this chaotic policy on the grounds that low rates are required for recovery from a recession whereas high rates are required to curb inflation. We have already seen that high interest rates cannot curb infla- tion. The same can be said about the use of low rates to revive the economy on the grounds that low interest rates boost consumption and investment. Specifically, low interest rates are supposed to encourage consumers to borrow and spend on consumer durables, households to borrow and invest in housing, and businesses to borrow and invest in plant and equipment as well as inven- tory. However, it seems that central bankers do not know that one can lead a horse to water but can't make it drink. This means that someone can be given an opportunity but cannot be forced to take it. Therefore, the central bank can reduce interest rates but it cannot force individuals and companies to borrow and spend. This policy will not work if financial institutions are not willing to extend credit to the private sector, fearing the risk of default. And it will not work if the private sector is not willing to borrow because the economic outlook is bearish.

A policy of ultra-low interest rates is harmful. When interest rates are extremely low, prudent savers are penalised and encouraged to take on more risk. If the policy is sustained over a long period of time, it provides support for over-leveraged inefficient companies that would otherwise fail. Low interest rates maintain bubbles in the housing and stock markets. On a macroeconomic level, the policy hurts economic growth because growth needs capital accumulation that is financed through savings. Households are reluctant to lend their savings to the government when Treasury bond yields are low, in which case the government finds it tantalising, perhaps inevitable, to go down the slippery slope of monetising the budget deficit by "printing" money and risking hyperinflation.

The policy of ultra-low interest rates has been criticised repeatedly. Tagliaferro (2019) is critical of this policy, suggesting that "lower interest rates have not been encouraging investment but rather share buy backs". In his outgoing speech upon leaving his job as the head of the European Central Bank, Mario Draghi said that interest rate cuts may not have the same power they once did (Schrager, 2019). More recently, Draghi has argued, "we are in a situation where low interest rates are not delivering the same degree of stimulus as in the past, because the rate of return on investment in the economy has fallen". Bill Gross, the founder of PIMCO, described a low interest rate environment as "money for nothing interest rate policies", suggesting that these policies have failed. Low interest rates, he noted, "may not cure a fever … they may in fact raise a patient's temperature to life threatening status" (Cox, 2015). The *Financial Times* (2020) argues that "today's ultra-low interest rates are anything but natural" and that "policymakers who have cut rates repeatedly should not be let off the hook so easily". In a letter sent to the *Financial Times*, Martin Allen commented on the article by saying that "low interest rates are the corollary of rising debt". He suggested that low interest rates are not conducive to the accomplishment of the stated objective of boosting the economy, particularly in 2020 and beyond, because the current problems in the world economy are the result of the aggregate demand and supply shocks produced by a pandemic.

In reality, a low interest rate policy is pursued for the benefit of banks and the corporate sector, helping them to finance parasitic activities such as stock buy-backs and venture capital. The minority who hold stocks, including billionaires, benefit because low interest rates boost the stock market by enabling these parasitic activities. Banks benefit from low deposit rates because they can still charge 20% on credit card debt. They also benefit by enticing more people to get mortgages, a business that has become perhaps more important than business lending in this era of financialisation (see, for example, Moosa, 2023a). Loan sharks benefit because they can borrow at 2% and lend at 5000%.

An extreme form of low interest rate policy is that of negative interest rates, a policy that is highly beneficial for commercial banks because they can still charge interest on loans. Some of them benefit even more by indulging in a scam called "negative interest mortgages" by offering a mortgage at −0.5% and hitting the borrower with 3% charges in the form of commissions and administrative fees. At an interest rate of −2%, banks earn 2% by charging depositors, 20% by charging credit card holders and some hefty percentage by charging those unfortunate enough to request an overdraft. The question is why would anyone want to hold deposits with banks at a negative interest rate? Perhaps security, particularly if the amount is big – in this case it is like paying for a safety deposit box. The government makes sure that the adverse effects of negative rates on banks do not materialise – these effects, as envisaged by Haksar and Kopp (2020), are: (i) the potential impact on bank profitability, and (ii) incentive to switch out of deposits into holding cash.

Negative interest rates, the war on cash and the bail-in legislation are three components of an elaborate scheme executed by the banking-government complex to enrich bankers and reward politicians when they leave public service. Negative interest rates are bound to encourage people to keep money under the bed or in a hole in the ground rather than with banks. This works against the feasibility of bail-in legislation whereby failed banks are allowed to confiscate depositors' money to finance the bonuses and golden parachutes given the executives who cause failure in the first place. So, how do governments retaliate against those "irresponsible" depositors who withdraw their money from banks? For one thing, governments and the banking oligarchy are waging a war on cash transactions, not to combat the underground economy (as they claim) but to force people to keep money with banks, so that the money can be confiscated to rescue failed banks. People are threatened with confinement behind bars if they use cash to settle transactions over a certain value (so much for human rights). But this is not all, as unscrupulous economists acting as "hired guns" have come up with some ingenious ideas to force people to keep money with banks. One idea is to cancel, by a random selection of serial numbers, 10% of the banknotes in circulation. Those who keep money at home will face an expected rate of return of −10% on their cash holdings, in which case they will be better off (or less worse off) by keeping their money with banks at the rate of −2%, hoping that a bail-in will not materialise (for details, see Moosa, 2022).

Like everything else in life, moderation is the name of the game. Interest rates should be neither too high, nor too low. The transition from low interest rates to high interest rates should be gradual. Interest rate policy is supposedly used to defend the economy against inflation and recession, but in reality it is intended to enrich bankers who benefit from high rates, low rates and from a speedy transition from high rates to low rates, and vice versa.

8.8   ALTERNATIVES TO INTEREST RATE POLICY AS AN ANTI-INFLATIONARY TOOL

As an anti-inflationary tool, interest rate policy is not only ineffective but also harmful. It is often portrayed as being a tool with no viable alternatives, but viable alternatives are available. The alternatives can be classified under three headings: (i) actions that suppress consumer spending; (ii) actions that boost the supply of goods and services; and (iii) actions that restrain prices directly. Policies classified under (i) and (ii) are intended to keep inflation under control, whereas those classified under (iii) are intended to deal with the negative consequence of eroding real income.

In 2022 a survey was conducted by the Economic Society of Australia, in which 48 economists were asked about the actions, other than raising interest rates, which policy makers can take to bring the inflation rate down (Martin, 2022). Table 8.1 shows some possible actions as suggested by the participants in the survey. Actions intended to restrain demand are counterproductive, not in the least because inflation in Australia is mostly cost-push inflation. This view was expressed by some of the participants who suggested that "suppressing demand wouldn't tackle the main reasons prices were climbing". One participant thought that much of the inflationary pressure had come from things such as oil prices that were beyond the power of policy makers to influence. Another participant put forward the view that inflation was mainly due to a series of short-term supply-induced price rises, making it hard to see how choking demand could do much good. Both suggestions for suppressing demand are counterproductive.

Actions taken to boost supply sound much more sensible, with the exception of increasing immigration, which is itself inflationary because it is a source of demand. However, it makes sense if, for example, immigration is targeted towards skilled labour, which may help reduce the skyrocketing costs of domestic services such as plumbing. Reserving a portion of Australian east coast gas for domestic use would help decouple Australia's east coast gas prices from sky-high international prices. This action has been taken in Western Australia, where 15% of the state's gas is reserved for domestic use.

Actions designed to restrain prices or reduce out-of-pocket expenditure are in general intended to deal with the consequences of inflation when it cannot

Table 8.1   Anti-inflationary actions

Restraining Demand	Boosting Supply	Restraining Prices
• Winding back spending on infrastructure and construction • Pushing for below-inflation wage rises in the Fair Work Commission	• Reducing supply chain shortages • Boosting productivity growth • Increasing immigration • Reserving a portion of gas and other commodities for domestic use	• Extending the temporary cut in fuel excise • Boosting childcare subsidies • Tax reform

Source: Author's own.

be controlled, and this is why they include subsidies and financial aid. The specific tax reforms suggested include the imposition of super-profits tax on fossil fuel producers to generate revenue that can be used to reduce the cost of services, which is good. The bad tax-related suggestion is increasing the income tax rate and using the proceeds to reduce the cost of services – this is bad unless it is imposed on high earners who are not suffering from the consequences of the cost of living crisis. Unfortunately, no one mentioned anything about a wealth tax or a tax on financial transactions. No one mentioned anything about boosting consumer protection to restrain profit-push inflation. Boosting childcare subsidies is a good suggestion, and so is curbing the tendency to privatise healthcare, which no one mentioned. In a resource-rich country like Australia, the ultimate action would be to nationalise the mining sector and use the proceeds to support welfare programmes. Naturally, no prime minister would even consider that, having witnessed the removal of Kevin Rudd as the prime minister in 2010 for daring to propose a resource super-profits tax. None of the participants suggested anything like wealth tax, mining tax, financial transactions tax, consumer protection or the nationalisation of natural resources, even though they are necessary and feasible, because no one wanted to give the impression that they think outside the box defined by neoliberalism and the free-market dogma.

    While Adrian and Gaspar (2022) believe that across-the-board fiscal support is not warranted, they call for governments to prioritise helping the most vulnerable to cope with soaring food and energy prices and cover other costs. They also call for investment in infrastructure, healthcare and education; fair distribution of incomes and opportunities through an equitable tax and transfer system; and provision of basic public services. This is thinking outside the box but Adrian and Gaspar would have been called "lefties" in a derogatory manner.

On the other hand, the Committee for a Responsible Federal Budget (2022) presents a menu of six ways to fight inflation in the US, most of which are intended to suppress demand. The six ways are the following: (i) refraining from adding to the federal deficit; (ii) reducing healthcare costs; (iii) reforming the tax code to raise more revenue; (iv) limiting discretionary spending; (v) promoting work and savings; and (vi) reducing energy, trade and procurement costs. This is thinking within the box because these proposals have a right-wing, neoliberal tune aimed at reducing the size of the public sector. The Committee proposes cuts in the deficit by walking away from a petrol tax holiday, student debt cancellation, expanded veterans' benefits, enhanced Medicaid payments to states, farm subsidies, and social security benefits. A better alternative would be to cut the Pentagon's budget by one-half and refrain from financing wars of aggression and proxy wars overseas. Reducing healthcare costs cannot be achieved "through payments to Medicare providers" but by providing universal healthcare and preventing medical bankruptcies. Tax reform should not be about raising taxes across the board and reducing subsidies but by introducing taxes on financial transactions and luxury goods and services.

I am surprised that those who suggested measures to restrain demand did not mention forced savings, a proposal that can be traced to the writings of J.M. Keynes in the 1940s. In his book *How to Pay for the War*, Keynes (1940) suggested that in a fully employed war-time economy, everyone who is capable of working can find an income-generating job, at a time when most resources are directed towards the war effort rather than supplying the usual amount of consumer goods. To stop income earners from using their purchasing power to compete over a limited stock of consumer goods and triggering inflation, Keynes considered two options: (i) transferring bigger chunks of people's incomes to the Treasury (by raising taxes) or banks (by raising interest rates); and (ii) postponing their ability to spend too much through mandated savings of some kind. Keynes favoured the second option on the grounds that it is fairer because it allows workers to keep their earnings. In his own words, Keynes suggested that "for each individual it is a great advantage to retain the rights over the fruits of his labour even though he must put off the enjoyment of them". Specifically, Keynes suggested that workers should have "deferred pay cards" that record the amount of pay that would be kept aside out of each pay packet. He also suggested that workers should have the right to choose where their deferred pay would be deposited. Once the war was over, the accumulated savings could be released back to workers "probably by a series of instalments".

This brilliant idea (which resembles compulsory superannuation) was described by Keynes's intellectual opponent, Fredrich Hayek, as "ingenious" (Hayek, 1939). It is what led Gruen (1999) to believe that there was no reason why compulsory super contributions could not be used to meet short-term macroeconomic stabilisation objectives by allowing some short-term variation in compulsory super contributions. This is how Gruen described the idea:

> Thus, when macro-economic policy required tightening, the requirement to contribute to superannuation could be increased. By contrast, where economic stimulus is called for, there may be occasions where temporarily lowering the superannuation contribution rate would be an appropriate instrument.

A similar idea has been proposed by McCall (2021) who notes that "with discretionary fiscal tightening on both the revenue and expenditure sides politically difficult, and conventional monetary policy inefficient, ineffective and inequitable, empowering central banks with an adjustable mandatory savings rate could prove an effective and politically feasible potential complement to the automatic stabiliser and sector-specific inflation management approach. Specifically, he suggests that the central bank should have the power to quarantine a small portion of people's weekly income in a separate system to compulsory super.

8.9   CONCLUDING REMARKS

The perceived benefit of raising interest rates is that such an action brings inflation down. The definite cost is aggravating the crisis by transferring more money from households to banks in the form of rising mortgage payments, and by contributing to inflation because interest payments represent a cost of production. As such, interest rate policy is a subject of the law of unintended consequences. This reminds me of the practice of local councils that charge people for disposing of hard rubbish by taking them to council-operated tips. The declared (perhaps not the real) reason for the charge is to discourage people from producing waste, thereby reducing environmental pollution. This practice produces unintended consequences that are exactly the opposite of the declared objective. Instead of producing less waste, people start dumping their waste in parks and bushland, thereby making pollution even worse. The same is true of interest rate policy as an anti-inflationary tool.

It is wrongly believed that central banks can readily control inflation, simply by manipulating interest rates. This is the wrong medicine administered because of a misdiagnosis of the problem. The resurgence of inflation has not happened because of too much demand, but rather because of too little supply. We are told that higher interest rates are warranted because cheap credit has allowed spending to overrun the economy's ability to produce what people want to buy. In reality, the figures show very slow growth in credit because low interest rates do not constitute a necessary and sufficient condition for debt-financed spending by households and business firms.

Another alleged reason for the use of higher interest rates is the fear of wage-push inflation or the wage-price spiral. Central banks blame the spiral on "greedy workers" who demand increasingly higher wages, thereby forcing firms to raise the prices of their products. In reality, businesses raise their prices to boost their profit margins when they can get away with it. Central banks are not concerned about the inflationary threat posed by higher profits for businesses or higher asset prices for investors because higher profits and stock prices are thought to encourage more investment, when in fact both of them are inflationary. Since (allegedly) workers are responsible for inflation, they are punished by channelling bigger portions of their incomes to banks via higher mortgage rates. In reality, workers may have once had some bargaining power over wages, but this is no longer the case.

Government officials who make vital decisions do not shy away from inflicting excruciating pain on ordinary people under the pretext of fighting inflation. When the British Chancellor of the Exchequer Jeremy Hunt was asked whether he was comfortable with raising interest rates, even at the risk of precipitating a recession, he replied in the affirmative. Keegan (2023) tells a similar story about a former chancellor, John Major, who declared the following during the 1990–92 recession: "If it isn't hurting it isn't working." When Major became prime minister, his chancellor, Norman Lamont, said the following: "Rising unemployment and the recession have been the price that we have had to pay to get inflation down", adding that the "price is well worth paying". For Keegan, "these were pretty insensitive statements". Even worse, the same statements remind me of Madeleine Albright, Clinton's Secretary of State, who once said that killing 500,000 Iraqi children was "worth it".

Papadimitriou and Wray (2021) describe the course of action followed by the Fed in fighting inflation as "the tail wagging the dog". Joseph Stiglitz mentions his dog, Woofie, while talking about the inability of central banks to control inflation (Stiglitz, 2023). What he says is hilarious but very true, as he draws a comparison between central bankers believing that they brought inflation down and his dog, Woofie, who seems to think that he scares off the planes flying over his owner's house by barking. Conversely, Woofie may believe that not barking aggravates the risk of the plane falling on him.

A very interesting view is put forward by Lapavitsas et al. (2023) who believe that governments collude with corporate interests to boost profit. However, if higher interest rates bring about recession, this cannot be in the interest of the corporate sector. They argue that recession or the fear of recession puts workers in a position not to negotiate for higher wages, thus preserving corporate profitability. The end result is a combination of inflation and recession, or stagnation, which gives stagflation. Again, this cannot be in the interest of the corporate sector, but it is the inherent contradiction of capitalism, which emanates from the fact that wage earners are themselves consumers. By minimising the wage bill, which may occur with the help of the government, firms also minimise the purchasing power of consumers. This is why the capitalist system prevailing today is inherently unstable and conducive to the occurrence of economic crises in general and cost of living crises in particular.

9. The way forward: rethinking public policy

9.1 RECAPITULATION

This book is about the cost of living crisis and its implications for economic theory and public policy. A thorough analysis was conducted in the previous eight chapters using actual and simulated data, coupled with economic theory and common sense. Formal econometric analysis was avoided for two reasons: to make the book accessible to potential readers without formal training in econometrics, and (more importantly) because econometrics is a con art that can be used to prove anything. For example, those using econometrics to test the relation between the money supply and the general price level use a cointegration test to find out if the two variables are related in the long run and a causality test to find out if they are related in the short run. These tests are bogus. Causality in economics is not the same as causality in physics – it is simply a test of temporal ordering, which gives any result one wants to see by playing around with the lag structure. Once upon time, cointegration testing was regarded as a contribution to human knowledge because it (allegedly) enables economists to distinguish between spurious and genuine correlation. This is nonsense because only economic theory, common sense and even intuition allow us to distinguish between spurious and genuine correlation. For example, it was argued in Chapter 7 that a causal relation from money to prices requires a transmission mechanism, which does not exist and that it is more plausible to envisage a causal relation from prices to money. Econometrics may lead us to conclude that the consumption of margarine causes divorce and some other bizarre findings. And like causality tests, cointegration tests can be used to prove prior beliefs. Econometrics and ideology represent a toxic combination.

A cost of living crisis has two dimensions: prices and wages (or incomes in general). It is defined as a situation that arises when real income declines over time (that is, when prices rise at a higher rate than incomes, irrespective of whether the inflation rate is high or low). A severe cost of living crisis would arise because of stagflation and hyperinflation. Even artificial intelligence is likely to cause a cost of living crisis as robots replace workers and reduce their real income to zero. We have to remember that a cost of living crisis does not affect everyone and not to the same extent. Even under a devastating hyperinflation, some people survive the crisis because they are, for example, self-sufficient in the production of food. This observation was witnessed during the German hyperinflation of the 1920s.

The current cost of living crisis has not been caused by Vladimir Putin or even a shortage of semiconductor chips, but rather by a combination of factors that led to the resurgence of inflation at a time when wages have been stagnant. This crisis is not the first, neither will it be the last of its kind, because in a neoliberal economic system these crises are bound to surface periodically. Neoliberalism and its offshoots (such as privatisation, deregulation, deindustrialisation and financialisation) have transformed economies in such a way as to become vulnerable and crisis-prone. Neoliberalism has enabled the transfer of income from labour to capital, reduced the ability of the economy to produce goods and services, led to a stagnation in productivity, deprived ordinary people of a social safety net, and reduced the ability of the public sector to provide basic services and offer financial assistance to those in need. The occurrence of cost of living crises will continue as long as the building blocks are there, and as long as neoliberalism is the guiding philosophy, the building blocks will always be there.

The crisis has implications for economic theory and public policy. One implication for economic theory is that the relation between monetary growth and inflation is tenuous and based on a number of unrealistic assumptions. Inflation did not arise in the heyday of quantitative easing when massive amounts of fresh money were created by central banks. Resurgent inflation has not been caused by monetary growth but rather by supply-side factors of two kinds: cost-push and profit-push factors. Another implication for both theory and policy is that interest rate policy is ineffective for curbing inflation. One of the conclusions we have reached is that higher interest rates intended to curb inflation do the opposite because interest payments represent a cost of production. These implications, however, do not mean that the money supply and interest rates do not matter. A monetary expansion resulting from the availability of cheap credit boosts asset prices, with all of its ramifications. Higher interest rates can create a recession without curing inflation as it is intended.

In the remainder of this chapter we examine some propositions pertaining to the way forward, particularly with respect to public policy reform. Specifically, we look at a list of potential policy actions that are conducive to the minimisation of the probability of the occurrence of a cost of living crisis or alleviate the impact of such a crisis on the poor and vulnerable. We have seen that the occurrence of a cost of living crisis is to be expected under an economic system that is based on the principles of neoliberalism. This is why the first proposition is the abandonment of neoliberalism.

9.2   ABANDONING NEOLIBERALISM

The current crisis has been caused by a weak supply side, resulting mainly from neoliberalism and its ramifications, such as deindustrialisation and financialisation, the effect of which is to reduce the ability of the economy to produce the goods and services that people want to buy. As a result of neoliberalism, Britain has been transformed from the workshop of the world during the industrial revolution to a deficit country that imports almost everything. This is how Lapavitsas et al. (2023) express this view without using the word "neoliberalism" explicitly:

> More broadly, the underlying weakness of aggregate supply in the UK is the result of trends and policies that have transformed the country during the past four decades. It reflects the loss of manufacturing industry, the resulting reliance on imports, the extraordinary scale of privatisation, and the dramatic changes in energy provision. It also reflects the further shift of the economy toward services, affording even greater power to the financial sector.

The cost of living crisis is a neoliberal crisis, not only because neoliberalism has weakened the productive capacity of the economy but also because an economic system based on the neoliberal principles (of privatise, liberalise and deregulate) boosts corporate power, facilitates the transfer of income from labour to capital, wipes out public services, and reduces the ability of the public sector to respond when it is called for the rescue. It follows that an appropriate step in the effort to avoid or reduce the intensity of a future crisis is moving away from a neoliberal economic system to a mixed economy in which the public sector plays a vital role and controls the production of the goods and services with a low elasticity of demand. These goods and services include healthcare, education, utilities and natural resources. Hillier (2022) calls for "taking every necessity (not only water, power and telecommunications but also shelter, staple food production etc.) out of the private market", arguing that "every good and service that we need to survive and to thrive should be taken out of the control of people who see in them only a means to augment their own wealth".

We are repeatedly told that there is no alternative to the currently prevailing economic system. Wolff (2012) debunks the myth of unavailability of alternatives as follows:

> Really? We are to believe, with Margaret Thatcher, that an economic system with endlessly repeated cycles, costly bailouts for financiers and now austerity for most people is the best human beings can do? Capitalism's recurring tendencies toward extreme and deepening inequalities of income, wealth, and political and cultural power require resignation and acceptance – because there is no alternative?

A large number of scholars have called for the abandonment of neoliberalism. Isaković (2020) suggests that neoliberalism has "depleted our public services, turned our education and healthcare into profit-driven businesses, hoarded profits at the expense of undervalued and underpaid workers, favoured profitability of a militarised world over human security and well-being, and aggravated inequalities between people and countries". Saad-Filho (2020) suggests that "neoliberal capitalism has been exposed for its inhumanity and criminality". Newfield (2021) sees the situation as follows:

> We're used to one-way neoliberalism, regardless of party, in which we keep getting more of its familiar features: public budget austerity, marketisation, privatisation, selective cross-subsidies favouring business and technology, precarisation of professional labour, and structural racism. But under the pressure of international social forces, neoliberalism is increasingly breaking down. These forces include the Covid-19-induced public health crisis, the climate emergency, multiple modes of racism and neo-colonialism, and the grinding effects of economic inequality.

We have already missed an opportunity to abandon neoliberalism in the aftermath of the global financial crisis, great recession and the pandemic as free marketeers kept bouncing back to tell and convince politicians that the road to salvation goes through a free market. The cost of living crisis is providing another opportunity to reconsider blind faith in the free market and its invisible hand. Stiglitz (2020) sums it up by suggesting that the way forward is to abandon the neoclassical economic model of competitive equilibrium and advocates the institution of labour legislation that protects workers and provides greater scope for collective action.

9.3 MINIMUM WAGES

One source of pain is that minimum wages have not kept up with inflation, which means that statutory minimum wages must be adjusted regularly. Reluctance to do so is typically justified by the corporate sector's proposition that minimum wages lead to unemployment, which is a myth. Minimum wages are intended to protect workers from unduly low pay that is tantamount to slave labour, and to reduce wage and income inequality.

The Minimum Wage Fixing Convention of the International Labour Organization (No. 131) stipulates that setting an adequate minimum wage level should involve social dialogue and take into account the needs of workers and their families as well as economic factors. It is recommended that minimum wages are set, on average, at around 55% of the median wage in developed countries and at 67% of the median wage in developing and emerging economies. Furthermore, a sufficiently frequent adjustment is crucial to maintain minimum wages at an adequate level (particularly if inflation is high), and a very low level often reflects failure to adjust rates regularly over time.

A minimum wage leads to an improvement in the standard of living of minimum wage workers, which would result in a higher level of morale, producing more tangible benefits for the firm, such as easy employee retention and lower hiring and training costs. Paying minimum wages could provide a boost to economic growth because the marginal propensity to consume of minimum wage earners is very high. An additional advantage of minimum wages is that they can alleviate inequality and poverty, which have been aggravated by the cost of living crisis. The availability of a minimum wage may also reduce crime, which has spiked as a result of the cost of living crisis. Minimum wages are conducive to a reduction of government spending on welfare. A minimum wage could go a long way towards improvement of public health and reduction in premature deaths. People who make the minimum wage do not use public services as frequently as the unemployed would. This would have a positive impact on the fiscal balance and put the economy in a better position to reduce taxes. Minimum wages could be beneficial for employers, in the sense that a minimum wage can be used as a reference point for wage setting.

Opponents of minimum wages are typically free marketeers who believe that the wage rate, like any other price, should be determined by the almighty market, not by the government. The opponents also see minimum wages as leading to inflation and unemployment, where inflation results from the rise in the costs of production, while unemployment follows from the setting of the minimum wage above the market equilibrium level. Another argument against is that minimum wages may lead to the aggravation of poverty and inequality as employers may cut working hours and therefore the take-home pay. Minimum wages, the opponents claim, may cause corporate failure and redundancies. They may also lead to more automation, thus replacing service employees. All of these arguments reflect an inherent contradiction in a market economy, resulting from the fact that wage earners are themselves consumers. The desire, of the corporate sector, to reduce the wage bill in order to maximise profit is counterproductive because when wage earners do not earn enough, they will not be able to buy goods and services by amounts that maximise profit.

The International Labour Organization (2020) recommends the adoption of "adequate and balanced wage policies, arrived at through strong and inclusive social dialogue" to mitigate the impact of the crisis and support economic recovery. The ILO elaborates on this recommendation as follows:

> Adequately balanced wage adjustments, taking into account relevant social and economic factors, will be required to safeguard jobs and ensure the sustainability of enterprises, while at the same time protecting the incomes of workers and their

families, sustaining demand and avoiding deflationary situations. Adjustments to minimum wages should be carefully balanced and calibrated.

The ILO believes that "in planning for a new and better 'normal' after the crisis, adequate minimum wages – statutory or negotiated – could help to ensure more social justice and less inequality". Tomaskovic-Devey et al. (2020) see the way forward in high minimum wages, universal healthcare and a strengthened labour movement.

Most of the available evidence indicates that minimum wages do not cause unemployment. A joint report published by the ILO, OECD, IMF and the World Bank reaches the conclusion that "an appropriate level of a statutory minimum wage is able to generate an increment in labour force participation at the margin avoiding adverse effects on demand which translate into a net positive impact on the labour market" (International Labour Organization, 2012). The OECD (2018) reaches the conclusion that as long as minimum wages are well designed and moderate, unfavourable employment impact can be avoided. In 2014, the IMF recommended an increase in the US minimum wage (IMF, 2014). In a landmark study conducted in the 1990s, Card and Krueger (1994) demonstrate, by using a natural experiment, that a rise in minimum wages can boost employment.

In a recent study, the OECD (2022a) examined the role of minimum wages in protecting the most vulnerable during the cost of living crisis. The study puts forward the proposition that "minimum wages can have a strong impact on wages at the bottom of the distribution and help preserving the purchase power of low-paid workers". In times of high inflation, it is argued, minimum wages must be revised regularly to ensure that they maintain their usefulness as a policy instrument. It is further argued that for minimum wages (irrespective of whether they are statutory or negotiated) to be more effective, it is essential that minimum wage policies be coordinated with tax and benefit policies in order to ensure that increases in minimum wages translate into higher take-home pay.

9.4   INCOME SUPPORT

While a rising cost of living hits people with a wide range of incomes, income support is particularly needed for low-income households. Untargeted support measures risk providing insufficient assistance to those who need it most. They can also raise fiscal concerns and feed future inflation. The OECD (2022b) argues that the discretionary support made available to offset the effect of higher energy prices has been poorly targeted, which can be attributed, at least in part, to the observation that on this occasion the cost of living shocks are felt more widely than in other economic crises, leading to calls for broad-based assistance. The OECD suggests that "some degree of targeting is possible with either price support or income transfers".

A question arises here about the merits and demerits of targeted income support (such as minimum income and benefits) as opposed to general price subsidies, universal basic income and broad-based transfer programmes (such as tax rebates and child benefits). Proponents of universal basic income argue that it does not involve exclusion errors, but those who prefer targeted programmes suggest that a universal basic income does not pay off in terms of costs and benefits, where the main benefit is reduction in poverty (see, for example, Majoka and Palacios, 2019). Another advantage of universal income is that it does not require a big bureaucracy to determine the eligibility criteria.

The proposition that targeted payments are more effective in eradicating poverty than universal income can be demonstrated with the help of a simulation exercise. Assume that five income groups are identified before the introduction of income support: Group 1 is 10% of the population with an average income of 500; Group 2 is 20% of the population with an average income of 750; Group 3 is 40% of the population with an average income of 2000; Group 4 is 20% of the population with an average income of 3000; and Group 5 is 10% of the population with an average income of 10,000. We assume that the number of people eligible for income support is 2,000,000 and that the poverty line is at income level of 1000, which means that, without income support, 600,000 people are below the poverty line. Consider first a plan whereby every one receives a universal income of 250. This will still leave 200,000 people below the poverty line. If, on the other hand, the total amount designated for payment as universal income is distributed only to people in Groups 1 and 2 (those living below the poverty line), each one in these groups receives 833, and no one is left below the poverty line. Figure 9.1 shows the Lorenz curve, which is a graphical measure of income distribution, without income support, with universal payment, and with targeted payment. We can see that under targeted payment, the improvement in income distribution is much more pronounced.

9.5   CONSUMER PROTECTION

In February 2024, the Australian Council of Trade Unions published a report which outlined the practices used by big business to make miserable people even more miserable in the absence of effective consumer protection. The report identifies the malpractices used by big business to raise prices and extract more and more consumer surplus. The main tactic used by big business to raise their prices is "excuse-flation" (otherwise known as "greedflation") whereby they use general inflation to raise prices without justification. Another tactic is "confusion pricing" whereby businesses establish "byzantine

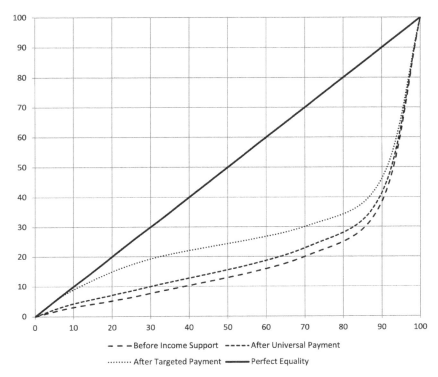

Source: Data simulation.

Figure 9.1   *Lorenz curve under three scenarios of income support*

pricing structures" that make it almost impossible to make price comparisons, thereby reducing competition. There is also "drip pricing" whereby businesses advertise only part of a product's price and reveal other prices later throughout the buying process. The term "rocket and feather pricing" is used to describe a situation where prices rise like a rocket as costs rise, but are incredibly slow to fall (like a feather) when conditions ease. Businesses also use loyalty schemes as a low-cost means of retaining and exploiting customers with schemes that are of dubious benefit and often poorly run (Australian Council of Trade Unions, 2024).

The problem is that a neoliberal government would feel that the market is the best in determining prices, which means that any act of consumer protection will distort market forces and lead to inefficiency, the same rhetoric that we always hear from free marketeers. Even worse, government agencies in charge of consumer protection advocate free-market pricing, when in fact there is nothing free about it – rather, it is oligopoly pricing. For example, the website of the Australian Competition and Consumer Commission (ACCC) says explicitly that "Australian businesses set their prices, influenced by supply and demand" and that "prices that people think are too high, known as price gouging, or a sudden increase in price are not illegal". This is why Rebecca Thistleton, Executive Director of the McKell Institute Victoria, expresses the following view (Thistleton, 2023):

> Practical solutions are needed, because the rising cost of living is hurting many, while businesses selling essentials report record profits despite difficult economic headwinds. The resulting inflation has been a burden pushed unfairly onto consumers through interest rate hikes.

A number of useful recommendations are proposed by Thistleton (2023) to ease pressure on consumers: (i) a curb on price gouging should be seen as part of the solution to rising inflation; (ii) price gouging preventions should be part of government work to improve resilience in the face of a crisis or natural disasters; (iii) empowering consumer protection agencies to scrutinise price gouging and profiteering; and (iv) identifying legislation that no longer serves the interests of consumers as markets and technology evolve. These recommendations must be taken seriously by policy makers as the way forward with respect to consumer protection. Unfortunately, this is unlikely to happen when deregulators, who believe in the power of the almighty market, are in charge of regulatory agencies.

9.6   THE CASE FOR UNIVERSAL HEALTHCARE

With or without a cost of living crisis, the case for universal healthcare (UHC) is strong. Health boosts human capital, which is conducive to growth, let alone the moral and ethical issues. The case for universal healthcare is even stronger under a cost of living crisis, because huge hospital bills or a medical bankruptcy are the last thing struggling people need. As argued earlier, healthcare should be kept away from profit-maximising business firms. It is a highly profitable business because the demand for healthcare is highly inelastic, allowing healthcare providers to charge exorbitant prices without losing their customers.

According to the World Health Organization (2019a), UHC means that all individuals and communities receive the health services they need without suffering financial hardship. The World Health Organization (2019b) defines UHC as "ensuring that all people have access to needed promotion, preventive, curative and rehabilitative health services, of sufficient quality to be effective, while also ensuring that people do not suffer financial hardship when paying for these services". UHC includes the full spectrum of essential, quality health services encompassing health promotion, prevention, treatment, rehabilitation and palliative care. It enables everyone to access the services that address the most significant causes of disease and death, and ensures that the quality of those services is good enough to improve the health of the people who receive them. The case put for UHC by the World Health Organization (2019a) is that "protecting people from the financial consequences of paying for health services out of their own pockets reduces the risk that people will be pushed into poverty because unexpected illness requires them to use up their life savings, sell assets, or borrow – destroying their futures and often those of their children". When people have to pay most of the cost of healthcare out of their own pockets, the poor are often unable to obtain many of the services they need, and even the rich may be exposed to financial hardship in the event of severe or long-term illness.

Apart from the fact that UHC serves a human right, the right to access healthcare without ending up bankrupt or dead, it has several other advantages. It reduces healthcare costs as the government controls the price of healthcare services through negotiation and regulation. It eliminates the administrative costs of dealing with different private health insurance companies. It forces hospitals and doctors to provide the same standard of service at a low cost. It creates a healthier labour force because preventive care reduces the need for expensive emergency room usage.

The arguments against UHC are typically free-market slogans, put forward by free marketeers who believe that it represents an aspect of the undesirable "nanny state". They invariably believe that healthcare is a commodity that must be paid for – and if you cannot pay for it, it is simply hard luck. For example, the argument that UHC forces healthy people to pay for others' medical care lies at the heart of neoliberalism where selfishness is considered a virtue while altruism is condemned as leading to inefficiency. A nonsensical argument is that with free healthcare, people may not be as careful with their health because they do not have the financial incentive to do so. I am yet to hear about anyone enjoying an ambulance ride or going to a doctor for a manual prostate test without a reason to do that and after hesitation.

The main argument against UHC is affordability. It is strange that military expenditure, which is used to kill life, is justified on the grounds of saving lives from "foreign aggression". If governments want to save the lives of their citizens, they must save lives, no matter what the threat is. We know very well that cancer, and other health problems, kill more people than Vladimir Putin, Xi Jinping and Kim Jong Un, put together. An exception to this proposition is that Tony Blair, George Bush and the latter's "dad" killed more Iraqis than disease, allegedly to save lives in America and Britain.

Why is it that military expenditure is affordable but healthcare expenditure is unaffordable? If UHC is affordable at certain times in certain countries, then it should be affordable in most countries if they get their priorities right (for example, putting healthcare before militarism). UHC can be financed by changing a twisted tax code that benefits the rich and by taking natural resources under public ownership. It is all a matter of choice, and the choice in a neoliberal system falls on leaving healthcare to a profit-maximising alliance of doctors, private hospitals, insurance companies and pharmaceutical companies. The fact of the matter is that UHC is opposed because healthcare is a very profitable business, and this has to change to enable people to cope with the next crisis.

9.7   RETHINKING THE PRIVATISATION OF UTILITIES AND NATURAL RESOURCES

One way to prevent energy and water companies from making profit out of the misery of ordinary people is to put those companies under public ownership by nationalising or renationalising them. This does not represent a move towards socialism or communism, but rather a move towards the creation of a vibrant mixed economy in which the private sector has a lot to make money out of without controlling the production of necessities such as electricity, gas and water. The private sector can make money, without hurting ordinary people, by organising sporting events, Taylor Swift and Miley Cyrus concerts, and by producing fancy handbags. Lapavitsas et al. (2023) argue against the wholesale privatisation of everything under the sun, by suggesting that "Britain has further suffered from the unprecedented and wholesale privatisation of services and utilities." The following is the core of their argument:

> Instead of the surpluses made in particular utilities or services, for example the railways, returning to the public purse to be reinvested in service improvements, health and safety measures, and price reductions, they have been used to line the pockets of their private owners. Public wealth that could have been used to increase productive capacity was wasted to pump up company directors' bank accounts.

Likewise, Collinge (2022) argues that "if we [the UK] had a nationalised energy company as France does, and had spent 20 years building nuclear power plants, we would likely be better off now". This is because, Collinge argues, energy security is important to the extent that "it clearly cannot be left to the market". The reference made by Collinge (2022) to France is valid because in February 2023, the lower house of the French legislature passed a resolution to nationalise the majority state-owned energy company EDF (Jenkinson, 2023). In the case of Australia, Wardle (2022) argues that huge increases in energy prices, caused by profiteering private corporations, represent a good enough reason to renationalise them. Unfortunately, the Labor government of Anthony Albanese even ruled out the imposition of a windfall profit tax on these companies. This is because, according to Wardle (2022), "like the Coalition, the Australian Labor Party is in the pocket of the oil and gas industry".

In a country like Australia, with a small population and huge natural resources, one way to finance government spending on welfare is to take natural resources under public ownership by nationalising the mining sector. This idea can be traced back to Thomas Paine who in 1780 published a pamphlet entitled *Public Good* in which he made the case that territories west of the 13 colonies that had been part of the British Empire belonged after the Declaration of Independence to the American government, and did not belong to any of the 13 states or to any individual speculators (Paine, 1780). A royal charter of 1609 had granted the Virginia Company land stretching to the Pacific Ocean. A small group of wealthy Virginia land speculators had taken advantage of this royal charter to claim title to huge swathes of land, including much land west of the 13 colonies. Paine argued that these lands belonged to the American government as represented by the Continental Congress, which made his wealthy Virginia friends rather angry (including George Washington, Thomas Jefferson and James Madison, all of whom had claimed huge wild tracts that, according to Paine, should have been government-owned).

Like Paine, it is beyond me why natural resources, which are supposed to be owned by the people, are given to individuals and corporate interests for them to extract and sell the resources for private profit without paying taxes. This means of financing will be suitable for a resource-rich country like Australia, but this is unlikely to happen. When a particular Australian prime minister came up with the idea of imposing a mining tax (let alone nationalising the mining sector), he was promptly deposed and replaced by his deputy in effectively a *coup d'état* (just imagine the outcry if something like this happens in Africa).

There has been resurgence in resource nationalism worldwide, triggered by the need to generate pandemic-related expenditure. In March 2021, a report published by risk consultancy, Verisk Maplecroft, indicated that "over the course of 2020, 34 countries had seen a significant increase in resource nationalism, with the pandemic exacerbating an existing trend toward government intervention" (Smith, 2021). Resource nationalism is represented by various forms of state involvement in extracting, processing and marketing natural resources. If anything, this means that when natural resources are put under public ownership, they generate lucrative financial resources, which can be used to alleviate the pain inflicted on people by the cost of living crisis.

9.8   RETHINKING THE TAX CODE

The current tax code encourages the accumulation of debt and favours the one per centers by providing numerous loopholes that enable tax evasion. As a result, most of the tax burden falls on wage and salary earners, those mostly affected by the cost of living crisis. The tax code contains loopholes that are intended to allow the rich and powerful to pay less tax than what they ought to pay. Furthermore, plugging loopholes in the tax code will provide financial resources that can be used to alleviate the pain inflicted by a cost of living crisis.

An idea that was floated during the pandemic was that of a wealth tax. In 2021, Senator Elizabeth Warren proposed the imposition of a wealth tax on those with net worths of more than $50 million (for example, Stankiewicz, 2021). According to Senator Warren's proposal, an annual tax of 2 cents is to be levied on every dollar above $50 million and 3% (or 3 cents) on every dollar above $1 billion. This means that the first $50 million is tax exempt, implying that this tax will only affect marginally 0.1% of the US population. The proposed tax would generate revenue that can be used to finance the budget deficit without causing any financial pain for the 0.1%. Senator Warren is right in saying that "most Americans won't mind being rich enough to pay it" and that "most people would rather be rich and pay 2 or 3 cents" (Stankiewicz, 2021).

Those calling for the introduction of a wealth tax are typically accused of being "socialists", "lefties", even "communists". The fact of the matter is that a wealth tax already exists but it is imposed on the wrong people. For example, the Australian state of Victoria has recently introduced a "land tax", which is not a tax on land but on properties apart from the main residence. This tax comes on top of the council tax, which is effectively wealth tax levied as a proportion of the market value of (not the equity in) the property. A pensioner who lives exclusively on income from a rental property has to pay land (wealth) tax but a billionaire living on a huge stock portfolio does not have to pay wealth tax. This is indeed a twisted tax code.

The tax code can be changed in several ways for a better and fairer system. First of all, it does not make sense to charge a young couple some $40,000 as a stamp duty on the purchase of a house financed by a heavy mortgage, but a billionaire buying $10 million worth of shares is not charged a stamp duty. A financial transaction tax would go a long way to make the system fairer while generating revenue to finance public expenditure. Another possibility is to impose an infrastructure tax on companies that make use of publicly financed infrastructure for free. The system will be fairer without causing hardship for anyone by imposing a special tax on luxury items, the demand for which is highly elastic. I am sure that someone who is willing to pay $1000 to attend a Taylor Swift concert would not mind paying $1500. Last, but not least, a tax on super-profit is warranted. For example, a company earning more than a pre-specified return on equity or assets should pay tax on any profit in excess of the pre-specified amount. Perhaps it will also be useful to impose a special tax on the extravagant bonuses paid to corporate executives, particularly after making redundant thousands of workers and low-paid employees.

9.9   RETHINKING FOREIGN POLICY AND MILITARISM

If the war in Ukraine is a cause of the cost of living crisis, then the last thing governments should do is to prolong this war, which is exactly what Western politicians are doing, aided and abetted by the corporate media. The money channelled to the military-industrial complex, under the pretext of defending democracy in Ukraine, can go a long way towards the alleviation of the pain endured by people living in the countries that back Ukraine. It will also be good for the Ukrainians themselves who have endured catastrophic losses as a result of a war prolonged by Joe Biden, Rishi Sunak, Olaf Scholz, Emanuel Macron and Ursula von der Leyen.

The situation is rather perplexing. We often hear that universal healthcare is unaffordable, social services are unaffordable, and anything that helps ordinary people is unaffordable. When it comes to war, however, money can always be found. In 2023, Australia committed to the controversial AUKUS alliance, as a result of which some $400 billion was allocated to the buying of nuclear submarines from the other partners in the alliance ("dangerous allies", as labelled by Malcolm Fraser, a former Australian prime minister). The US does not have the money to forgive student debt, which is less than the budget of the Pentagon for two years. The US spends about one trillion dollars a year on military activities that have nothing to do with defending America and everything to do with wars of aggression and conspiracies for regime change somewhere in the world. Britain resumed its bombing of a previous colony, Yemen, on the pretext of saving lives, when lives can be saved in Britain diverting the money paid for the bombs dropped on Yemen to welfare.

Let us go back to the war in Ukraine, which is a cause of the crisis. The corporate media and elected politicians running Western countries justify the channelling of financial resources away from domestic necessities to the "luxury" of fighting a proxy war, allegedly to counter the aggression of "mad-dog" Putin, otherwise known as "Vlad the Bad" and "Vlad the Mad". The war is portrayed and accepted by the naive as a battle of good versus evil, with the good being NATO and its proxy (Ukraine) and the evil being the modern "Soviet Empire" as reconstructed by Vlad the Bad. For those who readily accept this narrative, no analysis of the facts on the ground is necessary, and there is no need to look into the fundamental causes leading to the conflict. The actual geopolitical facts that have contributed to the eruption of war in Ukraine are largely ignored by the corporate media and those who are naive enough to believe the corporate media. Lamb (2023) identifies the facts on the ground as "a U.S.-led 'coup d'état,' the emergence of neo-Nazi military units incorporated into the Ukrainian army, a brutal civil war killing 14,000, the purposeful failure of diplomacy in the Minsk Protocol, and most importantly a U.S.-led NATO push towards the Russian border, which sparked Moscow's existential angst". Those who accept the corporate media's narrative are inclined to think that it is a bad idea to pursue peace talks. On the other hand, accepting a narrative based on historical facts, supported by much of the neutral world, leads us to believe that the way forward is peace through negotiation.

However, war is a profitable enterprise for those who are not affected by it, unlike the Russian and Ukrainian young men (and women) who are put in the grinder every day. The continuation of the Ukraine war allows for the consolidation of US transatlantic corporate interests over Europe, to the detriment of the average European. The destruction of the Nord Stream gas pipeline, as a result of an act of terrorism committed by some elite US forces (as revealed by Seymour Hersh), boosts US hegemony over Western Europe by denying it energy independence and integration with Eurasia. As a result, US energy suppliers, who sell their expensive fracked gas, have realised massive profits at the expense of the average Europeans who have to cope with gas bills that have doubled or tripled. The military "aid" going to Ukraine is predominantly used to enrich those in charge of the US military-industrial complex. The longer the war goes on, the greater is the profit generated by companies manufacturing means of mass death. Arms manufacturers enrich themselves, and so do politicians calling for "war until victory" who get rewarded handsomely after leaving public service. This happens at a time when the financial resources allocated to Ukraine cannot be used to alleviate the pain endured by wage and salary earners as a result of the cost of living crisis.

The Ukraine war should be put to a peaceful end through negotiations, using the Minsk agreements as a starting point. Putting an end to the war means reversing some of the cost-push factors that have contributed to the resurgence of inflation and the freeing of financial resources that can be devoted to the alleviation of the pain suffered by the poor and vulnerable.

9.10   THE ROLE OF ARTIFICIAL INTELLIGENCE

Artificial intelligence (AI) may not sound relevant here, but it is relevant in more than one way. The intersection of AI and contemporary political economy is a complex terrain marked by both promises and perils, as societies grapple with issues of economic transformation, labour displacement, power dynamics and ethical considerations. The relevance of AI to the cost of living crisis takes more than one form. The first is that AI itself may cause a cost of living crisis by depriving workers of their jobs and incomes. The second is that AI can be used for economic policy formulation, which may provide neutral guidelines for dealing with a future crisis, and perhaps to find out if interest rate policy can be successfully used to curb inflation. The third is that AI may put an end to the current economic system, which gives rise to frequent crises. This is because if people are replaced by machines, who is going to buy the output produced by the machines? These points will be discussed in turn.

9.10.1   AI as a Cause of Unemployment and Rising Inequality

Automation driven by AI has the potential to displace jobs, at least in certain sectors, leading to concerns about unemployment and income inequality. A widely held view is that AI will lead to a "jobs apocalypse" whereby mass unemployment becomes the norm (see, for example, Avent, 2016; Brynjolfsson and McAfee, 2014; Chace, 2016; Ford, 2015; Kaplan, 2015). Harari (2016) goes even further by arguing that AI will render a vast swathe of humanity "useless". For example, taxi drivers and truckers will lose their jobs once self-driving vehicles hit the road. However, some economists consider as a fallacy the view that robots will leave nothing for humans because economic history shows that automation creates new jobs around the new processes, and that these new jobs still require people. According to Bowen and Magnum (1966), "technology eliminates jobs, not work".

Irrespective of the extent to which people will lose their jobs as a result of automation, some will definitely lose their jobs. Look no further than the attendants of parking exits who have become a thing of the past because of automation. Samuels (2020) gives more examples of jobs lost to machines: "the spinning jenny replaced weavers, buttons displaced elevator operators, and the Internet drove travel agencies out of business". He refers to a study showing that about 400,000 jobs were lost to automation in US factories from 1990 to 2007. Likewise, Innis (2016) argues that "every industry has the potential to be automated", suggesting that fishing and farming can be done by drones and that "there's very little examples of a menial task that can't be done by a robot". Therefore, the threat is real: AI can cause a cost of living crisis by taking people's jobs and incomes.

We need to think about how to prepare for the eventuality of mass job losses as machines displace human workers. The potential solutions put forward range from taxing robots to decoupling incomes from jobs. There have also been calls for more substantial interventions, such as the state providing universal basic income to redistribute gains from the owners of the means of production who deploy AI to the vast army of the unemployed who are AI's victims. Some observers have suggested Nordic-style policies that provide benefits to individuals regardless of work status, in return for labour market liberalisation that gives business freedom to manoeuvre. Another possibility is that any worker replaced by a machine and who cannot find work should receive either unemployment benefits or a pension from the employer.

9.10.2   Using AI for Economic Policy Formulation

History tells us that economic crises are frequently caused by faulty policy, which is bound to happen when politicians are driven by ideology rather than the desire to serve the people at large. Under neoliberalism, politicians implement policies that serve the rich and super-rich and get economists to build models that prove the soundness of these policies. Look no further than the economic mess created by Liz Truss, the British prime minister with the shortest tenure ever, when she wanted to cut taxes in the midst of a cost of living crisis, a policy action driven by belief in neoliberalism and the free-market dogma (and intended to boost the wealth of the already wealthy). Examples of bad policies that either lead to or aggravate an existing crisis include quantitative easing, interest rate policies that lead to rapid transition from high to low interest rates, using interest rate policy to curb inflation and revive the economy, deindustrialisation, cutting taxes for the rich, and privatisation.

The idea that economic policy formulation is left to a computer algorithm may sound absurd. However, AI is used in numerous applications, including the writing of poetry which is as good as what a real poet can write. It has been demonstrated that AI is better than humans in many fields. Bejnordi et al. (2017) examine the discriminative accuracy of deep learning algorithms compared with the diagnoses of pathologists in detecting lymph node metastases in tissue sections of women with breast cancer. In a cross-sectional analysis of 32 algorithms submitted as part of a challenge competition, seven deep learning algorithms showed greater discrimination than a panel of 11 pathologists in a simulated time-constrained diagnostic setting. In the field of theoretical mechanics, Sagar (2019) demonstrates that neural networks are far superior in solving three problems than Newton's laws of motion and gravitation (numerical methods). It has also been found that AI beats professional poker players in their own game – for example, Coldewey (2019) shows that an AI agent decisively beats professional poker players in championship-style six-person games.

If AI can do better jobs than humans in various fields, that should also be true for economic policy formulation. One perceived advantage of leaving this task for machines is that a computer algorithm with no priors does not exhibit ideological bias or the tendency to confirm prior beliefs. Apart from ideological and self-preserving biases of economic policy makers and politicians, several problems are associated with model-based economic policy. The design and evaluation of economic policy cannot evolve as rapidly as real-world events, and cannot adapt to black swan events such as the COVID-19 pandemic. The specification and estimation of economic models involve many assumptions, some of which are unrealistic and counterintuitive, such as rational agents, the tendency of the economy to go back to equilibrium, and perfectly flexible wages and prices. Furthermore, estimation is often based on low-quality or faulty data. Even worse, economic models are typically specified and estimated in such a way as to produce results that favour an ideologically driven policy action (for example, cutting taxes for the rich and rejecting the idea of a wealth tax). They can also be used to prove that privatisation is always and under all conditions good for the economy at large.

AI, on the other hand, offers powerful algorithmic solutions to complex economic optimisation problems. This is why Salesforce, an American AI company, has developed an approach to economic policy design based on the use of reinforcement learning and economic simulations for fast and data-driven design and evaluation of new economic policy. Salesforce has introduced the concept of the "AI Economist", which allows an objective analysis of various kinds of economic policy (for example, Salesforce, 2020). Zheng et al. (2020) justify the use of AI on the grounds of "a lack of appropriate (micro-level) economic data and limited opportunity to experiment". They refer to AI-generated tax policies that can effectively trade off economic equality and productivity. In this sense, therefore, AI may be a positive factor in the endeavour to cope with future cost of living crises.

9.10.3 AI as a Threat to Capitalism

Several scholars believe that AI poses a threat to capitalism. For example, Zizek (2023) suggests that "AI capitalists don't realize they're about to kill capitalism", arguing that AI "will change capitalism so much that in the end we will be faced with a choice between two systems: a new form of communism or unchecked chaos". The reasoning is simple: machines that produce goods and services do not get paid and they do not consume the goods and services they produce. Human workers, on the other hand, produce goods and services, get paid, and use their incomes to buy the goods and services they produce. If those who lose their jobs as a result of automation are not provided with income support of some sort, they will not be able to buy the goods and services produced by machines. Entrepreneurs who introduce AI to boost their profit will encounter the opposite of the anticipated outcome. In this sense, AI may hasten the abandonment of neoliberalism, which is a good outcome.

9.11   CLOSING REMARKS

The current inflation, which is one dimension of the cost of living crisis, has not been caused by too much money or rising wages, but rather by supply-side constraints. This is why Lapavitsas et al. (2023) suggest a comprehensive plan to deal with the crisis, a plan that has a lot of merit. They start by suggesting that any action taken to deal with the crisis should aim at protecting the interests of the majority, as opposed to the desire to protect corporate interests. They call for "socially minded policies that will have the interests of workers, the poor, and the self-employed at the forefront". The plan they suggest has three pillars. The first pillar is wage indexation, which is required to preserve real wages. The second pillar is restraining big business profits, which cannot happen by persuasion and incentives, but rather by regulation and the provision of serious consumer protection. The third pillar is "dealing with the persistent malaise of aggregate supply" that lies at the root of the crisis. This requires a thorough rebalancing of the economy in favour of socially useful work rather than financial services, which implies a reversal of the two sides of the same coin: deindustrialisation and financialisation. In general, avoiding cost of living crises or alleviating their impact requires moving away from neoliberalism as a guiding philosophy and as the basis of policy formulation.

The sad side of the story is that of blaming the victim, wage and salary earners (who belong to the poor and middle classes), as the perpetrators of the crisis. High-ranking government officials are notorious for finger pointing, blaming workers and refusing to acknowledge the effect of skyrocketing corporate profit. In the UK, for example, senior Tory politicians have used the pretext of a "wage-price spiral" to deny public sector workers a pay rise that offsets the effect of inflation. The underlying argument is that when wages rise, companies are forced to push up the prices of their products, which in turn leads to workers demanding higher wages, forcing further price rises, and so on. The same argument has been used by the governor of the Bank of England, Andrew Bailey, when he called for workers to exercise "pay restraint" and to justify crushing people with high interest rates. Bailey, of course, can survive without exercising pay restraint, since he earns over half a million pounds in annual salary. His chief economist, who earns £190,000 a year, once demanded that households need to accept that they are poorer and stop seeking pay increases. Officials of the Reserve Bank of Australia have made similar remarks. I must add that the culture of blaming the victim is rife in Western society: the homeless are homeless because they like being homeless and the poor are poor because they are too lazy to seek the "American dream" or the "Western dream". The victims of the Bengal famine of the 1940s, which was engineered by Winston Churchill personally, were blamed for the famine because they "breed like rabbits", as Churchill put it.

The current cost of living crisis is yet another disaster caused by following blindly the principles of neoliberalism and the free-market dogma. We had an opportunity to change things following the global financial crisis, but nothing happened. We had an opportunity to do something drastic for the better following the pandemic, but nothing happened. Now, we have an opportunity to do something so that future crises can be avoided or alleviated. I doubt very much if anything is going to happen soon, unless a few Jeremy Corbyns are in charge. One Jeremy Corbyn was very close to being in charge, but (unfortunately for most people) a "coalition of the willing" toppled him in an elaborate conspiracy. Things can be much better if a few Cornel Wests or Jill Steins are in charge. Unfortunately, they will never be in charge in a phoney democracy, a two-party dictatorship where people choose between Tweedledee and Tweedledum. Cost of living crises will persist as long as the lunatics are in charge of the asylum.

References

Abate, T.W. (2020) Macroeconomic Determinants of Recent Inflation in Ethiopia, *Journal of World Economic Research*, 9, 136–42.

Adler, G., Duval, R., Furceri, D., Çelik, S.K., Koloskova, K. and Poplawski-Ribeiro, M. (2017) Gone with the Headwinds: Global Productivity', *IMF Staff Discussion Notes* No. SDN/17/04.

Adrian, T. and Gaspar, V. (2022) How Fiscal Restraint Can Help Fight Inflation, IMF Blog, 21 November.

Akinboade, O.A., Siebrits, F.K. and Niedermeier, E.W. (2004) *The Determinants of Inflation in South Africa: An Econometric Analysis*, Nairobi: African Economic Research Consortium.

Alcohol and Drug Foundation (2023) The Cost-of-Living Crisis and Alcohol and Other Drugs in Australia, 5 September.

Amaglobeli, D., Hanedar, E., Hong, G.H. and Thévenot, C. (2022) Fiscal Policy for Mitigating the Social Impact of High Energy and Food Prices, *IMF Notes* No. 2022/001.

Andrews, D., Criscuolo, C. and Gal, N. (2016) The Best versus the Rest, OECD Productivity Working Paper No. 5.

Andriantomanga, Z., Bolhuis, M.A. and Hakobyan, S. (2023) Global Supply Chain Disruptions: Challenges for Inflation and Monetary Policy in Sub-Saharan Africa, IMF Working Papers No. 039.

Applied Energy Systems (2023) Semiconductor Shortage Update: The State of the Industry Going into 2024, 31 October.

Ashcroft, S. (2023) Timeline: Causes of the Global Semiconductor Shortage, *Supply Chain*, 11 January.

Askew, J. (2023) Brexit Turbocharging Cost of Living Crisis, Says Economist, Euro News, 22 June.

Australian Council of Trade Unions (2024) *Inquiry into Price Gouging and Unfair Pricing Practices*, February.

Australian Institute (2023) OECD Report Shows Corporate Profits Contributed Far More to Inflation in Australia than Wages, Media Release, 8 June.

Avent, R. (2016) *The Wealth of Humans: Work, Power, and Status in the Twenty-First Century*, New York: St Martin's Press.

Baker, T. (2023) Cost of Living: "On Me Personally" if Inflation Isn't Halved, Says Rishi Sunak, Sky News, 7 June.

Bakker, J.D., Datta, N. Davies, R. and De Lyo, J. (2023) Brexit and Consumer Food Prices, *CEP Brexit Analysis* No. 18.

Balcerowicz, L. and Rzońca, A. (eds) (2015) *Puzzles of Economic Growth*, Washington, DC: World Bank.

Baltagi, B.H. (2002) *Econometrics* (3rd edn), New York: Springer.

Becchio, G. (2020) The Two Blades of Occam's Razor in Economics: Logical and Heuristic, *Economic Thought*, 9, 1–17.

Bejnordi, B.E., Veta, M., van Diest, P.J. et al. (2017) Diagnostic Assessment of Deep Learning Algorithms for Detection of Lymph Node Metastases in Women with Breast Cancer, *JAMA*, 318, 2199–210.

Benes, J. and Kumhof, M. (2012) The Chicago Plan Revisited, IMF Working Papers No. WP12/202.

Bentham, M. (2023) Cost of Living Crisis Threatens New Surge in "High Harm" Crime, *The Standard*, 17 July.

Berentsen, A., Huber, S. and Marchesiani, A. (2015) Financial Innovations, Money Demand, and the Welfare Cost of Inflation, *Journal of Money, Credit and Banking*, 47, 223–61.

Bernard, H. (2022) How Might the Cost of Living Crisis Affect Long-Term Poverty? *Economics Observatory*, 8 September.

Bisno, A. (2023) How Hyperinflation Heralded the Fall of German Democracy, *Smithsonian Magazine*, 23 May.

Bittman, M. (2014) Is It Bad Enough Yet? *New York Times*, 13 December.

Bivens, J. (2022) Wage Growth Has Been Dampening Inflation all Along – and Has Slowed Even More Recently, Economic Policy Institute, 12 May.

Bivens, J., Banerjee, A. and Dzholos, M. (2022) Rising Inflation Is a Global Problem: U.S. Policy Choices Are Not to Blame, Economic Policy Institute, Working Economics Blog, 4 August.

Blair, A. (2023) How Aussies Are Cutting Back as the Cost of Living Crisis Takes Hold, News.com.au, 29 November.

Blakeley, G. (2022) The Solution to Britain's Cost of Living Crisis is Higher Wages, *Jacobin*, 4 October.

Borio, C., Hofmann, B. and Zakrajšek, E. (2023) Does Money Growth Help Explain the Recent Inflation Surge? *BIS Bulletin* No. 67.

Bourne, R. (2023) Brexit Can't Be Blamed for Britain's High Inflation, The Cato Institute, 22 June.

Bowen, H.R. and Magnum, G.L. (1966) *Report of the National Commission on Technology, Automation, and Economic Progress* (Volume I). Washington, DC: United States Government.

Bowes, M. (2024) Divorce Stats Reveal Sad Cost of Living Truth, News.com, 9 January.

Broadbent, P., Thomson, R., Kopasker, D., McCartney, G., Meier, P., Richiardi, M. and Katikireddi, S.V. (2023) The Public Health Implications of the Cost-of-Living Crisis: Outlining Mechanisms and Modelling Consequences, *The Lancet Regional Health – Europe*, 27, 100585.

Brown, R., Wilson, C. and Begum, Y. (2023) The Price We Pay: The Social Impact of the Cost-of-Living Crisis, National Centre for Social Research, July.

Bruno, A., Dunphy, J. and Georgiakakis, F. (2023) Recent Trends in Australian Productivity, *Bulletin*, 21 September.

Bryant, M. (2023) Vulnerable UK Women Forced into 'Sex For Rent' by Cost of Living Crisis, *The Guardian*, 29 April.

Brynjolfsson, E. and McAfee, A. (2014) *The Second Machine Age: Work, Progress, and Prosperity in a Time of Brilliant Technologies*, New York: Norton.

Buchanan, M. and Burns, J. (2023) Numbers in Temporary Accommodation in England Hit Record, BBC News, 25 July.

Buick, A. (2017) Enoch Powell on Inflation (1971) https://socialiststandardmyspace.blogspot.com/2017/09/enoch-powell-on-inflation-1971.html.

Bureau of Labor Statistics (2014) One Hundred Years of Price Change: The Consumer Price Index and the American Inflation Experience, *Monthly Labor Review*, April.

Butler, P. (2022) Poor UK Households May Have to Spend Half Their Income on Energy, Says Charity, *The Guardian*, 18 January.

Cagan, P. (1965) The Money Stock and Its Three Determinants. In P. Cagan (ed.), *Determinants and Effects of Changes in the Stock of Money, 1875–1960*, Cambridge, MA: National Bureau of Economic Research.

Calnan, M. (2023) What Are the Costs of Privatisation in the UK's Healthcare System? *Economics Observatory*, 12 December.

Card, D. and Krueger, A.B. (1994) Minimum Wages and Employment: A Case Study of the Fast-Food Industry in New Jersey and Pennsylvania, *American Economic Review*, 84, 772–93.

Cerrato, A. and Gitti, G. (2023) Inflation Since COVID: Supply versus Demand, *VOXEU Colum*, 12 June.

Chace, C. (2016) *The Economic Singularity: Artificial Intelligence and the Death of Capitalism*, London: Three Cs.

Chakraborty, R. (2014) The Bengal Famine: How the British Engineered the Worst Genocide in Human History for Profit, 15 August. https://yourstory.com/2014/08/bengal-famine-genocide.

Chick, V. (1973) *The Theory of Monetary Policy*, London: Gray-Mills Publishing.

Chowdhury, A. (2020) Financialisation and the Productivity Slowdown, Australia Institute, 5 March.

Christian Action Research and Education (2022) Mums Turning to Prostitution to Cope with Cost-of-Living Crisis, 24 October.

Ciccarelli, M. and Mojon, B. (2010) Global Inflation, *Review of Economics and Statistics*, 92, 524–35.

Clark, D. (2022) Opinion on if Brexit Has Made Cost of Living Higher in UK 2022, 31 May. https://www.statista.com/statistics/1311116/uk-cost-living-brexit/.

Cochrane, J.H. (2021) What Makes It Hard to Control Inflation, *Chicago Booth Review*, 3 November.

Coldewey, D. (2019) AI Smokes 5 Poker Champs at a Time in No-Limit Hold'em with "Relentless Consistency", *Tech Crunch*, 12 July.

Collinge, T. (2022) Should We Nationalise Energy to Tackle the Cost of Living Crisis? *Progressive Britain*, 22 August.

Committee for a Responsible Federal Budget (2022) Six Ways to Fight Inflation, 30 June. https://www.crfb.org/blogs/six-ways-fight-inflation.

Corrigan, T.D. (2005) The Relationship between Import Prices and Inflation in the United States, WCOB Faculty Publications, Paper 18. http://digitalcommons.sacredheart.edu/wcob_fac/18.

Cox, J. (2015) Gross: Low Rates Are the Problem, Not the Solution, CNBC, 30 July.

Crime Investigation (2023) How the Cost of Living Crisis Could Impact Crime Rates in the UK. https://www.crimeandinvestigation.co.uk/articles/crime-and-cost-living-crisis.

Curry, S. (2023) A Shrinking Money Supply and Rising Rates Presents Liquidity and Capital Challenges for Banks, Endurance Advisory Partners, 19 August.

Dales, P. (2022) Cost of Living Crisis: It Was Far Worse in the 1970s and 2008, Inews, 19 January.

Daley, J. (2021) Gridlock: Removing Barrier to Policy Reform, Grattan Institute Reports No. 2021-08.

De Goeij, M.C.M., Suhrcke, M., Toffolutti, V., Van de Mheen, D., Schoenmakers, T.M. and Kunst, A.E. (2015) How Economic Crises Affect Alcohol Consumption and Alcohol-Related Health Problems: A Realist Systematic Review, *Social Science and Medicine*, 131, 131–46.

De Grauwe, P.D. and Polan, M. (2014) Is Inflation Always and Everywhere a Monetary Phenomenon? In P.D. De Grauwe (ed.), *Exchange Rates and Global Financial Policies*, Singapore: World Scientific.

Dodd, V. (2022) London Mayor Warns of Rise in Violence as Cost of Living Crisis Deepens, *The Guardian*, 17 August.

Dom, G., Samochowiec, J., Evans-Lacko, S., Wahlbeck, K., Van Hal, G. and McDaid, D. (2016) The Impact of the 2008 Economic Crisis on Substance Use Patterns in the Countries of the European Union, *International Journal of Environmental Research and Public Health*, 13(1), 122.

Duffy, C. (2023) Fears Cost-of-Living Crisis Worsening Child Poverty as Families Make "Impossible Decisions", ABC News, 2 May.

Duggan, W. (2023) Inflation Slows Again in November, *Forbes Advisor*, 12 December.

Elliott, L. (2023) This Isn't Wage-Price Inflation, It's Greedflation – and Big Companies Are to Blame, *The Guardian*, 20 April.

European Parliament (2022) Inflation as a Global Challenge. https://www.europarl.europa.eu/RegData/etudes/STUD/2022/733992/IPOL_STU(2022)733992_EN.pdf.

Fanta, F. (2013) Financial Deregulation, Economic Uncertainty and the Stability of Money Demand in Australia, *Australian Economic Papers*, 32, 496–511.

FAO (1996) Rome Declaration on Food Security and World Food Summit Plan of Action, World Food Summit, Rome, 13–17 November.

FAO (2006) Food Security, *FAO Policy Brief*, Issue 2, June.

Federal Reserve Bank of New York (2023) Global Supply Chain Pressure Index. https://www.newyorkfed.org/research/policy/gscpi.

Financial Times (2020) Today's Ultra-Low Interest Rates Are Anything but "Natural", 20 August.

Financial Times (2022) Low on Gas: Ukraine Invasion Chokes Supply of Neon Needed for Chipmaking, 4 March.

Financial Times (2023) Eurozone Money Supply Shrinks for First Time in 13 Years as Lending Slows, 28 August.

Fisher, I. (1907) *The Rate of Interest*, London: MacMillan.

Fitzmaurice, J. and Taylor, H. (2022) Spring Statement 2022: A Failure to Prioritise Support to Those Who Need It Most, Work Foundation, University of Lancaster, 23 March.

Fix, B. (2021) The Truth about Inflation: Why Milton Friedman Was Wrong, Again Evonomics, 24 November.

Fondeville, N. and Ward, T. (2011) Homelessness during the Crisis, *European Commission, Research Notes* No. 8/2011.

Ford, M. (2015) *Rise of the Robots: Technology and the Threat of a Jobless Future*, New York: Basic Books;

Friedman, M. (1963) *Inflation: Causes and Consequences*, New York: Asia Publishing House.

Friedman, M. (1969) *The Optimum Quantity of Money and Other Essays*, Piscataway, NJ: Aldine.

Friesen, G. (2021) No End in Sight for the COVID-Led Global Supply Chain Disruption, *Forbes*, 3 September.

Friesen, G. (2023) The End of the Supply Chain Crisis: A Relief from Inflationary Pressures, *Forbes*, 9 July.

Gencer, D. and Akcura, E. (2022) Amid Energy Price Shocks, Five Lessons to Remember on Energy Subsidies, *World Bank Blogs*, 13 May.

Gentilini, U., Almenfi, M., Iyengar, H., Okamura, Y., Urteaga, E.R., Valleriani, G., Muhindo, J.V. and Aziz, S. (2022) Tracking Global Social Protection Responses to Price Shocks: Version 1, World Bank Social Protection & Jobs Discussion Papers No. 2208.

Geopoll (2022) Global Cost of Living Crisis World Economy in a Fragile State, 13 October. https://www.geopoll.com/blog/cost-of-living-crisis/.

Ghelani, D. and Clegg, A. (2022) Uprating Universal Credit to Tackle the Cost of Living Crisis, Centre for Social Justice, 20 May.

Gill, A. (2022) The Cost of Living Crisis Is Deeply Impacting Victims of Domestic Abuse, Inside Housing, 7 October.

Goldin, I., Koutroumpis, P., Francois, L. and Winkler, J. (2022) Why Is Productivity Slowing down?, Oxford Martin Working Papers No. 2022-8.

Goldman Sachs (2023) Why the US Money Supply Is Shrinking for the First Time in 74 Years, 28 August.

Goodair, B. (2023) How Does the Outsourcing of Health and Social Care Affect Service Quality? *Economics Observatory*, 30 November.

Gordon, R.J. and Sayed, H. (2022) A New Interpretation of Productivity Growth Dynamics in the Pre-Pandemic and Pandemic Era U.S. Economy, 1950–2022, NBER Working Papers No. 30267.

Graham, A. (2023) Bank May Need to Spark Recession to Control Inflation, Economist Says, *The Independent*, 21 June.

Green, E. (2023) Australians Resorting to Petty Crime in a "Desperate" Sign of Cost of Living Crisis, NCA Newswire, 9 October.

Gregory, J. (2022a) The Cost of Living Crisis – Part 1: Bread in 1795, British Library, 19 April. https://blogs.bl.uk/untoldlives/2022/04/the-cost-of-living-crisis-part-1-bread-in-1795.html.

Gregory, J. (2022b) The Cost of Living Crisis, Part 2: Inflation in 1800, British Library, 12 May. https://blogs.bl.uk/untoldlives/2022/05/the-cost-of-living-crisis-part-2-inflation-in-1800.html.

Gruen, N. (1999) Avoiding Boom/Bust: Macro-economic Reform for a Globalised Economy, Business Council of Australia, Discussion Paper No. 2.

Haksar, V. and and Kopp, E. (2020) How Can Interest Rates Be Negative? *Finance and Development*, March.

Hambur, J. (2021) Product Market Power and Its Implications for the Australian Economy, Treasury Working Papers No. 2021-03.

Hamilton, E. (2023) The Global Supply Chain Consequences of the Russia-Ukraine War, University of Florida News, 21 February.

Hanke, S.H. and Krus, N. (2012) World Hyperinflations, Cato Working Paper. https://www.cato.org/sites/cato.org/files/pubs/pdf/workingpaper-8_1.pdf.

Hannam (2022) "Over-the-Top Alarmism": Economists Dismiss Concerns Wage Rises Cause Inflation, *The Guardian*, 16 July.

Hansen, N.J., Toscani, F. and Zhou, J. (2023) Europe's Inflation Outlook Depends on How Corporate Profits Absorb Wage Gains, IMF Blog, 26 June.

Harari, Y.N. (2016) *Homo Deus: A Brief History of Tomorrow*, London: Harvill Secker.

Harris, M. (2022) These 5 Charts Help Demystify the Global Chip Shortage … and Reveal Why Even Infusions of Cash from the U.S. and European Union Won't Solve It, *IEEE Spectrum*, 14 FEB.

Hatton, B. (2023) PM Says He Will Stick to His Plan on Reducing Inflation amid Calls for Tax Cuts, *The Independent*, 15 November.

Hayek, F.A. (1939) Mr. Keynes and War Costs, *The Spectator Archive*, 24 November.

Hayward, S. (2022) Thought for the Day: Milton on (Monetary) Paradise Lost, Power Line, 2 November.

HealthCare.com (2023) Federal Poverty Level (FPL). https://www.healthcare.gov/glossary/federal-poverty-level-fpl/.

Henderson, D.R. (2021) Inflation: True and False, Econlib, 12 May.

Heritage Foundation (2021) The Real Story behind Inflation, 2 November.

Herrity, J. (2023) Cost of Living: Definition, Index and Factors to Measure, 9 December. https://www.indeed.com/career-advice/career-development/cost-of-living-definition.

Hillier, B. (2022) How to Fix the Cost-of-Living Crisis, *REDFLAG*, 6 May.

Hofmann, B. and Bogdanova, B. (2012) Taylor Rules and Monetary Policy: A Global "Great Deviation"? *BIS Quarterly Review*, September.

Holtemoller, O. (2002) Money and Banks: Some Theory and Empirical Evidence for Germany, Humboldt University of Berlin, Interdisciplinary Research Project 373.

Holtfrerich, C.I. (1986) *The German Inflation: 1914–1923*, New York: de Gruyter.

Hoover, K.D. (1991) The Causal Direction between Money and Prices: An Alternative Approach, *Journal of Monetary Economics*, 27, 381–423.

Howley, D. (2021) These 169 Industries Are Being Hit by the Global Chip Shortage, Yahoo Finance, April 25.

Hutchens, G. (2023a) Is There a Better Way to Kill Inflation than Raising Interest Rates? ABC News, 12 February.

Hutchens, G. (2023b) One Reason Australian Wages Are Depressed? ABC News, 2 March.

IMF (2014) Article IV Consultation with the United States of America Concluding Statement of the IMF Mission, 16 June.

Indaily (2022) Business Warns of Economic "Death Spiral", 8 June.

Inman, P. (2023) Corporate Profits Drove up Prices Last Year, Says ECB President, *The Guardian*, 27 June.

Innis, H. (2016) Why AI Will Break Capitalism, *Chatbots Magazine*, 12 June.

International Labour Organization (2012) Boosting Jobs and Living Standards in G20 Countries: A Joint Report by the ILO, OECD, IMF and the World Bank.

International Labour Organization (2020) COVID-19 and the World of Work: Impact and Policy Responses. https://www.ilo.org/wcmsp5/groups/public/---dgreports/--dcomm/documents/briefingnote/wcms_738753.pdf.

International Labour Organization (2023) *Global Wage Report 2022–23: The Impact of COVID-19 and Inflation on Wages and Purchasing Power*, Geneva: ILO.

International Rescue Committee (2022) What the Cost of Living Crisis Looks Like around the World, 7 November.

IRI (2022) FMCG Demand Signals: A Return to 1970s and 1980s Behaviour as Inflation Fatigue Deepens. https://www.iriworldwide.com/en-gb/insights/publications/demand-signals-2.

Isaković, N.P. (2020) COVID-19: What Has COVID-19 Taught Us about Neoliberalism? https://www.wilpf.org/covid-19-what-has-covid-19-taught-us-about-neoliberalism/.

Itaya, J.I. and Mino, K. (2007) Technology, Preference Structure, and the Growth Effect of Money Supply, *Macroeconomic Dynamics*, 11, 589–612.

Jacobs, D., Perera, D. and Williams, T. (2014) Inflation and the Cost of Living, *Reserve Bank of Australia Bulletin*, First Quarter, 33–46.

Jenkinson, O. (2023) France Moves to Fully Nationalise EDF and Prevent Break-up, *Wind Power Monthly*, 10 February.

Jericho, G. and Stanford, J. (2023) Minimum Wages and Inflation, The Australian Institute, 27 April.

Jones, O. (2023) Wage Rises Are Driving Inflation? Don't Swallow This, *The Guardian*, 29 June.

Jones, S. (2022) Cost of Living Crisis: What Governments around the World Are Doing to Help, *The Guardian*, 7 September.

Joplin, T. (1826) *Views on the Subject of Corn and Currency*, London: Baldwin, Cradock and Joy.

Jung, C. and Hayes, C. (2022) Prices and Profits after the Pandemic, IPPR, 20 June.

Kaldor, N. (1970) The New Monetarism, *Lloyd's Bank Review*, 98, 52–3.

Kaplan, J. (2015) *Humans Need Not Apply: A Guide to Wealth and Work in the Age of Artificial Intelligence*, New Haven, CT: Yale University Press.

Kaushal, N. (2017) View: Inflation Is Not Always a Monetary Phenomenon, *The Economic Times*, 13 November.

Keane, D. (2022) Addiction Soars as Cost-of-Living Crisis Bites, *The Standard*, 1 November.

Keegan, W. (2023) It's Brexit that Cranks up Inflation. Don't Just Blame the Bank, *The Guardian*, 25 January.

Kelly C. and Butler, J. (2023) More than 1,600 Australians Pushed into Homelessness Each Month as Housing Crisis Deepens, Report Finds, *The Guardian*, 4 August.

Keynes, J.M. (1940) *How to Pay for the War*, London: Macmillan.

Kharpal, A. (2023) How the World Went from a Semiconductor Shortage to a Major Glut, CNBC, 27 July.

Kiganda, E. (2014) Relationship between Money Supply and Inflation in Kenya, *Journal of Social Economics*, 2, 63–83.

Kilgore, E. (2021) Joe Biden Is Not Jimmy Carter, and This Is Not the 1970s, *Intelligencer*, 16 October.

Kinealy, C. (1994) *This Great Calamity*, Dublin: Gill & Macmillan.

Konczal, M. (2023) Supply-Side Expansion Has Driven the Decline in Inflation, Roosevelt Institute, 8 September.

Konczal, M. and Lusiani, N. (2022) Prices, Profits, and Power: An Analysis of 2021 Firm-Level Markups, Roosevelt Institute, 21 June.

Lamb, K. (2023) Profiteering is a Key Driver of the Ukraine Conflict, CGTN, 8 March.

Lapavitsas, C., Meadway. J. and Nicholls, D. (2023) *The Cost of Living Crisis (and How to Get out of It)*. London: Verso Books.

Lee, J., Powell, T. and Wessel, D. (2020) What Are Inflation Expectations? Why Do They Matter? Brookings, 30 November.

Leggatt, J. (2023) Australian Inflation Rate: No Cost-of-Living Relief in Budget Update, *Forbes Advisor*, 14 December.

Lira, G. (2010) How Hyperinflation Will Happen, 23 August. http://gonzalolira.blog spot.com.au/2010/08/how-hyperinflation-will-happen.html.

Lopez-Garcia, P, and Szörfi, B. (2021) The Impact of the COVID-19 Pandemic on Labour Productivity Growth, *ECB Economic Bulletin*, 7, 46–51.

Lucas, R.E. (1980) Two Illustrations of the Quantity Theory of Money, *American Economic Review*, 70, 1005–14.

Lucas, R.E. (1996) Nobel Lecture: Monetary Neutrality, *Journal of Political Economy*, 104, 661–82.

Macfarlane, L. (2022) To Tackle the Cost of Living Crisis, We Must End the Great British Rip Off, *Open Democracy*, 9 February.

Madrick, J. (2022) The Supply-Side Causes of Inflation, The Century Foundation, 4 November.

Majoka, Z. and Palacios, R. (2019) Targeting versus Universality: Is There a Middle Ground? Social Protection and Jobs, *Policy & Technical Note* No. 22.

Makhlouf, G. (2023) Inflation and Monetary Policy: What to Expect, Central Bank of Ireland Blog, 2 June.

Marin-Guzman and Shapiro, J. (2022) Reserve Bank Warns of Wage-Price Spiral as Unions Push for Pay, *Australian Financial Review*, 6 May.

Market Monetarist (2023) This Is Why Inflation Is ALWAYS and EVERYWHERE a Monetary Phenomenon, 24 July.

Marshall, A. (1890) *Principles of Economics*, London: Macmillan.

Martin, P. (2022) "It's Important Not to Overreact": Australia's Top Economists on How to Fix High Inflation, Economic Society of Australia. https://esacentral.org.au/news/47852/its-important-not-to-overreact-australias-top-economists-on-how-to-fix-high-inflation/.

Massie, G. (2021) Major Chip Shortage Caused by Trump Trade War Blamed for PS5 Shortage, *The Independent*, 11 February.

McCall, L.C. (2021) Managing Inflation through Thrift, Not Usury, Modern Money Lab Working Paper No 3.

McLeay, M., Radia, A. and Thomas, R. (2014) Money Creation in the Modern Economy, *Bank of England Quarterly Bulletin*, First Quarter.

Mcrae, I. (2022) What Are Other Countries Doing about the Cost of Living Crisis? *Big Issue*, 18 November.

Mcrae, I., Westwater, H. and Glover, E. (2023) UK Poverty: The Facts, Effects and Solutions in the Cost of Living Crisis, *Big Issue*, 24 October.

Mehra, Y. (2000) Wage-Price Dynamics: Are They Consistent with Cost Push? *Reserve Bank of Richmond Economic Quarterly*, 86, 27–43.

Mind.org (2023) Mind Reveals Mental Health Toll of Cost-of-Living Crisis, with 2.7 Million People Considering Suicide Because of Financial Pressure, 27 October.

Mishel, L. (2015) Causes of Wage Stagnation, Economic Policy Institute, 6 January.

Mishel, L., Gould, E. and Bivens, J. (2015) Wage Stagnation in Nine Charts, Economic Policy Institute, 6 January.

Molina, G.G., Montoya-Aguirre, M. and Ortiz-Juarez, E. (2022) Addressing the Cost-of-Living Crisis in Developing Countries: Poverty and Vulnerability Projections and Policy Responses, UNDP, July.

Monbiot, G. (2016) Neoliberalism – The Ideology at the Root of All Our Problems, *The Guardian*, 15 April.

Money and Mental Health Policy Institute (2022) The Facts. https://www.moneyandmentalhealth.org/money-and-mental-health-facts/.

Monroe, J. (2022) We're Pricing the Poor out of Food in the UK – That's Why I'm Launching My Own Price Index, *The Guardian*, 23 January.

Moore, B.J. (1989) A Simple Model of Bank Intermediation, *Journal of Post Keynesian Economics*, 12, 10–28.

Moosa, I.A. (2007) *Operational Risk Management*, London: Palgrave.

Moosa, I.A. (2008) *Quantification of Operational Risk under Basel II: The Good, Bad and Ugly*, London: Palgrave.

Moosa, I.A. (2016) Blaming Suicide on NASA and Divorce on Margarine: The Hazard of Using Cointegration to Derive Inference on Spurious Correlation, *Applied Economics*, 49, 1483–90.

Moosa, I.A. (2017) *Econometrics as a Con Art: Exposing the Limitations and Abuses of Econometrics*, Cheltenham, UK and Northampton, MA, USA: Edward Elgar Publishing.

Moosa, I.A. (2020) *Controversies in Economics and Finance: Puzzles and Myths*, Cheltenham, UK and Northampton, MA, USA: Edward Elgar Publishing.

Moosa, I.A. (2021) *The Washington Consensus: A Critique of the Principles and Implications for Economic Development*, Singapore: World Scientific.

Moosa, I.A. (2022) *Fintech: A Revolution or a Transitory Hype?*, Cheltenham, UK and Northampton, MA, USA: Edward Elgar Publishing.

Moosa, I.A. (2023a) *Financialisation: Measurement, Driving Forces and Consequences*, Cheltenham, UK and Northampton, MA, USA: Edward Elgar Publishing.

Moosa, I.A. (2023b) Deindustrialisation and Financialisation: Two Sides of the Same Coin? ElgarBlog, 21 August. https://elgar.blog/2023/08/21/deindustrialisation-and -financialisation-two-sides-of-the-same-coin/.

Moosa, I.A. and Moosa, N. (2019) *Eliminating the IMF: An Analysis of the Debate to Keep, Reform or Abolish the Fund*, New York: Palgrave Macmillan.

Moosa, I.A. and Shamsuddin, A. (2004) Expectation Formation Mechanisms, Profitability of Foreign Exchange Trading and Exchange Rate Volatility, *Applied Economics*, 36, 1599–606.

Mukul, P. (2022) Explained: Why the Russia-Ukraine Crisis May Lead to a Shortage in Semiconductors, *The Indian Express*, 29 March.

Musgrave, A. (1981) "Unreal Assumptions" in Economic Theory: The F-Twist Untwisted, *Kyklos*, 34, 377–87.

Nagel, E. (1963) Assumptions in Economic Theory, *American Economic Review*, 53, 211–19.

Neely, C.J. (2023) The Rise and Fall of M2, Federal Reserve Bank of St Louis, *Economic Synopses* No. 11.

Nelson, E. (2008) Why Money Growth Determines Inflation in the Long Run: Answering the Woodford Critique, *Journal of Money, Credit and Banking*, 40, 1791–814.

Newfield, C. (2021) Universities after Neoliberalism: A Tale of Four Futures, *Radical Philosophy*, Summer, 77–86.

Nosrati, E., Kang-Brown, J., Ash, M., McKee, M., Marmot, M. and King, L.P. (2019) Economic Decline, Incarceration, and Mortality from Drug Use Disorders in the USA between 1983 and 2014: An Observational Analysis. https://www.thelancet .com/pdfs/journals/lanpub/PIIS2468-2667(19)30104-5.pdf.

Nunes, A.B., St. Aubyn, M., Valério, N. and de Sousa, R.M. (2018) Determinants of the Income Velocity of Money in Portugal: 1891–1998, *Portuguese Economic Journal*, 17, 99–115.

OECD (2018) *Good Jobs for All in a Changing World of Work: The OECD Jobs Strategy*, Paris: OECD Publishing.

OECD (2022a) Minimum Wages in Times of Rising Inflation. https://www.oecd.org/ employment/Minimum-wages-in-times-of-rising-inflation.pdf.

OECD (2022b) Income Support for Working-Age Individuals and Their Families. https://www.oecd.org/social/Income-support-for-working-age-individuals-and-their-families.pdf.

Oppenheim, M. (2022) Cost of Living Crisis Forcing More Women into Sex Work and Accepting Dangerous Clients, *The Independent*, 15 November.

Ostry, J.D., Loungani, P. and Furceri, D. (2016) Neoliberalism: Oversold? *Finance and Development*, June.

Ozili, P.K. and Ozen, E. (2023) Global Energy Crisis: Impact on the Global Economy. In K. Sood, S. Grima, P. Young, E. Özen and B. Balusamy (eds), *The Impact of Climate Change and Sustainability Standards on the Insurance Market*. Hoboken, NJ and Beverly, MA: Wiley and Scrivener Publishing. https://papers.ssrn.com/sol3/papers.cfm?abstract_id=4309828.

Paine, T. (1780) *Public Good*. https://www.thomaspaine.org/works/essays/american-politics-and-government/public-good.html.

Papadimitriou, D.B. and Wray, L.R. (2021) Still Flying Blind after All These Years, Levy Economics Institute, Public Policy Brief No. 156.

Parker, S. (2022) US Inflation Originates in Washington, Not Moscow, *The Daily Signal*, 15 June.

Partington, R. and Kirk, A. (2022) As UK Households Face Increasingly Squeezed Budgets, Six Charts Show the Scale of the Challenge, *The Guardian*, 3 February.

Patel, N. (2021) Why the Global Chip Shortage Is Making It So Hard to Buy a PS5, *The Verge*, 31 August.

Patrick, R. and Pybus, K. (2022) Cost of Living Crisis: We Cannot Ignore the Human Cost of Living in Poverty. https://doi.org/10.1136/bmj.o925.

Peetz, D. (2019) There's an Obvious Reason Wages Aren't Growing, But You Won't Hear It from Treasury or The Reserve Bank, *The Conversation*, 9 September.

Percy, N. (2023) Flash Mob Summer: How Can Retail Theft Stampedes Be Stopped? *Los Angeles Daily News*, 5 September.

Pilkington, P. (2014) Bank of England Endorses Post-Keynesian Endogenous Money Theory, 12 March. https://fixingtheeconomists.wordpress.com/2014/03/12/bank-of-england-endorses-post-keynesian-endogenous-money-theory/.

Porter, T.J. (2022) Cost of Living: What It Is, How to Calculate it and How to Compare, 18 July. https://www.bankrate.com/real-estate/what-is-cost-of-living/.

PR Newswire (2022) Blistering Cost of Living Crisis Brings Back 1970s and 1980s Shopper Behaviours: Consumers Experiencing Diminished Living Standards, 24 October.

Radzievska, S. (2016) Global Crisis, Financialization and Technological Development, *IEP*, 24, 124–54.

Rasool, H. and Tarique, M. (2017) Determinants of Inflation: Evidence from India Using Autoregressive Distributed Lagged Approach, *Asian Journal of Research in Banking and Finance*, 8, 1–17.

Rawlinson, K. (2023) UK Workers £11,000 Worse off after Years of Wage Stagnation – Thinktank, *The Guardian*, 20 March.

Remeikis, A. (2023) "An Economic Fairytale": Australia's Inflation Being Driven by Company Profits and Not Wages, Analysis Finds, *The Guardian*, 24 February.

Remes, J., Manyika, J., Smit, S., Kohli, S., Fabius, V., Dixon-Fyle, S. and Nakaliuzhnyi, A. (2021) The Consumer Demand Recovery and Lasting Effects of COVID-19, McKinsey Global Institute, 17 March.

Reserve Bank of Australia (2023) *Statement on Monetary Policy*, May.

Richards, H. (2022) What the 1970s Teaches about Today's Energy Crisis, *Energy Wire*, 4 December.

Richardson, D., Saunder, M. and Denniss, R. (2022) Are Wages or Profits Driving Australia's Inflation? The Australian Institute, Discussion Paper, July.

Ritchie, A. (2023) How Does Raising Interest Rates Curb Inflation? Rate City, 8 March.

Roberts, E. (2022) In the 1970s, We Didn't Have to Choose between Heating and Eating, *The Guardian*, 3 September.

Roberts, M. and Petchey, L. (2023) The Cost-of-Living Crisis is a Public Health Issue, LSE Blog, 3 February.

Robinson, A. (2018) Did Einstein Really Say That? *Nature*, 30 April.

Rolfe, B. (2023) Shocking Stats Reveal Toll of Country's Cost of Living Crisis, News. com, 7 September.

Roshan, S.A. (2014) Inflation and Money Supply Growth in Iran: Empirical Evidences from Cointegration and Causality, *Iranian Economic Review*, 18, 131–52.

Rother, B., Mirzoev, T., Kato, N., Luca, O., Miksjuk, A., Kazandjian, R., Kushnir, M. and Wang, J. (2023) Global Food Crisis Update – Recent Developments, Outlook, and IMF Engagement, International Monetary Fund, October.

Rouse, C., Zhang, J. and Tedeschi, E. (2021) Historical Parallels to Today's Inflationary Episode, CEA Blogs, 6 July.

Rowthorn, R.E. and Ramaswamy, R. (1997) Deindustrialization: Causes and Implications, *IMF Economic Issues* No. 10.

RSM (2022) UK Inflation: Running up that Hill. https://www.rsmuk.com/insights/real -economy/global-supply-chains/uk-inflation-running-up-that-hill.

Ryczkowski, M. (2021) Money and Inflation in Inflation-Targeting Regimes – New Evidence from Time–Frequency Analysis, *Journal of Applied Economics*, 24, 17–44.

Ryssdal, K. (2022) Fed Chair Jerome Powell: "Whether We Can Execute a Soft Landing or Not, It May Actually Depend on Factors that We Don't Control, Marketplace, 12 May.

S&P Global (2023) US Money Supply Falls at Unprecedented Rate, Possibly Cooling Inflation, 31 May.

Saad-Filho, A. (2020) From COVID-19 to the End of Neoliberalism, *Critical Sociology*, 46, 477–85.

Sagar, R. (2019) Newton vs Neural Networks: Exploring the Unsolved Three-Body Problem with ML, 4 November. https://analyticsindiamag.com/newton-vs-neural -networks-exploring-the-unsolved-three-body-problem-with-ml/.

Salami, A. and Kelikume, I. (2013) Is Inflation Always and Everywhere a Monetary Phenomenon? The Case of Nigeria, *International Journal of Business and Finance Research*, 7, 105–14.

Salesforce (2020) The AI Economist: Why Salesforce Researchers Are Applying Machine Learning to Economics, 29 April.

Salvation Army (2023) Surge in Australians Sinking into Extreme Poverty amid Cost-of-Living Crisis, 17 May.

Samuels, A. (2020) Millions of Americans Have Lost Jobs in the Pandemic – and Robots and AI Are Replacing them Faster than Ever, *Time*, 6 August.

Schmuecker, K. and Earwaker, R. (2022) Not Heating, Eating or Meeting Bills: Managing a Cost of Living Crisis on a Low Income, Joseph Rowntree Foundation, June.

Schnabel, I. (2022) The Globalisation of Inflation, European Central Bank, 11 May. https://www.ecb.europa.eu/press/key/date/2022/html/ecb.sp220511_1~e9ba02e127 .en.html.

Schrager, A. (2019) Has the Fed Lost Its Power to Influence the Economy? 31 October. https://qz.com/1736846/can-the-federal-reserves-rate-cuts-still-boost-the-economy/.

Shapiro, A. (2022) How Much Do Supply and Demand Drive Inflation? *Federal Reserve Bank of San Francisco Economic Letter*, 21 June.

Shivdas, S. (2021) Global Auto Recovery to Take More Hits from Japan Chip Plant Fire, Severe U.S. Weather, Reuters, 31 March.

Sigurjonsson, F. (2015) Monetary Reform: A Better Monetary System for Iceland, 10 March. http://www.forsaetisraduneyti.is/media/Skyrslur/monetary-reform.pdf.

Smith, E. (2021) Protectionism around Natural Resources Is Surging, and Could Spell Danger for Commodities, CNBC, 5 March.

Springer, S., Birch, K. and MacLeavy, J. (2016) An Introduction to Neoliberalism. In *The Handbook of Neoliberalism*, London: Routledge.

Stanford, J. (2023) Profit-Price Spiral: The Truth behind Australia's Inflation, The Australian Institute, 23 February.

Stankiewicz, K. (2021) Sen. Warren on Wealth Tax: "I Think Most People Would Rather Be Rich" and Pay 2 or 3 Cents, CNBC, 2 March.

Stedman-Jones, D. (2012) *Masters of the Universe: Hayek, Friedman, and the Birth of Neoliberal Politics*, Princeton, NJ: Princeton University Press.

Stephenson, M. (2022) Forced into Sex Work by Cost of Living Crisis, Channel 4 News, 1 December.

Stern, W.M. (1964) The Bread Crisis in Britain, 1795–96, *Economica*, 31, 168–87.

Stewart, A., Stanford, J. and Hardy, T. (2022) The Wages Crisis Revisited, The Australian Institute. https://australiainstitute.org.au/wp-content/uploads/2022/05/Wages-Crisis-Revisited-WEB.pdf.

Stiglitz, J.E. (2020) Conquering the Great Divide, *Finance and Development*, September, 17–18.

Stiglitz, J.E. (2023) How Should You Fight Inflation? *The Guardian*, 27 January.

Sumner, S. (2022) Persistent Inflation Is Always and Everywhere a Monetary Phenomenon, Econlib, 27 October.

Sweeney, M. (2021) Global Shortage in Computer Chips "Reaches Crisis Point", *The Guardian*, 22 March.

Tagliaferro, A. (2019) The Unintended Consequences of Ultra-Low Interest Rates. https://www.livewiremarkets.com/wires/the-unintended-consequences-of-ultra-low-interest-rates.

Taylor, A. (2022) 5 Problems behind the Global Cost-of-Living Crisis, *Washington Post*, 20 May.

Taylor, H. (2022) What Are Other Countries Doing to Mitigate against the Cost of Living Crisis? Work Foundation, University of Lancaster, 8 April.

Taylor, J.B. (1993) Discretion versus Policy Rules in Practice, *Carnegie-Rochester Conference Series on Public Policy*, 39, 195–214.

Teles, P., Uhlig, H. and Azevedo, J.V. (2016) Is Quantity Theory Still Alive? *Economic Journal*, 126, 442–64.

The Economist (2021) Crypto-Miners Are Probably to Blame for the Graphics-Chip Shortage, 19 June.

The Standard (2024) Houthis Vow Retaliation after UK-US Strikes as Rishi Sunak Pledges He "Won't Hesitate to Protect Lives", 13 January.

The Straight Times (2023) Cost of Living Stress Fuels Crime Wave in Australia, New Zealand, 27 September.

Thistleton, R. (2023) *Adding Value: Easing Cost of Living Pressures through a Price Gouge Crackdown*, Melbourne: McKell Institute Victoria.

Thompson, A. and Tapp, S.N. (2023) Criminal Victimization, 2022, US Department of Justice Bulletin, September.

Thompson, J.R., Baggett, L.S., Wojciechowski, W.C. and Williams, E.E. (2006) Nobels for Nonsense, *Journal of Post Keynesian Economics*, 29, 3–18.

Thwaites, G., Smietanka, P., Bunn, P., Mizen, P. and Bloom, N. (2021) The Impact of Covid-19 on Productivity, *VoxEU*, 18 January.

Timmins, B. and Thomas, D. (2022) Inflation: Seven Reasons the Cost of Living Is Going up around the World, BBC News, 20 January.

Tomaskovic-Devey, D. (2015) The Rise of Financialization Has Led to Lower Living Standards and Reduced Growth in the U.S., LSE Phelan US Centre Blog, 12 June.

Tomaskovic-Devey, D., Dominguez-Villegas, R. and Hoyt, E. (2020) The COVID-19 Recession: An Opportunity to Reform Our Low Wage Economy? Center for Employment Equity, University of Massachusetts Amherst.

Transport & Environment (2022) A Dereliction of Fuel Duty: Europe's €9bn Gift to Putin and the Rich, 22 March.

Trussell Trust (2023) End of Year Stats. https://www.trusselltrust.org/news-and-blog/latest-stats/end-year-stats/#factsheets.

TUC (2022) UK Set for "Worst Real Wage Squeeze" in the G7, 15 July.

UNDP (2022) Global Cost-of-Living Crisis Catalyzed by War in Ukraine Sending Tens of Millions into Poverty, Press Release, 7 July.

Unite the Union (2022) New Unite Investigation Exposes How Corporate Profiteering Is Driving Inflation Not Workers' Wages, 17 June.

United Nations India (2023) Secretary-General: A Global Cost-of-Living Crisis Is Affecting Billions of People, Press Release, 20 September.

Walker, L. (2022) Cost of Living Is the Biggest Risk to Suicide Rates, a Survey Found. Here's What Individuals Can Do about it, ABC News, 26 September.

Wang, X. (2017) The Quantity Theory of Money: An Empirical and Quantitative Reassessment, Working Paper, Washington University in St. Louis, 24 November.

Wardle, D. (2022) Australia's Gas Crisis Proves It's Time to Renationalize Energy, *Jacobin*, 25 June.

Wearden, G. (2023) Britons "Need to Accept" They're Poorer, Says Bank of England Economist, *The Guardian*, 26 April.

Wen, Y. and Arias, M.A. (2014) What Does Money Velocity Tell Us about Low Inflation in the U.S.? Federal Reserve Bank of St Louis, 1 September.

Williams, K. (2022) Back to the 1970s? Energy Prices and the Cost of Living Crisis, *Economic Bulletin*, March.

Williamson, J. (1990) What Washington Means by Policy Reform. In J. Williamson (ed.), *Latin American Adjustment: How Much Has Happened?* Washington, DC: Peterson Institute for International Economics.

Wohl, A.S. (1990) Racism and Anti-Irish Prejudice in Victorian England, The Victorian Web. https://victorianweb.org/history/race/Racism.html.

Wolff, R.D. (2012) Yes, There Is an Alternative to Capitalism: Mondragon Shows the Way. *The Guardian*, 25 June.

Woodroffe, J. and Ellis-Jones, M. (2000) States of Unrest: Resistance to IMF Policies in Poor Countries. World Development Movement Report. https://www.globaljustice.org.uk/resource/states-unrest-resistance-imf-policies-poor-countries/.

World Bank (2022) Fact Sheet: An Adjustment to Global Poverty Lines, 14 September.

World Bank (2023) *Food Security Update*, 18 December.

World Economic Forum (2022) The Cost-of-Living Crisis Is Having a Global Impact. Here's What Countries Are Doing to Help, 21 September. https://www.weforum.org/agenda/2022/09/cost-of-living-crisis-global-impact/.

World Economic Forum (2023) These Countries Have Been the Hardest Hit by Food Price Inflation, 21 February.

World Food Programme (2023) A Global Food Crisis. https://www.wfp.org/global-hunger-crisis.

World Health Organization (2019a) Universal Health Coverage (UHC). https://www.who.int/news-room/fact-sheets/detail/universal-health-coverage-(uhc).

World Health Organization (2019b) Universal Health Coverage and Health Care Financing Indonesia. http://www.searo.who.int/indonesia/topics/hs-uhc/en/.

Zheng, S., Trott, A., Srinivasa, S., Naik, N., Gruesbeck, M., Parkes, D.C. and Socher, R. (2020) The AI Economist: Improving Equality and Productivity with AI-Driven Tax Policies. https://arxiv.org/abs/2004.13332.

Ziady, H. (2023) The UK Economy Still Can't Cope with the Consequences of Brexit, CNN Business, 29 August.

Zizek, S. (2023) The AI Capitalists Don't Realize They're about to Kill Capitalism, *Worldcrunch*, 15 May.

Zolopa, C., Hoj, S., Bruneau, J., Meeson, J.-S, Minoyan, N., Raynault, M.F., Makarenko, I. and Larney, S. (2021) A Rapid Review of the Impacts of "Big Events" on Risks, Harms, and Service Delivery among People Who Use Drugs: Implications for Responding to COVID-19, *International Journal on Drug Policy*, 92, 103127.

Index